87 X

Imelda Marcos

Imelda
Marcos

Carmen Navarro Pedrosa

ST. MARTIN'S PRESS
New York

To all my countrymen
who suffered under
Marcos's martial law

Design by G. Laurens

All photographs courtesy of Carmen Navarro Pedrosa.

Library of Congress Cataloging in Publication Data

Pedrosa, Carmen Navarro.
    Imelda Marcos: the rise and fall of one of the
world's most powerful women

    1. Marcos, Imelda Romualdez, 1929–
2. Philippines—Presidents—Wives—Biography. 3. Marcos,
Ferdinand E. (Ferdinand Edralin), 1917–   . I. Title.
DS686.6.M36P43   1987   959.9'046'0924 [B]   86-26110
ISBN 0-312-00058-8

First Edition
10 9 8 7 6 5 4 3 2 1

Imelda Marcos

The Chink in the Image

IN THE EARLY MORNING of December 30, 1965, a few hundred Filipinos milled around the suburban residence of President-elect Ferdinand E. Marcos. They came in all manner of transport, from distant and nearby provinces, attracted by publicity on the celebrated beauty of the First Lady-to-be, Imelda Romualdez Marcos. She was, newspapers said, as beautiful as an actress and had once held the title Miss Manila. The spectators were mostly humble Filipinos who had sacrificed an hour's sleep to be ahead of the thousands who would be in historic Luneta for the inaugural rites. They perched on trees and scaled the concrete wall to get a good view of the courtyard where Marcos and Imelda were to make an appearance.

So determined were they on this immediate task that it would have been futile to persuade them to give some thought to the virtues of the man they had elected to be their President for the next four years. The spectators of that morning were archetypal common folk, with a reputation for lethargy in the most trying social and economic circumstances. They seemed doomed by fate not to care beyond what was immediate and to hand. That day they had come to see Imelda. This was the good show they preferred to remonstrations that there were other things more politically significant than the reputed beauty of a First Lady. This preoccupation by the masses with what is trite and shallow seemed their quintessential tragedy.

The curtains were about to be raised on a drama in which the beautiful Imelda, whom they had traveled miles to see, would play a stellar role. They had assumed the role of spectators, unaware that the plot of the story about to begin would be played out at their expense. When the end came, alas . . . the early birds would have much to regret about that seemingly innocent morning. But this is going years ahead. The task then was to secure the best vantage point to see the proceedings in the courtyard, which was partially shielded by the profuse foliage of an acacia tree.

Members of the Marcos and Romualdez families and their friends were gathered around an improvised altar decorated with white gladiolas. A German priest, Father Albert Gansewinkle, was saying mass exclusively for the family before the official rites. It was said that Imelda, mindful of tradition and family ties, chose him for the occasion. He was the former rector of the Divine Word University in Leyte, where Imelda had been a student and where her father was once the dean of law. The priest had been summoned from faraway Bonn for this auspicious morning. But a more significant historical touch was the choice of music to be played. This, too, Imelda had specially requested. It was "Plegaria" ("A Plea"), a song composed by Norberto Romualdez, her paternal uncle and the first Romualdez to achieve national fame. Though its music reached out to all, only Imelda and some members of the Romualdez clan understood its meaning.

After the mass Marcos went over his inaugural speech with a press aide while Imelda returned to her dressing room for a final touch-up. There was still no view for the public outside.

It was ten-fifteen, five hours after the first comers had perched on the trees beyond the walls, when Imelda and the three Marcos children, followed by the President-elect, emerged from the iron grille gates. The bodyguards skirmished with the eager crowds as they pushed to get a better view. Imelda paused and waved before she entered the car.

There have been many descriptions of Imelda from both those who have seen her and those who have not. There are also those who described her beauty before and after she became Mrs. Marcos. Their descriptions have been printed in countless magazines and newspapers both in the Philippines and abroad . . . the flawless complexion, long jet-black hair, the finely chiseled features that combined the best of her mixed ancestry, and a queenly bearing. These, coming from the very best sources, fell short of capturing Imelda's appearance that day in 1965 when she became First Lady of the Land. Imelda was radiantly and stunningly beautiful that morning.

For the inaugural rites she wore a plain sheath of embroidered *piña*, a silky Philippine fabric, and a fine veil over her head that she lifted when she faced the cheering crowd. A deceptively simple but expensive string of pearls framed her delicate face, which was barely touched by makeup. The glow of triumph shone through.

At the Luneta grandstand dignitaries and representatives from thirty-five countries, government officials, and Manila's elite stood in attendance as the Marcoses made their way to their respective seats. In the crowd were United States Vice-President Hubert Humphrey, Prime Minister Il Chung of Korea, Foreign Minister Thanat Khoman of Thailand, and Prime Minister Nobusuke Kishi of Japan.

Mr. Humphrey's presence underlined the importance of the Philippines to the United States. Although most Westerners have only a vague romantic image of this group of islands of some 115,000 square miles in the Pacific, the country is the site of the two largest military bases outside the United States. As such it is strategically important to the Western world. But more important, it holds the key to understanding America, for the Philippines, as it were, is the skeleton in its closet, the country that holds the distinction of being the only formal colony that freedom-loving America has ever had. From the time that Admiral Dewey docked his warship at Manila Bay

3

in 1898, and Americans took over the Philippines in 1899, millions of dollars have been poured by American entrepreneurs into these islands for the odd profit.

But the mercenary aspect had long been clouded by rationalization and evangelical zeal. Like the Spaniards before them, the Americans claimed they came to the Philippines to save poor Filipinos. The trouble was they never asked whether Filipinos wanted to be "saved." One-tenth of the entire Filipino population died, in what American historian Gore Vidal described as the first genocide in modern history before Hitler, resisting such "altruism."

The conquest of the Philippines was America's maiden imperialist adventure in the Pacific, and all major political events in that country thereafter spring from that fact. Yet through the years the memories of that brutal war have been repressed, reined in by declarations of special friendship, plenty of aid, and good deeds until it came to pass that some Americans believed that the granting of independence to the Philippines was an act of kindness and generosity to Filipinos rather than one of self-respect and self-preservation.

This distortion is at the bottom of America's ambivalent policy and attitudes toward the people of these islands. America has not quite come to terms with the fact that sometime in the past it had committed a grave mistake by using brute force to deprive a people of a victory that was rightfully theirs. But more tragically, when the mistake had been realized, it refused or was unable to cut and cut cleanly, to paraphrase a Republican senator apropos the end of the Marcos regime. Most Americans, and especially those who were in a position to alter the course of history, had allowed themselves to be deluded by their own subterfuges in holding on to the Philippines, belaboring the many good deeds they had done for the sake of the Philippines, forgetting perhaps that it was not goodness that Filipinos desired but their freedom and the opportunity to shape their own destiny.

Why did it happen? Why did a country founded on the great traditions of freedom and democracy succumb to the tempta-

4

tion of conquest? Until four months before the Spanish-American War, President William McKinley assured Congress that the United States would not annex Cuba, for "it would go against the American code of morality and it would be an act of criminal aggression." This, too, initially was the attitude toward the Philippines. Annexation was unanimously condemned by both the American people and their political and economic leaders.

Some believe that the yellow press, led by William Randolph Hearst's *Journal* and Joseph Pulitzer's *World,* contributed to reverse this attitude. These two newspapers started a campaign to tantalize Americans with the fruit of conquest. Before long, just as there had been near unanimity about the evils of imperialism, there was general agreement after Dewey sailed into Manila Bay that the islands should be kept at all cost. Senator Albert J. Beveridge of Kansas told an enthusiastic audience in Boston: "Fate has written our policy for us; the trade of the world must and shall be ours. . . . Our institutions will follow our flag on the wings of commerce. American law, American order, American civilization, and the American flag will plant themselves on shores hitherto bloody and benighted, but by those agencies of God henceforth to be made beautiful and bright. . . . The Philippines are logically our first target." Thus did the Philippines become America's colony.

The ultimate rationalization was expressed by President McKinley in what has become a classic: "I walked one floor of the White House night after night until midnight; and I am not ashamed to tell you, gentlemen, that I went down on my knees and prayed Almighty God for light and guidance more than one night. And one night late it came to me this way— I don't know how it was, but it came. . . . And then I went to bed and went to sleep and slept soundly. . . . The next morning I sent for the chief engineer of the War Department and I told him to put the Philippines on the map of the United States, and there they are, and there they will stay while I am President!" Contemporary American policy makers shirk from the hypocrisy of McKinley's manifest destiny rationale, but it is useful to recollect in trying to understand the frustrations of Filipino nationalists.

On that same spot where the grandstand stood, amid the ruins and devastation of Manila nineteen years ago, the United States formally relinquished the islands back to its people, in ceremonies that mocked the truth. For even the little that was saved from the war was grudgingly given, and the aid that was to help Filipinos to reconstruct the country was tied up with the onerous Laurel-Langley Agreement giving Americans parity rights in the development of its natural resources. To Filipinos, it was the war for independence of 1898 all over again. This time it would not be fought in battlefields but in legislative halls, front pages, and diplomatic missions. It would be played out in slow motion, devoid of cataclysmic surges but equally painful and destructive. No matter what was said in the name of freedom and democracy, what 1946 meant was that the Philippines were being set free so long as they remained under American control. True, there was formal political freedom, but this amounted to nothing in the face of economic hardship and need for American aid. It merely signaled a more subtle form of domination, as colonial as the pre-independence period, but this time Filipinos were deprived of even the indignation of revolt. From here on, if Filipinos botched up their chance to develop their country, they would have only themselves to blame.

At the inauguration, across the grandstand stood the monument to the country's national hero, José Rizal, who was executed by the Spaniards for fomenting revolution only a year before the Americans came. These historical facts were lost to most of the audience that morning, standing at attention during the ceremonies that would install the sixth President of the Philippine republic. There was not a cloud in the sky. But such are December mornings in this exotic city. It is the time of year with near-perfect weather.

Away from this convivial gathering were other Filipinos, the heirs of the recalcitrant revolutionaries of 1898 who viewed Presidential inaugurations with understandable reserve. They were not deceived by declarations of independence. They kept faith and waited anxiously for the day when the country would have leaders brave and bold enough to break away from the onerous special relationship with America. Paradoxically, it seemed such a leader would have to have the moral vision of a saint and the ruthlessness of a scoundrel, if there was such a man, to wean the country from its habits of dependence.

Press accounts of the President-to-be augured well for optimists, who saw in Marcos's character traits that might just fulfill the role. He was young, brilliant, and daring. There was some discomfiture that his reputed ruthlessness outweighed his moral qualities, but such doubts were cast aside. There had been "good" Philippine Presidents and they had been unable to deliver. The rationale was cultivated in those days that Filipinos might, after all, need a kind of devil to pull them out of the colonial morass, someone who knew the game of evil and would cope with it for their sake.

This mood for compromise was the cue on which publicists built an image of Marcos as a "crisis hero." What it really meant was that with Marcos's mediocre political record, they proceeded to fantasticate the legend—brilliant student, war hero, successful politician. Overnight, Filipinos were besieged by propaganda of a superhero combining the qualities of Audie Murphy and John F. Kennedy, who lived in their midst, unknown until the Presidential campaign of 1965. A book entitled *For Every Tear a Victory* documented this heroic life so preciously hidden from public knowledge. There was some grumbling that the over-enthusiastic portrayal of Marcos as a larger-than-life hero was being made at the expense of Filipinos. But even these objections were brushed aside as petty. The stakes were too high to quibble about propagandists' hyperbole. Marcos has always believed that it was this book that won him the Presidency. It had not been written, after all, for Filipinos but for Americans.

Also he had Imelda. She, too, proclaimed highly paid propagandists, was a paragon of virtue, the female complement to the modern-day superhero. She was rich, young, and beautiful, an Asian Jacqueline Kennedy. The souvenir program described her as the wealthy and well-bred descendant of one of the "mightiest political clans of the country." As she sat in animated conversation with Mr. Humphrey and former President Carlos P. Garcia on the Luneta grandstand, there was no reason to dispute the claims. To the public at large, and at a safe distance, she did exude the confidence and poise of an heiress.

But as with the image of Marcos, there were flaws in Imelda's media image. Manila is a small city. It is not possible to have the qualities the image makers proclaimed her to have and not be in the exclusive roster of Manila's four hundred most prominent families. Until her marriage to Marcos, Imelda was socially insignificant. Despite a famous name and a beauty title, Imelda was not, by the city's standards, an aristocrat or a society deb. More knowledgeable people kept their peace lest they be accused of envy. They viewed the image-making of the Marcoses as harmless fun. Moreover, Imelda was good copy, and prominent award-winning writers and editors, taken in by the aristocratic image, joined the cheering squad.

Yet it was Imelda who had, perhaps unwittingly, given away the clue that the image made for her by her publicists, and with which she concurred, did not hold together. Something about the portrait was askew, but the public was not prepared to question it for the moment. This had to do with her role in the 1965 Presidential campaign, which saw her rise as a political star in her own right.

Both friends and foes agreed that she had carried the brunt of the campaign. True, Marcos was a brilliant strategist, but it was Imelda who had had the stamina and determination to go through the demands of the campaign. It was one thing to have maps and plans for a journey but quite another to reach a destination. That was the unique role Imelda played, and this is confirmed by their closest colleagues. Marcos made the plans, but it was Imelda who implemented them.

The area of the campaign covered 1,700 municipalities, all of which had to be visited. It was Imelda who made sure that her husband's campaign reached the most obscure and remote parts of the country, hopping from airplanes, jeeps, and bancas. She remembered the names of political leaders and their families and circumstances. She knew who needed a new roof, who was celebrating a wedding anniversary, who mourned a recent death. For these myriad tasks, the most precious talent was sheer endurance, a virtue not often found in aristocrats. Sleepless, determined, energetic Imelda fulfilled the role to the chagrin of Marcos and sturdier colleagues. Her reputation as an accomplished political arm of Marcos during the campaign was well deserved, and the President-elect conceded that she was responsible for a million votes, the margin that made him victor. It also established her as a political figure by an indirect mandate. Later Imelda's political role would be amplified by groups in the Marcos camp who would use her to further their own political fortunes.

This was the chink in the demure and aristocratic image of the sixth First Lady of the Philippines, and some people saw through it. She was his ally in the longest, dirtiest, and bloodiest Presidential campaign. She sat on that platform composed, beaming, with a sense of quiet triumph. Although it was Marcos who was being installed as the sixth President of the Philippines, the inauguration rites that morning were different from any other, because of Imelda. The delicate, innocent beauty hardly betrayed a character that had the subtle glint of fine steel. A foreign correspondence in an inspired moment called her "steel butterfly." The label stuck and deepened the mystery of Imelda Marcos. What made her run? Why did she act so compellingly? She told friends it was for "the love of Ferdinand." For him, she said, she would do anything, even climb a mountain. And for a long while the public believed her.

This public declaration of love enhanced the idyllic image of the Marcoses and heightened expectations of Filipinos yearning for forceful leadership. Indeed, in 1965 it had seemed they were blessed not just with one heroic leader but two, with the surprise bonus of a wife who shared the new President's commitment to the country.

In October 1966, barely a few months from that morning's inauguration rites, the Marcoses paid the customary state visit to America. As with past Philippine Presidents, the personal call to Washington was high on Marcos's agenda. This was the occasion for horse trading, in which both countries reiterate the special relationship and proceed to iron out the details of quid pro quo in civilized, diplomatic parlance. The result of such bargaining, as in the past, only exposed the dependency of the Philippines. There was no reason to expect that Marcos would radically depart from the paths taken by his predecessors. Still, nationalists and more politically perceptive Filipinos hoped that Marcos, known for his brazen character, would put up some kind of stand for his country's sake. They were to be disappointed.

The American government was preoccupied with the war in Vietnam, with government and diplomatic activity concentrated on portraying the war as a Southeast Asian concern. President Lyndon B. Johnson laid out the red carpet in pursuit of a commitment and public declaration from Marcos to support America's role in the war. The Philippine President was asked to repudiate public opinion in the Philippines and reverse an electoral promise of noninvolvement in the war. To this, Marcos readily acceded. Indeed, the famed Marcos ruthlessness caved in in the face of the mighty American dollar. There was talk of plentiful aid in return, but whether it was for the Marcoses or for the country was not yet clear.

The publicity that was generated by the state visit added to the luster and glory of the youthful couple who now ruled the Philippines. "A photographer's delight," American journalists said of Imelda as they trailed her from the White House to the Metropolitan Opera House to the Rockefeller estate, noting every change of gown and accessory. She had brought trunkloads of clothes, saying that her wardrobe was prepared like an album, with each gown in a suitcase with its matching shoes and accessories. At the National Press Club in Washington, D. C., it was Imelda's eye-catching black and white pearl earrings and brooch; at the Metropolitan Opera House opening, a white-over-pink *terno* (a Filipino national dress); at breakfast with Cardinal Spellman, a stunning polka-dotted gown.

She sprung a surprise on 1,400 guests at the return reception for President and Mrs. Lyndon B. Johnson at the Shoreham Hotel in Washington when she stood up and sang "Dahil sa Iyo," a Filipino love song. The act was unprecedented for the wife of a head of state on an official visit, but Imelda broke tradition, convinced that it added to rather than diminished the luster of the occasion. She did not think that the Washington establishment was any different from Filipino poor folk whom she had persuaded to vote for her husband by singing. She had a beautiful voice, and she would use it against any rule of protocol. At that time her boldness was described as "charming."

The New York Times featured Imelda Marcos on its front pages. The reporter of the London *Evening Standard* wrote from New York about her super coolness, and put her in a league with Queen Elizabeth, Princess Grace, and Jacqueline Kennedy. Echoing Filipino publicists, the *Standard* reporter said that Imelda, too, was from a socially powerful family of great wealth.

Back in the Philippines, Imelda gave a press conference, and her off-the-cuff remarks were published in the October 16 issue of *Woman and Home,* a weekend supplement of a Philippine national daily, which revealed a bit more of what motivated this remarkable woman.

"The Met—it was fabulous—those chandeliers, those paintings, the audience . . . my God, the Rockefellers, the Du Ponts, the Fords, the Magnins, the Lindsays, the painter Marc Chagall—you know he wanted to paint me but he was reluctant—would my husband allow him to do so?

"And the jewels the women were wearing—it is a good thing I decided not to wear any diamonds—because those that the Americans were wearing—wow!—strands and strands of them around their necks. My, in America when they're rich, they're really rich . . . when I came in wearing my pearls, I was so thankful I chose them because everyone else was wearing diamonds. . . .

"The contacts we made can be very useful—this is why I would like to set up a secretariat to follow up the people who have been so willing to help us.

"One very interesting person I met was Mary Lasker—who is considered America's most useful woman. She is responsible for beautifying Central Park, building museums and [is] a patron of art . . . and she is a very good friend of Mrs. Blair [wife of the then United States Ambassador to the Philippines, William McCormick Blair], so when I went to her house— wow! you never saw anything so fabulous—I never in my life saw anything like it—her collection of Matisses, Pisarros, Monets, Gauguins—and especially Matisse—really fabulous— and the ten minutes I was supposed to stay dragged on to almost three hours. Really fascinating.

"The Rockefeller estate was another place we visited. Imagine an estate right in the heart of New York . . . with its own golf course, an orchard of rare fruits, flower gardens of the best blooms . . . and stables—beautiful horses and they did not even stink! These were cared for so well. Inside, more paintings and art collections . . . but after lunch, when Mrs. David Rockefeller asked me what I wanted to do, I just said, "Sleep!" So I was given a room upstairs and had a good rest."

And on Air Force One she said, "This is the Presidential plane which was given for our use for our trip to Tokyo. Beautiful, with beds as wide as this dining table, telex machines, movies, telephones that can call Manila or any place in the world, and outlets for a flatiron, which I found very handy.

"Everywhere I had a chance to talk to the leaders of both political parties in America I put in my two cents' worth. Like I told them—leaders like Javits, Romney, Brown, and Lindsay —you have to see for yourself what we in Asia are going through, so your decisions must be based on reality.

"Take a man who is unclothed—when it rains he feels it

immediately. But when you put a rich man fully clothed, furred, and rain-coated, he will not feel a single drop . . . this is why when you say that Asians are a crazy bunch, too sensitive, it is because we are poor, we are deprived, we are in want. . . ."

It was during this trip, when the communiqué was being prepared, that President Johnson allegedly said three times, "Don't forget Mrs. Marcos's three and a half million dollars. This was for the cultural center, but since the funds for that are already adequate, I shall divert it to the Social Integration Program." Her singing did pay off.

And more. Imelda's assessment of that trip is also recorded for posterity: "It was a big hit. . . . I was told that never in the history of Washington did a reception last on and on and on. . . . As for President Johnson—he kept on signing cards for me, and on the ninth menu card he said, 'To Mrs. Marcos, with A and A.' So I told him, 'Mr. President, I am a little bit dumb. Can you tell me what this means?' And he said, 'Admiration and affection.' And I replied, 'Oh, I just wanted to make sure.' "

Not long after this candid public report of the visit, there was to be another "press conference," another laying down of heart, but this time it would be closed to all but the Romualdez family. Imelda invited everyone who carried a Romualdez name, even cousins she normally would not invite to the Palace. One cousin pointedly asked Imelda why she should be so privileged as to be invited. They were being invited, Imelda said, to get "a firsthand account of the trip."

For the occasion Imelda brought to the fore her story-telling talents and narrated to awed near and distant cousins the triumph of the state visit and how she was acclaimed "the star of the show." She told them how Marcos tutored her, made her read all the books on America so she would be knowledgeable when she spoke to American officials. By the time she spoke to President Johnson, she knew his favorite color, his favorite perfume, his favorite food, as well as the trade figures between the United States and the Philippines and a general outline of the military bases agreement. She told them about the panic that engulfed her when Marcos insisted she had to know all the information required for the next day's conferences and how she drove herself till the wee hours of the morning. The following day Marcos drilled her on foreign policy, like a teacher, question-and-answer style, until her answers were perfect.

The rest of her story covered what the relatives had already read in the newspapers. And before she went on and on, one impatient cousin asked whether this was the firsthand account they had come for. "It is still to come," Imelda replied.

Imelda's flair for drama is not unknown, and she endowed the occasion with the importance she wanted her relatives to treat it with. In hushed tones she told them that after a reception for the Johnsons was over, she waited until Marcos was asleep. She tiptoed out of her own suite and sought out her favorite brother, Benjamin. Taking his arm, she led him to a dark corner by a window overlooking a spectacular view of New York. The roomful of Romualdez kin were stone silent as she said there were tears in her eyes when she asked him to look down below. "Kokoy, that is the world beneath us. Think of it. What we came from, and now the world . . . the whole world beneath us."

To a cousin, this was the part of the story they had been asked especially to come to hear, not the "firsthand account of the trip." It was a message, a warning, if one wishes, that she was now in a position of power, and notice was being served to the other members of the Romualdez clan.

Loreto Romualdez Ramos, first cousin of the First Lady, historian, musician, daughter of Norberto Romualdez to whom the clan owed its first fame, had a foreboding that Imelda was about to commence a war of attrition against their side of the clan and that this was the first salvo. When the Palace released the official bio data of Imelda, Loreto had wished to tell her to put a stop to the foolish "aristocratic image" they had made out for her. "I wanted to tell her that she could not get away with it, nor was it right that she should distort the truth, if only for her own sake." Loreto was especially concerned about the glossing over of her maternal side which seemed to have had Imelda's complicity. But Loreto never got around to doing it. Instead she cajoled aides and friendly press agents whenever she had the chance for the gigantic hoax they were playing on the Filipino public on Imelda's origins. The truth, she said, was so much better than the lie. Imelda was no aristocrat, but her life story was nevertheless remarkable. Why she chose to hide it was the puzzle.

CHAPTER ONE

The Untold Story of Imelda Marcos

IMELDA REMEDIOS VISITACION ROMUALDEZ, born at dawn on July 2, 1929, entered a family basking in rising wealth and national prominence, much of it due to her uncle, noted jurist and nationalist leader, Norberto Romualdez. Imelda's father, Vicente Orestes, had a flourishing law practice which supported a young second wife and a brood of five growing children by his first. Shortly before Imelda's birth, her father's house on Calle General Solano, in a prestigious section of Manila, only a stone's throw from Malacanang Palace, was remodeled to add a garage for the car he had recently bought on the installment plan from the only car dealer in Manila, the Jewish-owned Estrella del Norte. The car was a Berlina, a prized possession in those days.

At first, the car was more than a status symbol for the Romualdezes. It was a godsend when Imelda's mother, Remedios, had to be rushed to the San Juan de Dios Hospital on the evening of July first. Taxicabs in Manila were scarce at that late hour, and the brand-new limousine could not have been more needed.

Vicente Orestes, eager to display his new wealth and success, called for two physicians and reserved a suite that cost twenty-five pesos a day, a small fortune at the time. By all standards, then, Imelda was born into luxurious circumstances. Her father, with prophetic vision, had told relatives that the expense was justified because "this child will be important." Imelda, as the first child of his second marriage, offered him a second chance at life, a bridge to the future.

From birth, Vicente Orestes's important child was an extraordinarily beautiful baby, with rosy cheeks and limpid skin, according to the doting aunts and cousins who saw her. Like most prestigious Filipino families, the Romualdezes were strict, no-nonsense Roman Catholics, or in Spanish parlance, *catolicos cerrados.* They went strictly by the book. They would not let twenty-four hours pass with the newborn child still a pagan. Imelda was baptized at San Miguel Church the morning after her birth. Her name was registered as Imelda Remedios Visitacion Romualdez, in keeping with the Catholic tradition for naming children. The first name was a choice, the second to honor a predecessor, her mother in this case, and the third represented the feast celebrated on her day of birth, the visit of St. Elizabeth to her cousin, the Virgin Mary.

Although the memories of that day have dimmed with time, one relative who attended the baptism attests to its lavish style, in keeping with Vicente Orestes's regard for his child. The grand matriarch of the Romualdez clan, Doña Trinidad Lopez de Romualdez, was present at the baptism and fretted at her son's indulgence. In her time, such excessive exultation over the birth of a child was inconceivable—so much gross vanity. A newborn baby represented an additional mouth to feed, financial worries, and sometimes even the specter of a domestic crisis. A new child could necessitate moving to another town in search of more income.

When Imelda was born, Doña Trinidad was an old woman, her life almost over. She was a tireless voice from the past whose moral authority held together the vast Romualdez clan. So long as she was alive, no conflict or crisis within the clan remained unresolved for long. She was a strong woman, and it is said that Imelda owes her dogged character to her. At the time of Doña Trinidad's death on April 6, 1932, at eighty-nine, Imelda was three years old.

In the 1870s there were no Romualdezes of Leyte. The Romualdezes were originally of Pandacan, a dusty suburb of Spanish Manila. Like most families with middling importance, they took pride in being city folk. One of them, Imelda's grandfather, Daniel Romualdez, was a *cabeza de barangay,* a petty town official, and a teacher at age twenty. While these were not accomplishments that brought national fame, he was regarded as a man with a promising future. Unfortunately, this talented youth was soon afflicted with tuberculosis, then an incurable disease, and his hopes for a bright future were dashed. He abandoned work and instead joined the ranks of believers in the miraculous powers of the Child Jesus of Pandacan.

In 1852 an earthquake devastated large parts of the city, including the church that housed the image of the Child Jesus. Written accounts of Franciscan friars narrate how the entire community of men and women worked night and day to clear the ruins to build another church. As a reward for such devotion, it is said that a group of boys, while clearing the ruins, found the image of the Child Jesus intact and unscarred. The image was immediately turned over to the archdiocese of Sampaloc, which had jurisdiction over the parish of Pandacan. But soon after, the image mysteriously returned to the spot where it was originally found. Stories of the miraculous feats of the image of the Child Jesus abound in the Philippines. One theory holds that idolatrous worship of the image enabled Filipino culture to shift from paganism to Christianity. When Imelda became rich and powerful a century later, she would build an "ancestral house" with a multimillion-peso shrine in honor of the Child Jesus. Such devotion came from the past.

The return of the image was deemed a miracle, and the parishioners built a small chapel and a fountain on the spot where people afflicted with all sorts of diseases flocked to the healing waters. Daniel was a frequent visitor to the fountain.

Although the waters may not have done much for Daniel, it was while on a visit to the fountain that he saw Trinidad Lopez. He fell in love with her instantly. She was tall and fair, with European features, deep-set eyes, and an aquiline nose. He later learned she was the daughter of a Spanish priest residing at the parish. Daniel began his pursuit of Trinidad by seeking the good offices of his father confessor, who obliged. Before long, in 1872, Daniel Romualdez Arcilla, and *cabeza de barangay* of Pandacan, Manila, married Trinidad Lopez y Crisostomo Talentin, a friar's daughter.

This watershed year in Imelda's history also marked the beginning of the Filipino revolution against Spain's colonial government. Three Filipino priests, Mariano Gomez, José Burgos, and Jacinto Zamora, who had advocated equality between Filipino secular priests and Spanish friars, were charged with insurrection and executed in Luneta, Manila. They were later to be known as the "Martyrs of 1872" and would inspire the nationalist movement that would grow into a full-blown revolution twelve years later. To Imelda's ancestors, rebellious priests were out of their ken. The significance of the date referred to personal fate. For indeed, had Trinidad refused marriage to the tubercular and dying Daniel, it is highly unlikely there would have been Romualdezes of Leyte or the myth of Imelda.

Trinidad had initially refused Daniel's marriage proposal, in favor of becoming a nun. But the confessor priest had shrewdly advised her against such an ambition, arguing that marrying and seeing a man through his difficult days required exemplary devotion. She could make a nunnery out of the marriage, too.

This larger-than-life figure in Imelda's past soon faced the formidable task of overruling Daniel's relatives, who would not listen to suggestions that she bring their ailing relative to the backwoods of Leyte. The Romualdezes of Pandacan believed that they had to protect their social status in Manila and were aggrieved that this new member of the family would not acknowledge that she had married well. She had the effrontery to belittle their pretensions at being "city folk"! She, too, was a rebel. With keen foresight and nothing more, she stood firm in her decision to begin life in rural, backward Burauen, Leyte, hometown of her mother where she believed that the abundant sunshine, sea air, and *tuba* (local wine) would restore her husband's health.

In pushing for the move to Leyte, Trinidad relied on her father's prominence in the region. A parish priest, he had administered the town of Burauen capably for twenty years, and like most Spanish friars was both loved and hated for it. Trinidad correctly estimated that her father's stewardship of the small town, in which he was sole and undisputed ruler in the affairs of both soul and body, was superior to the minuscule reputation of Daniel as a *cabeza de barangay* in Manila. With uncommon perspicacity, she chose a locale where the Romualdez name and fortune would flourish.

Thus did the friar's daughter and her ailing husband begin the much-vaunted Romualdez dynasty when they sailed for Leyte in 1873. It would reach its apex with the rise of Imelda's political star in 1975. But more than a hundred years ago, Trinidad had to work very hard indeed, using the skills she had learned in Manila to provide a living for her own family as well as for her brothers and sisters. She taught, sang, and embroidered, much to the delight and surprise of her provincial neighbors.

In the years preceding the birth of Imelda's father, Vicente Orestes, Trinidad drove herself to exhaustion, attempting to preserve her family. At one point the young family with firstborn son Norberto was forced to return to Manila by Daniel's relatives. When Daniel suffered a nearly fatal relapse, Trinidad succeeded in returning the Romualdez family to Leyte for good.

After nursing Daniel back to health, Trinidad again took the helm and moved her family to Dagami, a bigger town than Burauen, in order to earn more money. Trinidad gave birth to a second son, Miguel, on September 29, 1880. In later years he would become the wealthiest of her three sons.

But Trinidad had pushed too hard for her own good. In 1885, while pregnant with Vicente Orestes, she suffered a nervous breakdown. Years later, recalling that episode in her life, Trinidad told her son Norberto, "I almost lost my mind." She would wake up nights screaming, unable to bear the sound of the wind. When it rained she imagined that their little house was being washed away. "Even little insects frightened me," she said.

In those days nervous disorders had an "infallible" cure—baths in the sea. It was believed that the salty seawater and the rhythm of the waves pacified the troubled mind. Trinidad would later recall with humor how she was brought to the sea to bathe under a mosquito net cover held by her brothers.

To aid Trinidad's recovery, the family once more moved in search of a town by the sea. Their search led them to Tolosa, an idyllic spot on the eastern coast of Leyte, whose shores are washed by the Pacific Ocean.

Trinidad's breakdown and the move to Tolosa would deeply affect her youngest son. Vicente Orestes grew up under the doting care of a broken woman who filled him with romantic notions and who instilled in him none of the drive or ambition that characterized his older brothers.

After she became First Lady, Imelda would attempt to rewrite her family's history by building a sumptuous summerhouse, called "Kalipayan," the Waray word for "happiness," in Tolosa. Imelda's publicists would describe Tolosa as a town founded by the prestigious Romualdezes of Leyte. Diplomats, foreign dignitaries, and high government officials who visited the little town by the sea were regaled by Imelda's tales of her aristocratic ancestry. In reality, the only contribution the Romualdezes made to Tolosa was to live there.

At this time, Daniel, then fully recovered, took over the running of the household, and the family's finances improved. Trinidad's brothers (all Lopezes) organized a family orchestra called Orquesta Lopez. The young Norberto Romualdez was flutist and violinist for this orchestra, and this provided a good source of supplementary income for the family. It was a creditable musical group, and latter-day Romualdezes recall its popularity with pride. "It was in this town by the sea that our family life blossomed," Norberto wrote of Tolosa.

No longer dependent on his wife, Daniel Romualdez assumed his rightful place as the man of the house. He was a towering man, and his sons spoke of the fear he instilled with the "thunder of his voice." He returned to his first love—politics—and was often in the streets and the town plaza where the menfolk gathered to discuss local and national events.

This was the period of revolutionary ferment, and no Filipino, however insignificant, missed the excitement generated by the nationalist "Propaganda Movement," a campaign initiated by Filipino intellectuals who sought reforms from the Spanish colonial regime. It lasted from 1872 to 1892 and is considered the golden age of Filipino nationalism, producing the very best artists, poets, and leaders.

Daniel Romualdez, as a *capitán del barrio* of Tolosa, had only a marginal role in this nascent nationalist movement. It was his eldest son, Norberto, who would break away from obscurity and make the family's name famous throughout the country.

Trinidad, the indomitable friar's daughter, was tamed after her nervous breakdown. When Imelda's father, Vicente Orestes, was born on July 3, 1885, she was a changed woman and quietly slid into the role of wife and mother. Freed from the responsibility of breadwinner, she devoted her time to the house and the new baby. Vicente Orestes received the undivided attention of a mother whose character was prone to excess. Her devotion to the child was no less than her devotion to the task she had set herself when she married sick Daniel in 1872. Vicente Orestes grew up under the protective wing of a strong and willful mother, and this relationship would set in motion a series of disasters that would ultimately cause the poverty that his important child, Imelda Romualdez, would suffer in her childhood and early youth. Trinidad, unwittingly perhaps, had cast Vicente Orestes into a role that would make it difficult for him to match the later successes of his brothers. He was forever to be the ward of his mother, unable to care for himself or his own family. Unfortunately, she would not always be there. Like his mother, he would also be enamored of the sea, the cure-all for pain and difficulty. He would keep coming back to Tolosa, a whim that would shape the fate of his children.

Trinidad lived to see her three sons establish families and make lives of their own in Manila. Norberto, the offspring of a heroic attempt to restore her husband's health, lived up to the promise of his talents as a young boy and became an eminent scholar at the time of her death. Miguel, the child of Dagami, a period in which the family bravely sought wealth in an ugly town, became a wealthy man after his tenure as mayor of Manila. But Vicente Orestes, the child of a nervous breakdown, who, Trinidad realized, would always need a caretaker, was never able to strike roots, and in 1938 when his law office collapsed, would be forced to return to a humbler life in Leyte.

Even as adults with families of their own, the three Romualdez sons revered their mother. A niece who was present at the time of her death in 1932 says she was no less theatrical than she had been when alive. On her deathbed, where she had lain for many months, she closed her eyes and prayed Ave Marias with great fervor. Her fingers fumbled over the beads of the rosary, but she summoned all that was left of her energy to create meaningful drama. She said, a few minutes before death, "Now it is time, let me lie down." Although gasping for breath, and obviously in great pain, she continued to give orders: "Light the candle by the altar. Remove this pillow. Remove the blanket. Call the priest. My hair," she commanded, "it has to be combed." Then she straightened her body and extended her hands in a beckoning gesture and called for her sons, Norberto, Miguel, and Vicente Orestes. Not one of the sons dared to come near her.

That was how strong a woman Trinidad was. Although her sons loved her, they were too frightened, too awed by the drama she played at her moment of death. Norberto stood at the top of the stairs, in tears, but with his back turned on her. Miguel locked himself in an adjacent room. Vicente Orestes

23

was farthest from the deathbed. Their children and wives were sent instead to keep watch in the death room on the second floor. As she called their names, Trinidad laid her hands crossed over on her breast in the fashion of peaceful deaths, as taught to her by priests. Then she closed her eyes and died.

She was the first Romualdez of the south. Had she not lived, there would have been no powerful political dynasty of Romualdezes from Leyte. Imelda hardly knew this woman, but it would seem that it is to her that she owes much of her gift for endurance. Trinidad was the archetypal figure of indomitable will for generations of Romualdez women to emulate.

As with most mothers, Trinidad presumed she had laid the groundwork for the future of her sons, and that they and their children would live in harmony as she wanted them to. She lived to see Vicente Orestes's fortunes begin to flounder, but she had rested on the word of Norberto that he would always look after his younger brother.

In keeping with Norberto's promise, Vicente Orestes was taken into the Romualdez law offices. The Romualdez name and prestige, at about the time of Imelda's birth, was enjoyed by all their children without distinction. But the peace and prosperity of the early 1930s did not last.

There were Filipinos, the Romualdezes among them, who had their own Wall Street collapse and an economic depression which deprived them of their wealth and tested their characters. It was during this economic crisis that Vicente Orestes went under; even Norberto's kindness could not save him. He was forced to abandon his Manila law practice and return to Tolosa, where a simpler way of life would enable him minimally to support his family.

The contrast between Norberto's success and Vicente Orestes's failure led to a lethal family feud lasting up to the time of the Marcos regime. Trinidad's concern for her youngest son had led her to commit the blunder of making him dependent on Norberto, which was all very well within their immediate family. But Vicente Orestes's children felt otherwise; the second-class status Imelda and her siblings experienced later turned into resentment and, ultimately, into hatred. Thus did Imelda become a poor relation of the rich Romualdezes, a development which would fuel her lifelong obsession to achieve fame and fortune, and to appoint herself leader of the Romualdez clan. Paradoxically, Vicente Orestes's other brother, Miguel, took off on his own, and his children remained friendly with the poorer Romualdezes.

Norberto, the exemplary son, made his mark quite early as a struggling student in Manila in the 1880s. As soon as the family's finances improved, his parents sent him off to Manila to enroll at the Ateneo Municipal de Manila, a school geared to the country's elite. Norberto and later his brothers were classified as poor students from the provinces, although Daniel made sure that they had some funds. Imelda's image makers would later use the city schooling of the Romualdezes as proof of their wealth and aristocracy, but Norberto himself was proud to say that as students at the elite Ateneo their poverty stuck out like a sore thumb. His poverty, however, did not deter him from pursuing academic excellence.

When the Revolution broke out in 1896, Norberto and his brothers returned home, as did thousands of provincial students whose schools were closed. To many Filipinos, those were glorious days when for a brief period they savored the struggle and the success of bringing down what had seemed an invincible master. No sooner had they ousted the Spanish, however, than they had to contend with the American conquerors, promising benevolence and ultimate freedom. There were those Filipinos who were eager to get on with life and were easily appeased by the American promises, but for others, the American occupation simply represented another delay for Filipino independence. The former were to be known as the Federalistas, and the latter the Nacionalistas. The Philippines, briefly united in war, returned to a conquered and divided nation under the American eagle.

In 1900 Norberto opened a school in Leyte and began to study law on his own. Eventually he was able to buy a house in Gran Capitán, the capital city's high street, cheek by jowl with the richest families in Leyte. Soon after, he opened a law office in Manila. At this time he also bought several pieces of land, some of which, a daughter later claimed, were put in his parents' names. These lands would later be a bone of contention in the clan.

Norberto married Beatriz Buz soon after the death of his first wife, María Marquez. It was a happy marriage, and Norberto's personal fortunes continued to rise. A keen grammarian and philologist, he published several scholarly books. President William Taft appointed him provincial prosecuting attorney in 1906.

In 1910 Norberto brought his family to Manila and was named assistant city attorney there. He also bought property in a posh Manila neighborhood. The Manila house and the house in Leyte gave the Romualdez family entree into privileged Filipino society. Norberto's successes continued to ensure the fame of the Romualdez name. He was also a politician and a nationalist, a delegate to the Constitutional Convention of 1934 and assemblyman for the 4th district of Leyte from 1936 to 1941. Like his mother, he was devoted to Leyte and laid the foundation for Romualdez political influence in that province.

In contrast, Vicente Orestes remained a poor younger brother. In keeping with Filipino family tradition, Norberto was a generous elder brother. He withdrew money from the bank accounts of his own children when his two brothers needed the money for their bar examinations. When Norberto became justice of the Supreme Court, he handed over the Romualdez law offices to his brothers. But it was Vicente Orestes to whom he was most generous. For a long time, Vicente Orestes and his family lived with Norberto in the Manila mansion. When Norberto built a new house, he gave the use of the old one to Vicente Orestes and his family. He was always on the side of his little brother.

With the division of the Romualdez properties, Trinidad specified that the best of the properties should go to her youngest son, who would need it the most. But it was a favor that would do him little good. A succession of misfortunes would befall Vicente Orestes.

Imelda's father did achieve a measure of success during the short period he lived in Manila. He was able, for example, to buy his own house in 1926 in a prestigious district called San Miguel. It was a fine house on Calle General Solano, where very rich Manilans lived. Vicente Orestes Romualdez's house was only a modest version of such mansions, with decorative woodwork and graceful grilled windows in the Antillean style. There were rows and rows of such houses in San Miguel. It was a good address and, more importantly, it was his first purchase. The lot was bought on the installment plan, and he mortgaged the land to construct the house. The house was only a few minutes' walk to Malacanang Palace, where his daughter would one day hold court.

Unhappily, soon after the house was finished, Vicente Orestes's wife, Juanita Acereda, died of leukemia. Very little is known of this first wife, except that she was buried in a crypt in San Miguel Church, across from the Romualdez house on Calle General Solano, and that she had dark Moorish features. Like Doña Trinidad and Norberto's wife, Beatriz Buz, she was a friar's daughter. Her death devastated Vicente Orestes, who had a need for strong women, like his mother. He was left to care for five children, whose ages ranged from nine to seventeen.

This was the tail end of the prosperous and frivolous 1920s, of carnivals and the heady days of Pancho Villa, when the first Miss Philippines, Anita Noble, was the toast of Manila. For a while nationalism seemed to have been forgotten. Filipinos were in the grip of Americanization, and those who wanted to survive had to jump onto the dizzying carousel of a new language, new politics, new ideas, and a new culture. The challenge of change was everywhere, and both Norberto and Miguel responded. But not Vicente Orestes. He was an intensely private person, soft and perpetually romantic. His terms of success in life were quite modest. He longed for the peace and quiet of Tolosa, and he remained impervious to the rise in wealth and fame of his elder brothers. He could have learned English to acquire more clients, but he did not.

At this time, a woman named Trining served as Vicente Orestes's constant companion, nurse to his children, and resident domestic. It would have been a suitable arrangement, given Vicente Orestes's temperament and his children's opposition to his ever remarrying following their mother's death. But Doña Trinidad, already a widow and living in Manila, was dismayed. She determined to put a stop to the affair, and in consultation with her son Norberto devised a plan to find a respectable wife for her lonely son.

Norberto knew that the question of a remarriage for his younger brother was bound to come up. The old lady was vehement about the way her son Vicente Orestes was wasting his life. To her, it was a simple matter of finding a suitable woman for him, never mind what he had to say. Thus was Imelda's mother found.

In those days the last strongholds of conservative Spain—the convents—were still the places to find the "best girls." These girls were similar to au pairs: students who paid for their board and lodging by helping in the convents. Their tasks ranged from teaching to cooking, embroidering, or whatever else the nuns assigned to them. As most convents had their mother houses in Spain or other countries in Europe, they represented pockets of the Old World in a country now opening to modern American culture.

Although most of the convents ran orphanages, not all the girls were orphans. Most of them had families of their own in the provinces; if they chose convent life, it was to acquire the skills to become perfect housewives. Their education centered on mundane and practical subjects, such as cooking and sewing, with one crucial difference: the convent girls lived and were trained as nuns, honed to the virtue of perfect obedience. Most of the girls eventually became nuns. But a few did get married and it was said that such ideal girls were coveted by reputable families who wanted "good wives" for their sons.

It was Norberto's idea to search these convents for a bride for Vicente Orestes. Norberto organized a committee of three women, consisting of the grand matriarch herself, Doña Trinidad; his wife, Beatriz; and a cousin, Mariquita Lopez-Mota, mindful that he needed some consensus for so delicate a task. First choice in the list of convents was La Concordia, his wife's former school, but the nuns there had stopped the system. The reply at a second convent was also negative, but Doña Trinidad would not give up. The third try, at the Asilo de San Vicente de Paul, was more encouraging. The Asilo was a well-known orphanage in Manila, and it has survived to this day, albeit with diminished esteem. But at that time, it was still a convent of note. The kind Mother Superior, Sor Modesta Zubillaga, received the committee graciously and without batting an eyelash fell in with the plan. However, she warned there were rules that had to be strictly observed. The rules followed the Spanish-Filipino tradition of *delicadeza,* a roundabout system of mores that implied subtlety and delicacy in the conduct of all affairs. The nuns would not openly line up prospective brides; rather, they would permit would-be bridegrooms to observe the girls without stating the purpose of their visit.

The nun rang a tiny bell and a little girl came in, who was then asked to call one of the five candidates to hand her the key to the pantry. After the girl had left, the nun provided information about her family background, general behavior, and character. Another girl was called to bring in the refreshments, another a mantle, and still another a pitcher. To the nun's delight, the guests selected two from among the five. One, Alice Burcher, had the dark Moorish looks of Juanita, Vicente Orestes's first wife, and Doña Trinidad chose her in the hope that a look-alike might help him recover from his loss. The other, Remedios Trinidad, was a typical Filipino beauty, with a golden-brown complexion and soft features.

29

She was tall, though slightly built, and while not beautiful, she exuded grace.

On their way home the three ladies agreed it was the girl with the Spanish looks who had the edge. Still, it was up to Vicente Orestes to make the choice—with the proviso that he consider his family's opinion, and especially the committee's choice.

The next Sunday a *merienda*, the equivalent of an English tea but with Spanish sumptuousness, was prepared for the two leading bridal candidates. The whole Romualdez clan was present, but only the adults were allowed into the living room. The two girls were dispatched by the clever nun, ostensibly to carry an important note to Señor Norberto. They were to await his reply, should there be one. The note, in a tightly sealed envelope, was a blank piece of paper.

For the occasion the Spanish-looking girl donned a pretty party dress, but Remedios simply wore the native Philippine costume. After delivering the note, the girls were invited to eat with their hosts. It was the custom at such Romualdez reunions to hold a musicale—a time when every Romualdez had a chance to show off with a song, a violin piece, a piano rendition. After the family had performed, Norberto, acting as toastmaster, turned to the girls and requested that Alice Burcher sing. She demurely turned down the request, saying she did not know how to sing. What about the piano? Or the violin perhaps? The answer was still no.

The audience was disappointed. How could a prospective Romualdez bride not know anything of music! Then Norberto turned to the Filipina beauty, who hesitated a moment, then gracefully gathered her long skirt about her and sang "Ako'y Ibong Sawi," a classic Filipino love song depicting the tragedy of a felled bird. It was a memorable performance.

The performance over, she was applauded enthusiastically by her audience. Don Norberto then sent the girls back to the convent, with a reply to Sor Zubillaga—an equally blank piece of paper.

Remedios Trinidad returned to her untroubled life at the

asilo. A contemporary at the convent describes her disposition as one of joy and serenity. To her friends, she had a character that was as soft as her beauty. She was industrious and did her work without fuss, cleaning, cooking, and embroidering. She had not a word of complaint or ill feeling against anyone. She was popular with her contemporaries, but she kept a lot to herself. As for the cunning nun who maneuvered the Trinidad-Romualdez match, she was well-known and appreciated by both the wealthy families and the poor of Manila. Through the doors of the *asilo* passed both those who had an abundance of possessions and those desperate for the smallest of mercies. Her roster of benefactors included Mrs. Aurora Quezon, wife of the President of the Philippines, as well as the Zobels, Roxases, Elizaldes, and other top-drawer Filipino families. These rich women came to the convent to buy the embroidered sheets and pillowcases which the boarders did so well. They came, too, for gold chasubles, for wedding dresses, first communion dresses, and matching embroidered layettes for babies. Remedios Trinidad was one of the best embroiderers then. She was also a superb cook, and her delicious sausages and meat loaves were coveted by the moneyed customers. To her friends, she was a gem of a woman who did everything well. But her most precious talent was her voice. Customers who knew of her talent, when they came to buy embroidered clothes, sometimes begged her to sing. Everybody regarded her as a woman worthy of esteem.

Remedios came from a humble background and belonged to working middle-class people without pretensions to wealth or distinction. Her widowed mother was a jewelry vendor from a southern province who traveled to various parts of the country selling her wares. Remedios also had a brother in Manila, but he was a bachelor and it was inappropriate by the rules of those days that she should live with him. Another sister was also a traveling vendor, mostly selling foodstuffs from Capiz. In terms of income, it could be said that her people were better placed than some families of note, including some of the Romualdezes. But trading was viewed with disdain. Upper-class Filipinos, mimicking their Spanish masters, favored artistic and intellectual pursuits.

Nevertheless, Remedios wanted to improve herself and took voice lessons at the conservatory of music of the University of the Philippines. As for her social life, although she was not wealthy, she had some well-placed friends who introduced her to rich Filipinos. She often spent weekends with the Ricaforts, who lived on Evangelista Street in Quiapo, then an upper-class residential district. Through them she met and fell in love with a son of the rich Tinio family. The family regarded her as unsuitable for their son and soon sent him away to the United States for further schooling. Remedios had been snubbed and would have pined away, waiting for his return, if, that fateful day, she had not sung a love song at the Romualdezes'. Even then she still awaited letters from her lover, but these soon became more and more infrequent.

When Vicente Orestes initially pressed his suit, Remedios rejected him. She was engaged, she said, although her fiancé was abroad. The pursuit of an elderly widower with five children was not an attractive offer.

Sister Zubillaga closely watched the courtship and, seeing the match she had so carefully nurtured turning sour, advised Remedios, perhaps much as Trinidad Lopez had been advised by her father confessor, about a life of sacrifice. The nun coaxed Remedios to take on the challenge of caring for the widower and his five children. Here was an opportunity to serve God, to prove how truly unselfish she was if she agreed to marry this lonely man.

After a year of courtship Remedios Trinidad consented to marry Vicente Orestes. A life of sacrifice was the ultimate good to a woman trained and disciplined in the ways of the *asilo.*

Unlike other brides preparing their trousseau, Remedios assembled an array of household articles for Vicente Orestes's children. She embroidered personalized sets of clothes and linen for them and told her prospective in-laws how eager she was to please the children and how she hoped they would like her. The wedding was to take place at the San Marcelino Church at six-thirty on the morning of May 21, 1928. Afterward the newlyweds would host a banquet at the convent's social hall.

But on the appointed day Remedios was roused from her sleep at three o'clock in the morning and told to dress as quickly as she could. Alarmed that there had been some mistake or mishap, she was assured that the wedding was still on. It was being moved ahead by three hours and she was not to ask questions until it was over.

Ever obedient, Remedios Trinidad donned her wedding gown and rushed to the church. The sky was still pitch-black and the windows of the church were still shut when she found the Romualdez clan clustered around the priest. As soon as she arrived, the ceremony began; it was over in minutes.

She was later told that Vicente Orestes's mistress had threatened to disrupt the wedding. Sympathetic neighbors of San Miguel had told Don Norberto of the scorned woman's threats and it had been decided to move the wedding ahead. The woman had warned that Vicente Orestes would marry only over her dead body.

Fate, indeed, unravels mysteriously but if the scorned woman had had her way, she might have done a multitude a favor. For the Trinidad-Romualdez match was not written in heaven. The tragedy was that it was not just another unhappy marriage. It was the mold on which a woman, who would wield power over fifty-four million Filipinos four decades later, shaped her view of the world. Imelda spent the first nine years of her life in the shadow of the unfortunate marriage between Remedios and Vicente Orestes.

While it is true that marriage to the Romualdez widower with five growing children was a formidable challenge, Remedios was optimistic that she would fulfill the role so nobly set up for her by the kindly nun. There was also comfort in the knowledge that the Romualdezes were a staunchly Catholic family, wealthy, and socially eminent. Remedios had improved her social status, and friends at the *asilo* regarded

Vicente Orestes as a good catch. The Romualdez women—wives of Vicente Orestes's brothers and their daughters—were all friends, and to them Remedios confided how she looked forward to her role as wife and mother.

Remedios's first sight of the filth and squalor of the Romualdez household came as a big shock. "Garbage, wastepaper, empty food cans, and assorted litter were swept under beds and chairs. The floor hadn't been scrubbed for weeks. Dirty plates were stacked up with clean plates in the pantry," Remedios told Beatriz, Norberto's wife. There could not have been anything farther removed from the spotlessness of the convent.

Remedios had gravely miscalculated the hostility of her stepchildren. She had thought that she could, like the nuns in the convent, lead her stepdaughters, then in the prime of their adolescence, into the ways of "true womanhood" and that together they would create a happy home. But her attempt to instruct Lourdes, the eldest daughter, in housekeeping was taken as an affront. The young girl, said to be as headstrong as Doña Trinidad, told Romualdez relatives that Remedios would never be welcome in their home. But the key reason stemmed from the fact that Vicente Orestes had not consulted his children about the marriage. Remedios, appearing at the door in the arms of their father, was a nightmare to them. They were not asked to come to the wedding. From the start, their father's new bride was an enemy, and her attempts to befriend them were doomed. Lourdes led her pack of brothers and sisters in rejecting their father's young bride, her nicely embroidered clothes, her cooking, her housecleaning, her convent ways, and her good intentions. She was not their mother and nothing could change that.

This was the life of sacrifice Remedios had been enjoined to take up, and she turned the other cheek to her stepchildren's insults, hoping that her goodness would ultimately triumph. Vicente Orestes was kind to her, and she clung to this fragile crutch in her battle for acceptance in General Solano.

She did not tell him of her difficulties with Lourdes, thinking that they would resolve themselves in time.

She was encouraged anew by her pregnancy with Imelda and, like Vicente Orestes, hoped that the child might bridge the two families. No wonder she was an important child. But the birth of Imelda did little to bring peace between wife and stepchildren, and later between husband and wife.

In the early days of the marriage, Remedios had devised all sorts of schemes to win her stepchildren's love, but these were consistently rebuffed. She even tried to give the girls a livelier social life, warning Vicente Orestes that the girls, then nearly in their twenties, had few male friends. Vicente Orestes, the classic Filipino male of Spanish and aristocratic Manila, believed human needs were his prerogative. His daughters should be content with home life and his loving care. Remedios found this attitude unnatural and chided her husband for being too strict. She was able to persuade him to allow her to take the girls to her hometown in Bulacan for the Barasoain church festival, where young people of both sexes met and made friends. When one of the girls, frustrated with unrequited love for a priest, broke down and created a scandal in San Miguel by running around with too little clothing, it was Remedios who nursed her stepdaughter back to health and enabled her to return home.

But such kindnesses were in vain. She was not the children's mother and nothing could alter that. There were two persons, nonfamily members, who witnessed life at the Romualdez household from Imelda's birth until she was ten years old. They were Marcelo Carpio Cinco and his wife, Estrella Cumpas. They lived with the family in General Solano during those years, and their memories of the rivalry between Lourdes and Remedios are remarkably vivid. As domestic help, they could not intrude or ask about the causes of the fights. But they could not help hearing the angry voices, screams, banging of doors, and muffled crying, which at times lasted through the late hours of night.

Marcelo, called "Siloy" by members of the household,

came to Manila on June 12, 1929, a month before Imelda was born. He was to have been employed in the household of Don Norberto, who had promised to help him continue his schooling in Manila.

It was a common practice then among wealthier Filipinos to employ their poorer relatives or townmates as household help. The workers were given free board and lodging, and some help with school fees, in lieu of wages. The practice benefited some but more often was an occasion for abuse. When Siloy arrived he was told by Don Norberto that he would be of greater help to his brother, Señor Vicente Orestes, who needed a servant in San Miguel.

"I was seventeen years old when I came to Manila," Siloy recalls. "My first impression of the city was that it was so big and full of promise. I felt important knowing I was to live with the Romualdezes. It was well known in Leyte that the family was now wealthy and important in Manila. I did not mind for whom I worked, whether for Señor Norberto or Señor Orestes. The house on General Solano was big and impressive, and they did look prosperous. When I first arrived there were other members of the household besides myself. When I came, Señor Orestes enrolled me in second year high school at the University of Manila."

Siloy studied for a year—the only formal schooling he would receive while employed by the Romualdezes.

When Imelda was about five months old, Remedios went to Leyte and returned to Manila with Estrella.

"I was only ten years old," Estrella relates. "My father was the caretaker of the Romualdez properties in Tolosa. I remember that Señora Remedios had seen me while I was playing in my father's yard. They were talking about conditions on the property. At ten, I did not think I would be of much help to her. I was a young girl with curly hair, and she thought I was very cute. Later she said she just liked me. She told my father that she would take me to Manila and treat me as one of her own." The conditions under which Estrella joined the Romualdez household were even vaguer than those promised

36

Siloy. It was not clear whether she was hired help, adopted daughter, or friend. This often happened because country cousins were so eager for a chance to live in the city. Estrella's parents had complete trust that it was in their daughter's interest to let her go to Manila with Remedios. Estrella gained little from the decision to go to Manila, except perhaps for the satisfaction that she had served Imelda's mother well and that she was loved and cherished in return.

In the first months of Siloy's and Estrella's stay with Vicente Orestes's family, there was no foreboding that the household would plunge into terrible economic misfortune. Nor were they aware of any hostility between Lourdes and Remedios. There was constant bickering, but these arguments were mostly about little things in the course of daily life. Soon, however, these issues mounted to a point where the two women became irreconcilable.

"What I remember distinctly was that Señora Remedios was a fastidious housekeeper," Estrella observed. She wanted the floors soaped and scrubbed and brushed and waxed until they sparkled. When the laundress had finished ironing the clothes at the end of the day, Señora Remedios would go up and fix each of the children's closets. She would put underwear in one row, housedresses in another, and sleeping clothes in still another. When the children left for school in the morning, she would supervise the maids making the beds. She would count the towels, pillowcases, and bedsheets and keep a list to see how many could still be used. When they became worn, she would order bolts of cloth and make new sets since she knew how to sew."

From Estrella's account, Remedios emerges as a model wife in the old Spanish tradition and a credit to the nuns at the convent. Her housekeeping was impeccable. Her humble background and poor education, to Estrella's eyes, were concealed by the elegance of her manners.

Like Remedios, Vicente Orestes's daughters were convent-bred, but the school they attended was no longer of the conservative Spanish tradition. The Holy Ghost College, where

Remedios's three stepdaughters studied, was among the progressive schools geared toward developing a woman's intellect. Lourdes ultimately took up medicine; Victoria, law; and Dulce, education. Dulce later became the superior of her alma mater.

The clash was inevitable. Their upbringing with their own mother, a farm girl from Barrio Tanghas, was not up to the rigid standards Remedios had learned from the Spanish nuns. The girls had grown up surrounded by maids to do their bidding. To them, Remedios's concern for cleanliness and order reflected her servile education at the convent, which did not match their concern for arts and sciences. But all this was rationalization. They were bent on turning her best efforts into failure. When she tried to teach them to make their own beds, they ran, hid, and giggled to mock her authority. Such conditions were tolerable only so long as there was plenty of money to hire help. In later years Imelda's image makers would show similar distaste for Remedios, erasing her from Imelda's life story, in keeping with Imelda's wish to re-create her background and her life.

Vicente Orestes was blissfully ignorant of the growing bitterness between his daughters and Remedios. Siloy recalls that he was a carefree and pleasure-loving man. He was happiest at a picnic by the sea. "Since Imelda's birthday is on July second, Señor Orestes's on July third, and mine on July fourth, they decided on one grand celebration for the week," Siloy recounts. On his birthday the whole family attended mass together, had a sumptuous lunch and the usual family concert. Vicente Orestes played the piano, Remedios sang, and Victoria, a younger stepdaughter, accompanied with the violin. Such a life was what Vicente Orestes wanted—money to spend and time to enjoy it. He preferred leisure to work, romance to reality. He had said many times that if it were only possible, he would prefer a life by the sea. That he was in Manila was not entirely his wish. He had been brought there by the tide of success of his elder brothers and the fact that Doña Trinidad did not want him left behind in provincial Leyte.

Imelda was an innocent victim in the deadly struggle between Remedios and her stepdaughters and husband. Imelda was barely two years old, and although her mother gave her all the care and love possible, her first world could not have been a happy one. Indeed, it was not unlikely that she shared her mother's grief but had only the silent language of a child. Remedios's second child, Benjamin, was born on September 24, 1930, a year after Imelda was born. Relatives and friends ascribe the special friendship of brother and sister to this period when both were allies in their mother's grief.

Between 1931 and 1932 the fortune of the Romualdezes in San Miguel began to decline, delivering the final blow to the marriage and dooming Imelda to a childhood of physical and emotional want. "Maids began to leave, one by one, until there were only Estrella and me," Siloy has said of those early days of impoverishment. "Señor Orestes told me I would have to stop going to school and help in the house. Estrella took care of Imelda and Benjamin. I had to do the marketing and cleaning. Señora Remedios did the cooking and Estrella the washing."

The crisis began with the Bar Questions Leak scandal of 1930. In those days when Philippine public officials were expected to be pillars of moral rectitude, the scandal made big news. Estela Romualdez, daughter of Miguel, the second son of Trinidad and Daniel, was accused of using her office to leak questions of the bar exams. The trial was a long, drawn-out court battle and was covered continuously by the press for more than a year. The Romualdez law office suffered a loss of prestige and clients as a result. Moreover, most of the cases being handled by Orestes at the law office involved former clients of his brother Norberto. Most of them had already been settled, and the firm needed to acquire new clients to keep it going. The scandal made this difficult.

Although Norberto resigned as justice of the Supreme Court and emerged unscathed by the charges against his niece, public confidence in the Romualdez law office was undermined. Miguel, too, had other interests and was well on his way to bigger political and economic success. But not Vicente Orestes. The Romualdez law office was his bread and butter. If there was anything he could not afford, it was a scandal such as Estela had created. He was up to the hilt in hock. He had bought the lot of his house in San Miguel on time and had subsequently taken out two large mortgages. Fees for his children's education, three of whom were in college, had become astronomical. And then he had taken on a new family. He had thrown his last dice on Imelda's birth, with a new garage, a new car, and the best medical care and a luxurious suite for his second wife. By 1932 poverty lay at Vicente Orestes's doorstep.

Without money, the feuding increased in the General Solano household. The stepchildren remained adamant in their disdain for housework, and they did not feel obliged to lessen Remedios's burden. Clashes between stepmother and stepchildren became a daily ritual, and to avoid it Remedios would leave the house as soon as Vicente Orestes had left for work. She took Imelda and Benjamin with her as she sought refuge in Norberto's house, where she poured out her heartache to Beatriz, her sister-in-law and confidante. There she would stay until it was time to return home and pretend once more that all was well with Vicente Orestes.

Beatriz remonstrated with her for not letting her husband know of her problems. This was not what a marriage should be, Beatrix said. In her own, which was a happy one, problems were mutually shared. It was advice Remedios took and would later have cause to regret. Vicente Orestes was unsympathetic. Either she was not able to convey the gravity of her problem or he acted blind to it.

"Whatever unhappiness Remedios had was her own doing," Lourdes says. The harsh judgment is not without truth, for Remedios was a gentle woman. Her softness was her undoing. Had she been more forthright and more demanding, she might have just survived her unhappy marriage.

One night, Estrella recalls, she heard raised voices in the master bedroom and the loud thuds of clenched fists hitting the walls. She heard Vicente's voice first, then Remedios's crying. "Imelda and Benjamin were restless and we were still awake when it happened," she said.

There are few things more disturbing to a child than hearing parents fighting. Nor does it help a child's confidence to see her mother in tears. For nine years Imelda saw her mother cry.

The next morning Remedios told Estrella to pack the children's things. They went to Norberto's house in Ermita and spent the night at the family's summerhouse, no more than a thatch-and-wood structure used by Norberto's family for picnics. The open-air hut was completely exposed to the cold night wind. This was to be the first of many times that Remedios would attempt to flee Calle Solano.

The fight that pushed Remedios to leave the house centered on a relatively minor point. Remedios had put her picture on top of the desk of Orestes's desk in his study. When Lourdes arrived and saw the picture there, she removed it and insulted Remedios. She did it, she said, because her own mother did not display her pictures, so why should her usurper do so? This fact is contradicted by Estrella, who says there were four pictures of Juanita Acereda in Vicente Orestes's study, two of them life-sized. It would have been merely another silly quarrel if he had not taken Lourdes's side. It was Vicente Orestes's nonchalance and open partiality to his daughter that broke Remedios.

To relatives, Orestes's attitude was consistent with his need for a strong woman like his mother. Lourdes was strongwilled, and it was to her that he left the disbursement and accounting of household expenses, to the dismay of his wife. On many occasions, Estrella recalls, her master preferred the company of his daughter and would often take her to the movies without taking his wife. It was this open partiality that finally estranged husband and wife.

Separation was not a course of action casually taken in Manila in those days, especially not by a woman of Remedios's upbringing and temperament. As for Vicente Orestes, he feared damage to his name and respectability. That Remedios took this step was a good indication of how badly she had been treated. Lourdes was unrepentant and said that if she went away, it was her own fault; no one sent her away.

Remedios, Imelda, Benjamin, and Estrella stayed in Norberto's summerhouse, more properly described as a birdcage, for three months. Remedios's mother visited her there and saw the pitiful conditions in which they lived. She coaxed her daughter to give the marriage another try while Norberto talked to Vicente Orestes.

Remedios and Vicente Orestes were reconciled but only for a short time. Remedios was to leave again and hoped distance would make it more permanent. This time she went to Capiz, a southern province where her sister lived. Remedios and her children stayed there for three months.

There was not a day in their Capiz exile that Remedios did not cry, and at night she would let her children sleep with Estrella. "I could hear her crying until early in the morning," Estrella says. Remedios bitterly regretted her marriage, and she tried a number of times over the next years to begin a new life. Had she lived in another country at another time, Remedios would have had the support she needed as a single mother. But this was the Philippines, and the 1930s was a difficult time.

On her return from Capiz, Remedios rented a flat not far from Calle General Solano, but she did not let Vicente Orestes know they were in the city. He soon found them, however, and visited her from time to time. He seemed to have accepted the separation. Soon Remedios moved her little family to a cheaper flat, lugging with them their meager belongings: a wooden cabinet bought in Capiz, a living room set, some tables and chairs bought from a sidewalk vendor. They had no bed.

Estrella, the ever-faithful helper, had become dear to Remedios. Their positions had reversed. Remedios now owed her helper a debt of gratitude; the child she had taken to educate in Manila became her sole aid and comfort. Estrella took care of Remedios's children when she was unable to pay attention to them. Through her years of service Estrella was not paid, nor did she ask to be. She was a member of the family, and she thought she would always be treated as such.

Remedios visited the nuns at the Asilo de San Vicente de Paul and tearfully told them of her broken marriage. She asked for their help so she could support her children. The nuns assured her that there should be many customers for the embroidered dresses, sausages, and meat loaves she made so well. Remedios would bring her wares to the convent and sell them to the nuns' rich clients. Soon the convent was deluged with orders for Remedios's products. Her income increased again when she began selling her embroidery to the then-new department stores.

Estrella handled the money, the housekeeping, and the children so Remedios could devote her time to the business. In a few months their bank account held a substantial amount of savings. Remedios was at last successfully on her own, freed from the shackles of an unbearable marriage.

But one afternoon Vicente Orestes showed up at her door once more, accompanied by Remedios's brother, Ricardo Trinidad. They had not seen each other for some time. "I don't know what they talked about," Estrella has said, "but Remedios was crying, Vicente Orestes looked sorrowful, and Ricardo was making motions, trying to bring them together. The two visitors soon left the house. A bit later Remedios dressed up, and I waited until midnight for her to return home."

The following day Remedios told Estrella to pack their things again. They were to return to the house in General Solano. She asked Estrella for an estimate of their savings and some jewelry she had bought recently. When they reached the house, they found that the electric power had been cut off, Siloy was the only servant around, and the house was as filthy as when Remedios had first seen it. From Remedios's and Estrella's hard-earned money, they paid the water and electric bills and the matriculation fees for Vicente Orestes's children.

A long reconciliation followed, but it would be fatal to Remedios. During this time Remedios bore three children: Alita, on January 3, 1933, Alfredo on July 16, 1934, and Armando on March 6, 1936.

Of all her children, Remedios lavished her affection on Imelda. She was her child of woe. She took Imelda to friends, to the nuns, to relatives when her marriage failed. Imelda was the child pitied, held, and coddled by friends as Remedios spoke of her sadness. She was called "Remedios's cute child," who clapped her hands when her mother laid out the *chorizos* and embroidered baby clothes to sell. "Remedios dolled up Imelda on those errands," Estrella reports. "She would heat a piece of iron metal, test its heat on paper, then roll Imelda's hair on it so it would curl. It was a tedious process, but Remedios did it each time they went out. All Imelda's pretty lace dresses were made by Remedios." In those years of anguish Remedios made a poignant if futile attempt to shield her beautiful daughter from pain.

The money which Remedios brought into the Solano household during this reconciliation did not buy the peace she had wished for. To the first family, she and her children remained outsiders and Remedios's renewed efforts to be accepted were rejected. The two families lived as two camps, those of the first marriage and those of the second. Vicente Orestes, in despair, described to a relative that his life was "between two hells." Try as she could, Remedios was unable to provide a normal childhood for Imelda and her other children. To the children of the first marriage, Imelda, too, was the enemy. Although she attended the same school as her stepsisters, she and her brother Benjamin were brought to school separately by Estrella.

In the meantime Vicente Orestes's finances had not improved, yet he refused to allow Remedios to return to her business while she lived as his wife. He did not, however, object when she volunteered to go to Leyte to try to save a piece of property on Calle Real that was about to be foreclosed for nonpayment of its mortgage. Rents from the tenants were not being turned in by the overseer, and the woman in charge had diverted rent monies to purchase her own properties. The notice to foreclose came abruptly, and there was no time to arrange where they would stay.

Imelda was seven years old when Remedios took her and Benjamin to Leyte. They lived in an empty nipa hut close to the tenants so Remedios could collect the rents. Estrella remembers the hut as no more than a pigeon cage, without even the most basic facilities.

During that year Imelda celebrated her first Holy Communion. She was in the second grade at the time and is recalled by a nun at school as a quiet and very well-behaved child. A picture taken of Imelda in her communion dress, sewed by Remedios, was sent to her aunt with the dedication, *"Sinceremente dedicado a mi Mama Beatriz*—Meldy." A dozen other copies of the photograph were sent to friends and teachers.

With the payments on the property on Calle Real brought up to date, Remedios and the children returned to Manila in 1937. Estrella recalls that Remedios did not want to miss the International Eucharistic Congress in 1937 in Luneta Park. There was considerable excitement over the event, which promised to make Manila an "international" city. As a fervent Catholic, Remedios was anxious for Imelda and Benjamin to witness the historic event. Monsignor Denis Cardinal Dougherty, Archbishop of Philadelphia, presided over the four days of ceremonies. An imposing cross on the Luneta drew thousands of Filipinos from all over the country to kneel in prayer with representatives from fifty-nine countries. Remedios took Imelda and Benjamin there every day of the congress.

Upon her return, Remedios underwent a drastic change. It seemed she had given up hope of ever being accepted by her stepchildren. Nor did she think again of leaving. That, too, had been tried. She had grown tired and weary.

When trouble broke out once more between her and the stepchildren, she asked Vicente Orestes if she could live in the garage and be left in peace, separated from her stepchildren in the big house. She told Estrella that if anything should happen to her, it would be best that the children be near their father.

The tiny garage where Imelda's family moved was dismal, with only a cement floor about a foot from the ground and one small window. The weather was very humid, and the once-plush Berlina that had transported Remedios to the Hospital for Imelda's birth blocked any air or sunshine. Estrella remembers the car had no tires and was missing parts of its engine, but it was kept in the garage until Vicente Orestes's creditors could haul it away. The garage had been used by former maids whom Vicente Orestes had been unable to pay. There were no beds in this garage. Remedios used a table as her bed, while the children had to sleep with Estrella on boards propped up by milk boxes. But Remedios moved in with complete indifference.

Early each morning she would send Imelda up to the big house to ask for the family's daily allowance. There were days when there would be nothing. Creditors, too, often came to the house, and it was Remedios who was often made to face them.

Vicente Orestes, true to his character, seemed to have accepted this arrangement. After dinner with the children from his first marriage, he would go down to the garage to visit Remedios. It was in that garage that the last of their children, Conchita, was conceived. It was puzzling behavior for those who lived closely with Remedios. Estrella could not understand why she did not pick up sewing again or why she persisted in staying in the garage. Remedios kept to herself and did not want to go out or see friends. "At night I could hear her crying and I understood why she did not want the children near her."

Siloy, the other helper, had left the Romualdez household in 1935 and had taken a job at the Silver Dollar Café, a restaurant patronized by Americans. He earned good money from wages and tips. Siloy often visited Estrella, whom he was then courting, and was privy to the miserable conditions at the garage. He often bought foodstuffs for Remedios and her children. Once he bought a new pair of shoes for Imelda after he saw how worn her old pair was. In later years this pair of shoes would be multiplied three thousandfold. Next-door neighbors, too, were touched by the plight of the family in the garage and often passed them food through the fence.

"One evening it rained so hard that even the Silver Dollar Café was under water," recalls Siloy. "I heard from customers that all of Manila and the suburbs were flooded. I quickly left work and hurried to Calle General Solano. If Manila was flooded, the garage would be under water. I thought the children must be cold. When I got there, the water was knee-deep, but no one in the main house had bothered to find out. So I knocked until Señor Orestes woke up and let Remedios and the children in."

Remedios by then was immune to pain. She followed Estrella's advice that she should break out of her self-imposed seclusion in the garage. She cut her hair and visited friends. She put her troubles aside and wore a happy face. Friends who visited her at this time recall her lightheartedness. She even allowed her children to play in the main house. Little did anyone know that this was the prelude to Remedios's final act of defiance.

But first she had to undergo a poignant visit from her former suitor—the Tinio son whose family had rejected her because of her humble origin. For the occasion, it was arranged that Remedios would go up to the main house to pretend that all was well in her marriage. Estrella recalls that Remedios was initially excited, but that she soon held her feelings in check. The meeting between the ill-fated lovers, under Vicente Orestes's watchful eyes, was politely cordial. Why the lover had returned to open a wound after so many years was a mystery. But the visit is remembered by those who loved Remedios because it seemed timed by fate, just before she died.

Shortly after her former lover's visit, Remedios gave birth to Conchita, her sixth and last child, alone. On December 1, 1937, when she felt her first labor pains, she dressed, walked to the corner, and hailed a taxi. This infuriated Vicente

Orestes. She had acted to spite him, he said. He sent the rebellious Lourdes to scour every hospital in the city to look for her stepmother, but she failed to find her. Remedios had succeeded at last in wounding Vicente Orestes's pride by defying his god of convention. She went to the Philippine General Hospital and registered in the free ward, among the poor and the dirty, where no Romualdez would have been expected to deliver a child. She stayed there for three days.

She did not wish to see Vicente Orestes on her return. Her recuperation from this last delivery was slow and painful. To Estrella, who saw her deteriorate, her face had a strange glow of anticipation despite the evident agony. While many Filipino women had by then taken to wearing short dresses copied from American magazines, Remedios persisted in wearing only the native Filipino costume whenever she visited friends after the birth. Alice Burcher, the other girl considered for Vicente Orestes's bride, saw Remedios and was shocked to discover she was living in the garage. She offered to help Remedios find a job, suggesting that she would make a good radio singer.

But Remedios was poised on a final leavetaking. When April came, the garage was stiflingly hot. Imelda, Benjamin, and the rest of Remedios's children tossed about on the wooden boards at night. Sometimes they could not sleep until ten o'clock. When the children were finally asleep, Remedios and Estrella would walk around the block to get some fresh air. They talked about Estrella's forthcoming marriage to Siloy. Remedios had wanted to make a wedding gown for her, but she had been too ill.

On the evening of April 5, 1938, Remedios was restless. They took their usual walk, but Estrella remembers how strangely she behaved. She talked about her life, her sorrows, her disappointments, and her regrets about her marriage. "I still remember how she took my hand and thanked me for my loyalty and service. She said she was sorry that I had not been able to study and that I had not been given any money for some time. She asked me to take care of her children, for she did not think they would be as unfortunate as she had been.

She said, 'If they become important and successful someday, they will look back with gratitude for what you have done for them.' "

Within an hour of their return to the garage, Remedios was tossing back and forth and shaking. When Estrella touched her, she was burning with fever. Vicente Orestes was called, and Remedios was taken to Singian Clinic across the street. She died of double pneumonia on April 7, 1938, less than twenty-four hours after entering the clinic. But to all who knew of her sufferings, her true cause of death was a broken heart.

Before Remedios died, the elder Romualdezes motioned to Lourdes to lead the rest of her sisters and brothers in asking for forgiveness from their dying stepmother. Lourdes hesitated. When she at last touched Remedios's hand, Remedios turned her head away and died. Imelda was not at this death scene.

When she walked with a handful of relatives to her mother's burial site, Imelda was about to turn nine years old—her first world shaped by the unrelenting misery of her parents' failed marriage. Although Remedios had tried to give Imelda as much normal nurturing as was possible under the circumstances, the central drama of Remedios's life was the conflict with her stepdaughter and later with her husband. Attention to her children played a secondary role. So Imelda's formula for looking at the world was marked by the sadness of a child coping with a grieving mother and a distant father.

Sadly, Imelda would claim to remember none of her tragic childhood. This denial of her past would bring grave consequences—first, to the Filipino people; and second, to Imelda and her husband, Ferdinand Marcos. Imelda and her sisters and brothers—the vanquished—moved to the enemy camp. They were handed over to the care of Lourdes, who was not expected to encourage memories of Remedios. For years Remedios would be a forgotten woman, found only in other people's albums, until Imelda became First Lady of the Philippines.

CHAPTER TWO

The Rose of Tacloban

REMEDIOS'S DEATH FORCED VICENTE ORESTES to face the truth—the city and the rat race were not for him. The game of playing rich Romualdez was up. In November 1938, almost seven months after Remedios's death, the General Solano house was put up for sale. Ironically, the buyers who enabled the Romualdezes to save the property from foreclosure were Remedios's close friends, the Ricaforts, from whom she had often sought comfort. Named as the sellers in the deed were Vicente Orestes Romualdez, who owned one half of the property, and the rest of his children by the first marriage, each having a share of the other half. The furniture, except for a long narra table, was also sold. The Berlina was finally towed away by the car dealers.

On the brink of bankruptcy, Vicente Orestes returned his family to Leyte. The move sealed the fate of his branch of the family and cast them forever as poor relations to the rich Romualdezes of Manila. This change in family status would be critical to Imelda's development and would set her ambitions even more firmly.

Vicente Orestes's aim was to live in semiretirement, oversee the Romualdez properties in Leyte, and live off the harvest revenues from the coconut farms. The economic prospects of this enterprise were dim, for no matter how large the properties in Leyte, coconut farming could hardly ensure a large income. The yield of the land was as much at the mercy of typhoons in the monsoon season as at the whim of the tenant farmers.

The only bright spot in the family's return to Leyte was their use of Norberto's elegant house in Gran Capitán. But this comfort, too, would not last. During the next ten years Vicente Orestes would be forced by financial difficulties to keep his family moving until they finally settled for good in a Quonset hut in Calle Real. There Imelda would blossom from the sad child of General Solano to the Rose of Tacloban.

Imelda's neighbors in Tacloban beam with pride when they speak of her childhood among them. A carpenter who outlived several wars and wives in Calle Real recalls her fondly: "What a sight Imelda made then! She wore dresses that reached down to her ankles. Those dresses must have been her mother's, because they were four or five sizes too big for her. She was a happy young girl and always in the streets with her hair all rumpled. Her cheeks were ruddy with too much play under the sun. She climbed guava trees and played boys' games. Even as a child she was energetic. It was a sight to see her walk to and from the school. How different she was from her elder stepsisters! They were snooty. They did not talk or mix with us neighbors. But not Imelda. She was a friendly kid." The carpenter also saw Imelda as First Lady, with her magnificent clothes and jewelry and a retinue of security guards, accompanied on visits to Leyte by wealthy and powerful people. It was inevitable, he says, to compare what he saw long ago with what she became. To him, it was a beautiful rags-to-riches dream. He was happy to catch even a whiff of her car's tires as she passed through town.

For much of her youth Imelda passed by this carpenter's house on her way to the Holy Infant Academy, a convent school run by Benedictine Sisters. The old wooden structure of the school with its Spanish *barandillas* still stands today about four blocks away from the Romualdez house. At this provincial school, Imelda was a mediocre student. She is remembered best for her voice and was always called on for solo numbers, but was considered a social outsider among the hard core of brilliant and active students.

Home to Imelda then was a ramshackle wooden hut, lacking the basic amenities, as did most of the neighboring houses on Calle Real. Imelda often joked about their primitive toilet system and the shed they used for a bathroom. When the Americans landed in Leyte during World War II, Vicente Orestes and Imelda went to the army camp to ask for surplus materials to improve the house. They may not have been much, but the improvements gave the Romualdez family in Calle Real some comfort. Plywood was used to make room partitions, galvanized iron went into a new roof, and landing mats served as the kitchen floor.

Imelda often spoke of her poverty, but only to close relatives. She described how her mouth would water whenever she saw neighbors who had margarine with their bread for breakfast. In her home breakfast was limited to a native roll and black coffee. The roll would not wait for late wakers, either. Food was strictly rationed, and any child who wanted more was reprimanded with "only those who work should have meat." She remembers that her father used to save his coins in a bamboo pole so he could afford a leg of ham when Christmas came. "If we had a slice of ham, then it was a feast."

As president of the neighborhood association, after the essential provision of rice, sugar, and salt had been rationed out to the different families, Vicente Orestes would often ask for the leftovers for his big family, a colleague recalls. The children, too, were wont to ask favors. It was Imelda who was often sent to buy food for the family from a store just a few yards from their home. The owner still remembers her, carrying a rusty lunchbox and pleading for a little extra each time she bought food.

At school, too, Imelda had to face the fact of their humiliating poverty. She was frequently among the students who had to apologize for late payments. The registrar's office was located in a central hallway of the school. It was the practice then to post a list of students who had not paid their tuition at the end of each semester, and Imelda's name was often on it. Once, her younger sister, Alita, was absent for almost a week, and a nun decided to visit the family. "As soon as the door opened, I could feel a mutual embarrassment. I could not believe this was where the Romualdez girls lived. Imelda did not ask me to come in, and I understood," the nun recalls.

After this visit the nun saw why Imelda did not often participate in activities that involved money and why she avoided the company of the wealthier students.

Happy and spirited to a carpenter, shy and painfully self-conscious to the nuns, Imelda in Tacloban lived the life of millions of Filipino children in the provinces. The difference was that she was a Romualdez. The name was both shield and scourge. Prying townfolk were in a quandary about the Romualdezes of Calle Real. If they were Romualdez, then they could not be too poor, but how come they seemed so poor? Imelda herself has often said, not without bitterness, that they were very poor. If there was ambivalence about their status in Leyte, the responsibility lay with Vicente Orestes. He had retained an honored position in the community because of his name and legal profession, while keeping himself detached from the "commercial" activities of Leytenos. Even when many families of merchants prospered after World War II, Vicente Orestes would have nothing to do with such mundane activities. He sat leisurely reading throughout the Japanese occupation, a typical gentleman of the old school. Even his deanship at the local university was largely honorary. Although English was the medium of instruction, his classes in legal history and legal bibliography were conducted in Spanish. He was a true romantic whose view of life did not include regard for wealth and power, but rather a deep appreciation for rustic life. "I remember how Papa loved picnics," recalls a younger sister of Imelda. "Almost every weekend we would take a jeep and go to the family beach in Tolosa. We were always a big group of girls with the inevitable train of admirers. Papa would ask the caretaker to broil fish. We swam all day and feasted on the fish, *palawan* [tuber] and *silot* [young coconuts]. We sang our voices hoarse. We slept in a nipa hut by the beach and returned to Tacloban the following day." As First Lady, Imelda would build a palatial summer home on the same beach to which Vicente Orestes had brought his children.

Vicente Orestes would be miserable when they returned to Tacloban the next day. Work, competition, and the acquisition of wealth was to him utter folly, and that in part explains why his family remained poor, despite their considerable land holdings. Back in Tacloban he faced the scrutiny and judgment of the world. Very soon even his honorary position would become precarious.

Shortly before the war broke out in 1941, Norberto died of a heart attack in Palapag, Samar. Consequently the house in Gran Capitán was formally transferred to his widow's estate. Vicente Orestes wrote to Beatriz to say he was willing to pay a small sum as rent to cover at least the taxes due just so his family could continue to live there. The request was granted. Unfortunately, he did not explain to his children the special arrangement under which they lived in Norberto's elegant house.

In 1946 Norberto Jr. wrote his mother that he wished to build his future in Leyte. Beatriz immediately informed Vicente Orestes of her son's plan so he would have sufficient time to vacate the house. The request came as a thunderbolt to Vicente Orestes and his family. Characteristically, he made no effort to move, hoping that Norberto Jr. would not come. When he did arrive with his family, they had to pack both families in the house. This uncomfortable situation sparked open hostilities between the two branches of the Romualdez clan. To Imelda, it was garage time once more, but the face of the enemy had changed.

Not only did Norberto Jr. lay claim to his father's house; he also claimed his father's excellent reputation in Leyte. Norberto's son, who would later become governor of Leyte, displaced Vicente Orestes from his honorary position as town patriarch. His return to Leyte was traumatic for Imelda. Leyte, like the house in Gran Capitán, was too small for two Romualdez families to claim supremacy.

But Imelda kept her bitter feelings about Norberto Jr. well-hidden. Imelda was breaking out of her cocoon; during those deceptively unchanging days in provincial Leyte she became aware that she, too, had a weapon—her beauty. When General Douglas MacArthur landed in Leyte, she was a budding beauty of sixteen, and it did not take long for her townmates to recognize this asset among them. She had the most beautiful face in town, and she was tall—an uncommon combination in the far-flung province. But to those who saw her in those days, it was the softness and innocence of her face that were most appealing. A schoolmate of Imelda at that time, Mary Chapman, of a Filipino-American family, wrote from San Francisco:

> We all called her "Meldy." She was soft-spoken and very feminine. I think she did come along to the many army camps we visited. She sang and was very popular among the Tacloban music lovers. I do not remember names of camps. But an American chaplain chaperoned us.
>
> One event I remembered very well was the anniversary parade on October 20, 1946, of the liberation of the Philippines—the landing at Leyte of the U.S. forces. Imelda was "Miss Philippines" and I was "Miss America." We rode together on a float.
>
> Meldy looked radiant as "Miss Philippines." Little did I know that she would be First Lady in later years.
>
> One thing that is so clear in my mind was Meldy's beauty. Her skin was silky white and I always envied her because of that (me with my freckles!). Also she had the striking quality of the truly beautiful woman—simplicity. With her features, no makeup was needed. Her face was "serenely lovely . . ."

Imelda stepped from the shadows into stardom as the Rose of Tacloban. At sixteen, she enthralled battle-weary American GIs with her singing. The camps were located in the northern fringes of Tacloban, in a district called Quarry. There was hardly any town fiesta, civic parade, or fund-raising benefit to which she was not asked. She was the much-in-demand singer at weddings. When politicians and dignitaries came, Meldy was the girl to represent the town and present the lei. Even then she came close to becoming the First Lady when President Elpidio Quirino was the guest of honor at the Divine Word University. Imelda had sung in the program given in his honor, and the elderly widower, enchanted, confided his interest in Imelda to his secretary of finance, a Leyteno.

Her popularity and assets did not escape a cousin who was running for congress. Danieling Romualdez, son of Miguel, shrewdly put her on his side in the campaign. He belonged to the Nacionalista Party while his cousin Norberto Jr. was in the Liberal Party. When Danieling came to Leyte to campaign, he brought Imelda with him to visit political leaders and made her sing at political meetings. Her political education was under way.

Indeed, Imelda learned her first political lesson when she ran for president of the student council at St. Paul's College, where she was to graduate with a bachelor of science degree in education. That was 1951, only three years before her marriage to Marcos. It was a mock competition, her rival from the school of law said, because Imelda had the election all sewed up. The Department of Education had eight hundred students and the Department of Law had only two hundred. She was the most popular figure on the campus, and he was put up as a scapegoat. The school had riotous fun, and when Imelda won, her first "achievement" was to hold part of the three-day college feast celebration in Tolosa, a first in the school's history.

Her ascendancy into town beauty and official greeter had given Imelda the needed boost to gain self-confidence. The bitterness that had arisen from Norberto Jr.'s return to Leyte was momentarily shelved.

At this time Imelda had her first intimations of a sense of destiny, for as soon as she became the Rose of Tacloban, she began to be dissatisfied and to doubt what future provincial Leyte could offer her. In an autograph book dated February 8, 1946, Imelda wrote that her favorite motto was "To try is to succeed." Her ambition then was more modest. She wrote that all she wanted to do was "any desk work or to be a ----" (four spaces which presumably meant wife). Her hobbies were singing, reading, going to movies, letter writing. Her favorites were Ingrid Bergman, the song "You Belong to Me," the rhumba, the musical piece "Rhapsody in Blue," fried chicken, ice cream, and the colors pink and blue. What on earth made her write that her favorite subject was lovemaking, no one really knows. What was revealing was the dedication she wrote to the owner of the autograph book:

Dearest Polly,
Keep that smile on your lips, but always keep that tears (sic) in your heart!

Love,
Meldy

To a close friend, Imelda opened up her heart and spoke of how important security would be to her in deciding whom to marry. She had a long line of suitors, who could by Leyte's standards give her the security she yearned for. Among them were a rich Chinese merchant and the owner of the local sawmill, both of whom offered her a comfortable provincial life. But Imelda turned them down. The security she aimed for was beyond them. At the same time, she did fall in love with a doctor who fitted the description of her ideal man—he was tall, dark, and handsome with deep-set eyes. The romantic part of her, like a true daughter of Vicente Orestes, hankered for a quiet life by the sea, a loving husband, and four children. But the man was Protestant and she was unable to convert him to Catholicism as her family required.

Fate was drawing her away from sleepy Tacloban. Friends and relatives from Manila constantly reminded her of the opportunities that awaited a woman of her beauty and talent in the big city. In 1947, when her cousin Loreto visited Tacloban, she suggested that Imelda study singing in Manila. It was only a question of time.

Imelda's opportunity came in the shape of an unwanted suitor and concrete offers from Loreto and Danieling to help her get started in the city. Without these factors, Vicente Orestes would never have allowed Imelda to leave Tacloban. The suitor, a man several years Imelda's senior, who had lavished the family with gifts and threatened violence when she turned him down, had taken to watching for her at the gate of the Chinese school where she taught. Alarmed, she told her father about it. It was then decided that Imelda should go to Manila. Loreto's offer to arrange singing lessons for Imelda was accepted. Danieling, who happened to be in Tacloban at the time of the suitor's threats, assured Imelda's father he would find a job for Imelda and said she could stay with him in the meantime. A shrewd politician, Imelda would have many uses for him.

Thus did Imelda leave Tacloban, the small town that made her queen, that helped her bury the memory that she was Remedios's deprived child. It was time to go. Leyte had nothing more to offer Imelda. Little did Danieling realize that the trembling country cousin he accompanied on the fateful journey to Manila, with five pesos in her purse and a dirty *tampipi* (a poor native suitcase), carrying only a few skirts and blouses, held the formula for one of the most remarkable success stories in Philippine political history.

Not even Imelda knew then what power she was capable of achieving. She was twenty-three, an age when most Filipino women are under great social pressure to marry. Although women are highly regarded in Filipino culture, a good marriage was and is the most certain step up the social ladder. So while the matter was left unsaid, marriage was uppermost in Imelda's mind, particularly because she was now aware that her beauty could be put to considerable use in Manila.

But Imelda was ambitious not just for herself but also for her brothers and sisters, Remedios's children. Though they were on peaceful terms with the Vicente Orestes's first family, they remained the "other family," the garage people, whose future and fate depended on what Imelda, the eldest child of Remedios, made of herself. Some of her stepbrothers and stepsisters were already established in the city, but Imelda's siblings could expect no help from them. Remedios's children, as they had been when she was alive, were very much on their own.

Imelda had no notion of how she would break through and make a fortune in the city. Manila in the 1950s was a highly structured society, with sharp divisions between the very rich few, a struggling middle class, and the masses of poor. Manila's Four Hundred consisted of top-drawer families with political dynasties, such as the Zobels, the Aquinos, and the Cojuangcos. Members of the middle class with varying degrees of wealth also aspired to be part of Manila's elite. As for the poor, they did not count at all.

When Imelda arrived in Manila in 1952, the hot topics involved a political murder scandal and the controversy over permitting cockfights in Manila. Two decades after independence the nation seemed to be going in futile circles, unable to take hold of itself and to tackle the urgent task of developing a viable economy to feed, clothe, and house its millions. The nation's politicians were perpetually locked in conflict, unable to agree on what was best for the nation. The political divisions of the country between federalists and nationalists, between pro-Americans and anti-Americans in the 1900s, and the split on parity rights in the 1940s had diverted the best Filipino minds from the task of nation-building. Without true purpose, Filipinos substituted a false sense of well-being for hard work, preferring to look nice rather than to create wealth. It was an artificial society destroying itself by conspicuous consumption while paying lip service to the poor.

Imelda lived at this time at the home of Danieling Romualdez, who was then a considerable politician, representing one of the most populous districts of the country. This was the rich and socially prominent side of the Romualdez family, and Imelda considered herself lucky to be asked to live with them. Or so she first thought.

Danieling's house in suburban Manila dazzled her. It was grand in the manner of Manila's elite, with luxurious furniture, winding staircases, air-conditioned bedrooms, modern kitchens, and even a bathroom suite—a world away from Calle Real's primitive toilet and kitchen with steel matting on the floor. Imelda ardently wished to belong to the rich Romualdezes of Manila. But such dreams were rudely checked on her arrival. Danieling's wife, Paz, of the wealthy Gueco family, received her cordially but promptly put her in her place. Imelda was shown the room she was to share with another poor relative (on the Gueco side), who acted as housekeeper and nurse to the children. Imelda was to Paz Gueco, perhaps with finer distinction, more or less what Estrella had been to Remedios—she was a country cousin seeking accommodation with rich relatives in Manila. Such cousins were not treated as servants or hired help, but neither were they considered part of the family. Paz was related to the wealthy Aquinos of Pampanga, a relationship that would have later significance in Imelda's life. In greeting Imelda, Paz had unconsciously touched a raw nerve from Imelda's past. She was an outsider once more.

She told other cousins how Paz showed her the cabinets and told her that if they were too narrow for her clothes, she could use the children's cabinets in the next room. Imelda wondered what clothes she was referring to, since she was holding only her small *tampipi* with a few skirts and blouses. But her hostess persisted. If she had any jewelry or money, she should give it to her for safekeeping, Paz continued. It was a most generous gesture, but Imelda did not know whether to laugh or to cry. "Instead I kept my dignity. I smiled, waved my hand, and nodded. Despite my poverty, I was still a Romualdez," Imelda later recalled with humor to cousin Loreto. At the time she felt hurt and resentful, but she suppressed her feelings. She allowed this incident to pass, as she did many others. She was the sweet daughter of Remedios who knew her place and how not to seem to take offense. Whatever Paz, Danieling, Loreto, or any other Romualdez of Manila had to say, she was too engrossed to care, too bent on making good for the sake of her family.

As Danieling had promised, a job was found for Imelda the very next day, at the P. E. Domingo music store in downtown Escolta, then Manila's commercial center. The job was as a receptionist–salesgirl. Imelda fit the bill with her good looks and lovely singing voice. Customers invariably asked her to play the piano as well as sing the lyrics of a particular piece before they bought anything from the shop.

She took on the modest job enthusiastically. Being in the Escolta meant being in the center of activity. It was a beehive of banks, swanky department stores, and prestigious offices. Anyone of any importance did business on the Escolta in Manila of the 1950s. Politicians, journalists, and industrialists were drawn each morning to the coffee shop of the fashionable Botica Boie, a two-story drugstore owned by the prominent Araneta family. Over a cup of coffee, as a popular newspaper column described it, these men made news in their midmorning tête-à-têtes. Indeed, seven years after the war, it could be said that the Escolta was the lifeline of Manila, and by corollary, also of the country. It might have been a lowly job, but Imelda first got her bearings in this music store.

One afternoon, while Imelda stood waiting for customers by the window, she saw a face she immediately recognized. It was Estrella. They had not seen each other since Remedios's death and their departure for Leyte. Estrella had heard through the Romualdez family grapevine that Imelda was working in a store in the Escolta. Since she did not know exactly which store, she had peered through all the store windows.

More than ten years had passed since Estrella and Imelda had last seen each other, but what they shared was beyond physical change and could not be blurred by time. Estrella, who was now thirty-four, looked old and haggard and had six children. Her husband, Siloy, the other faithful helper in General Solano, had lost his job in the Silver Dollar Café and was struggling to support his family with odd jobs. To Estrella, Imelda had changed radically from the little girl she had once held in her arms. She had become a ravishing beauty at twenty-three, a far cry from the child her brothers used to tease as flat-nosed.

It was an affectionate reunion. Imelda asked Estrella to wait on one of the shop's stools until five o'clock so they could have a long chat at one of the local snack bars. They talked of old times, but Estrella clammed up when the conversation veered toward the bitter memories of life with Imelda's mother. They talked of happier things and happier times, each shielding the other from the hurt that inextricably bound them together. Imelda described her life in Tacloban and how she had come to Manila. They would have gone on and on, but it started to get dark.

"Imelda exclaimed she had to go because Danieling's house was far away and she had to take two jeepney rides," Estrella recalls. She lingered a while to watch Imelda go until she was lost in the crowd of thousands of office workers leaving the Escolta. She did not know at that moment that she had lost Imelda forever, that she would never come so close to her again.

Had she known, Estrella said, she would have talked to Imelda about her mother's sufferings and Remedios's last words—that should her children be successful, they would repay Estrella for the sacrifices she had made for them. Estrella could neither read nor write, having spent her learning years coping with the sorrows of Remedios Trinidad in General Solano. At the time, however, Estrella was more concerned with Imelda's stories of life in Leyte than with sad memories. She and Siloy were planning to return to the province. At least they would not starve in Leyte, with the sea to fish in and the fields in which to plant rice.

Commuting was the lot of city folk, and in Manila, it was hell in the overcrowded jeepneys and buses. But if Estrella had given up the fight, Imelda had just begun, and she was prepared to suffer any hardship to succeed.

Her career as a salesgirl on the Escolta did not last long. Vicente Orestes, eager to know how his daughter was faring in the city, decided to visit Manila. Typically, he found the job degrading and was appalled that Imelda had to sing for customers. "Are you trying to sell my child?" was how he confronted his nephews. To appease the old man, Danieling and Eduardo quickly found Imelda a clerical job at the Central Bank. What Vicente Orestes would not know was that Imelda would also be made to sing by colleagues in the bank in exchange for dinner invitations. The bank's older employees and staff supervisors would joke and boast about the Romualdez girl working under them. Imelda had no way of getting to know the right people in Manila, although there were a number of eligible bachelors in the bank. Her circle of friends at first were the other clerks or visiting Taclobanos.

Imelda had relied too much on the help of the Romualdezes of Manila to give her the break she needed. It took her only a few months to realize that she was very much on her own and that she had to create her own opportunities. For sympathy and support, she turned to Ricardo and Adoración Reyes, friends of her cousin Loreto. Every day after work, Imelda would go to their house in scruffy Sampaloc, an inner Manila district that had seen better days. There, Adoración gave her voice lessons and hope and dreams. After a few lessons Adoración was convinced Imelda had talent and persuaded her to enroll at the College of Music and Fine Arts at Philippine Women's University, under a special arrangement that would put her on the register while Adoración would continue to give her free lessons.

Adoración was enchanted by Imelda's beauty and lack of affectation at the time she met her. She looked forward to helping her develop her talent and thought she could become a famous opera singer.

Other music students at the conservatory where Imelda went for her voice lessons with Adoración recall how she kept

63

apart and never lingered to make friends. Here, too, as a special student, she was an outsider. Among students at the university, Imelda left behind fragmentary impressions of herself: . . . beautiful but unexciting . . . did not want to discuss any relatives or family except the Danieling Romualdezes . . . always reading . . . wore old-fashioned dresses and slippers . . . tried hard to sound like a city girl but ended up being corny . . . Imelda once said to a fellow student, "If she married, he would have to be a very intelligent man." During this period Imelda sang only once onstage, in the intermission at a cousin's recital. But she was grateful for even such a small chance, and she prepared for it as if it were her own recital. The Reyeses saw Imelda's usually hidden tenacity, and it moved them deeply. "I really admired her, but at the same time I pitied her," recalls Adoración. "It was sad to see this strong desire to be a success in such a young girl. I am, after all, conservative at heart. When I looked at Imelda, I thought what she really needed was to be loved and protected. But the sort of ambition she had was frightfully serious—it should be only for men, tough men."

Soon after the recital, Imelda appeared on the cover of the Valentine's Day issue of *This Week* magazine, the Sunday supplement of the Manila *Chronicle,* a national daily. The caption accompanying the picture read, "The lass from Leyte—Imelda Romualdez." It was a big event in Imelda's life, and she wrote to a sister that the editor had discovered her while walking along Aduana Street. The editor would later deny that this was the manner in which he met his cover girl, but it revealed Imelda's penchant for dramatizing her experiences to family and friends. "Imagine, taking a picture of me, as though I were some person, when I am only a country girl from Tacloban," she wrote.

One morning thereafter, Adoración's husband read an announcement soliciting entries for the Miss Manila contest. The winner would represent the city as Miss Philippines at the International Fair Exposition. In an inspired moment he submitted a photograph of Imelda dressed in a polka-dot dress, with her hair gathered in two knots and tied with ribbons, just as she had looked when Adoración first met her on the Escolta. He enclosed a letter signed by him and his wife as representatives of the candidate, Imelda Romualdez.

Imelda acquiesced to Ricardo's idea, and did everything she could to see the project through. She tried to get some support from her rich cousins, Danieling and Eduardo, but each declined, reflecting the ambivalence of Manila's elite toward such events.

By the 1950s beauty contests had lost some of their social cachet and were the game of both the rich and the would-be rich. If a really rich girl won the title, she endowed it with the prestige of her name and her wealth. But if a social climber won the title, there was reluctant if polite acceptance. It took a long time before upstarts in Manila were truly accepted by the top families, a fact that would dog Imelda long after she was the wife of the President. In keeping with this ambivalence the rules governing beauty contests were quite vague. Ostensibly the Miss Manila competition involved both the acquisition of the highest number of votes (which had to be bought, requiring a lot of money) and selection by a committee of judges (when, hopefully, standards of beauty came into play).

At this point the Reyeses began to have second thoughts and realized the whole idea might be folly. They did not have the resources to support Imelda's candidacy, and they had expected the Romualdezes to pitch in. Despite the odds, Imelda decided to stay in the contest. This was a revelation to Adoración. Although she was aware of how ardently Imelda wanted to succeed, she did not know the extent of her ambition. It would take some time for Adoración to realize it had no limit. She was unable to reconcile this grit and single-mindedness with the shy provincial girl whom she met in the Escolta. They asked her to reconsider, but Imelda was adamant. "Her eyes were red, and her lips trembled, but she said she did not care if the Romualdezes did not help her. She would not back out, and she pleaded with us to help her," recalls Adoración. In this battle Imelda showed unusual tenacity and willingness to overcome all obstacles—a pattern she would continue throughout her career.

Thus did Imelda and her two kind friends embark on the campaign to win the title of Miss Manila, a victory that would mark a major step in her ascendancy to political power. For it was the publicity and the controversy that accompanied her participation in the beauty contest that brought Imelda to the attention of two persons who would change her life.

The plan was to make a list of friends who could be called upon to help in their campaign. Imelda rightly calculated that they would have to rely on people with a wide circle of friends, preferably with connections at City Hall or the mayor's office. Among those whom Imelda asked to help in her campaign were the medico-legal officer of Manila's City Hall, a senator, an educator, and a prominent businessman. Curiously, it was not clear whether one had to win the contest with a majority of votes or whether it was simply at the mayor's discretion. This confusion would benefit Imelda.

At the outset of the campaign, the candidates were told they would have to be sponsored by some organization, preferably a school. Adoración was dismayed. How could they ask Philippine Women's University to sponsor Imelda when she was not even a regular student? Adoración recalls spending sleepless nights worrying how they would meet the requirements, much less find the time and money to join in the social functions and public appearances of the candidates. The school was owned by the Benitezes, a prominent and wealthy Filipino family. They, too, would be future recipients of Imelda's largesse as First Lady. To Adoración, they were her bosses and she dreaded asking for their help. But there was no turning back.

Adoración and Imelda approached the head of the department of music, hoping that she could mediate with the Benitezes. There was some embarrassment when Imelda was introduced as Miss Romualdez. Why could she not ask for her relatives' help? When it was explained that she was only a poor relative from the provinces, the school bosses looked her up and down. But if the country girl did not own even a single gown, how could she compete with Manila girls? Imelda put on her sweet and silent face. This was not the time to fight back. She was there to win, and she had to hold on. When the insults were over, Mrs. Francisca Benitez, then the president of the school, agreed to sponsor Imelda, but sternly refused any help other than use of the school name. Imelda was told to borrow a gown from the collection in the costume room.

The rest was up to Imelda and the Reyeses. It meant arduous days of soliciting votes, knocking on the doors of friends and acquaintances. Imelda was her own best advertisement in making personal calls and pleading her own case. Adoración remembers those days with trepidation as she often had to leave her young children behind while she and Imelda toured the city. "Sometimes we would wait hours in the sun and eat in dirty restaurants. Imelda always offered to pay for the meals, but we knew she was hard up, so we turned it down. A sandwich or two, coffee—that's what we used to have. It was literally a hunger campaign. But we were happy to help the girl who had become dear to us. Oftentimes the Romualdez house in suburban Manila would be locked by the time we finished vote soliciting and Imelda had to spend the night with us."

But their ragtag enterprise failed to muster victory. A not so pretty and less glamorously named coed, Norma Jimenez, gained the most votes. The brief announcement in the Sunday newspapers described Miss Jimenez as the daughter of a government prosecutor and a member of several student organizations from various universities and colleges. Imelda was in tears, but she would not accept defeat. She shed her provincial shyness, and the genes of Doña Trinidad in her came to the fore as she prepared for her final battle. On her behalf, the Reyeses filed a protest claiming that no representative of the mayor of Manila had been present at the canvasing of votes, and that the winning candidate had powerful backers who had rigged the contest. A friend at City Hall further advised them to see the mayor personally.

On the day they were to meet with the mayor, Adoración's baby fell ill. It is a cardinal rule in the unwritten Filipino code of conduct that women, particularly single women, do not go on their own to ask a man for a favor. It was bad form and perilously so in the case of a mayor whose keen eye for beautiful women was well-known. Adoración was downhearted and expected that they had finally reached the end of the battle, that at this point Imelda would have to give up. To her surprise, Imelda went alone. Even then, her granite will was in place and equal to the test.

At the mayor's office Imelda used the infallible weapon of tears to get the mayor's sympathy. She cried as she told him how hard they had worked and that it seemed so unfair that she should lose. The chivalrous mayor, always accommodating to women, melted. This was no ordinary woman. Before him was a beauty in tears; he did not have the heart to refuse her.

The next day the newspapers published the mayor's decision: "Mayor Lacson yesterday disowned the choice of the International Fair Board and named Imelda Romualdez of Philippine Women's University as Manila's official candidate for Miss Philippines." In a letter to the director of the International Fair, Lacson charged that certain rules of the International Fair Contest were violated and that as mayor of Manila he would nominate the city's candidate for International Fair.

The beauty contest committee named by Mayor Lacson adjudged Miss Romualdez winner of the Miss Manila title with 655 points, Norma Jimenez and Amparo Manuel tied for second place with 453 points each. His action upheld a protest previously filed on behalf of Miss Romualdez before the Fair board of directors by Dr. A. Singian, Dean H. Quesada, Adoración Reyes, and Lilia Garcia.

The International Fair Board, however, would not be shoved aside by the blustery Manila mayor and refused to accept his ruling. Their reply to the mayor in the continuing press war was to declare Manila an unchartered city for the purpose of the beauty contest, meaning that the mayor of Manila, unlike the mayors of other cities, could not choose his city's candidate. Miss Jimenez had received more votes than Miss Romualdez, and hence had been declared winner.

Thus, both Miss Jimenez and Miss Romualdez were present at the International Fair presentation. The former represented the International Fair and the latter Mayor Lacson.

The public, however, was more interested in the major candidates than in the squabbling between the Miss Manila candidates. Little did anyone know that the event would be Manila's first model for the political maneuvering at which she would become so adept.

It did not really matter to Imelda whose winner she was or how she had won. She was in the limelight at last, and the publicity generated by the controversy only added to the curiosity about the beautiful Miss Romualdez. Two figures who would alter Imelda's life came to know of her through this controversy: Harvard graduate Ariston Nakpil, an architect, and a young congressman, Ferdinand E. Marcos.

Of the two, Architect Nakpil had the upper hand, by Manila's social standards. He had all the qualities that made for acceptance in Manila's highly stratified society at that time— old wealth, a respected name, a dashing figure, an overseas education. He had just returned from studies in modern architecture at Harvard University, the Cranbrook Academy of Arts, and the Fontainebleau School of Fine Arts in France. He was a top-drawer figure and eligible bachelor—a good catch for anxious Filipino maidens. The Juan Nakpils gave a huge dinner dance in honor of their newly arrived son, and it was duly documented in the newspapers as an affair of the affluent and the celebrated in Manila society, a world still closed to Imelda.

As Muse of Manila, however, she was soon invited to model at fashion shows, and organizers of civic gatherings kept her on their invitation lists. Not long after the Nakpil party, Imelda was asked to be an usherette at the Grand Derby, another red-letter event in Manila's social calendar. Ramon Valera, a top couturier, asked her to model some of his gowns, and, thinking she was a rich Romualdez, offered her the gown at half price. She politely turned it down, even at the ridiculously low price of two thousand pesos. "Where would I get that kind of money with my salary of two hundred and fifty pesos a month?" she asked a cousin. At this point, she was on the fringes of Manila's exclusive elite, but being only a poor relative of the Romualdezes, she lacked the wealth to be fully accepted. She still had to find the fortune that would buy her way in to this rarified company. She soon had many suitors from Manila's population of bachelors and dated quite a number of them, including the precocious journalist and budding politician Benigno Aquino Jr., a cousin of Danieling's wife, Paz.

When Ariston met Imelda, his curiosity had already been aroused by the beauty contest controversy. Ariston's mother, the beauteous Anita Noble, was herself the first Miss Philippines, so his interest in Imelda was in keeping with a family tradition. Imelda was as beautiful as he had expected, but also, as he put it later, "quite raw." However, Imelda's lack of sophistication did not deter Ariston. It made no difference to him that she was provincial or only a poor cousin of the rich Romualdezes. For this she was grateful, and Imelda confided in him. "Given a chance, she impressed me as a person who would work hard to get herself out of the rut," Ariston recalls. "Looking back, I would say that was perhaps her outstanding character trait—willpower."

To Imelda, Ariston was her key to social acceptance, the factor that would at last put her on a par with the rich Romualdezes and Manila's top-drawer society. She spent weekends on the Nakpil farm in Batangas and went on her first trip to Baguio during that summer of 1953. The Nakpil party stayed at the Pines Hotel, where a year later Imelda would be engaged to Marcos. Then, however, it was only Ariston who mattered, and she excitedly told relatives and friends about him.

The couple wanted to marry, but there was an impediment. Ariston had married a complete stranger while dazed with alcohol, and was trying to get an annulment at the time he courted Imelda. The Romualdezes soon came to know of his marriage and considered Imelda to be "having an affair with a married man," and brazenly so. Never mind what the circumstances of the marriage were or that Ariston had never lived with the woman concerned. He was married. Imelda's cousins were anxious about what would happen if Vicente Orestes learned about the affair. When confronted, Imelda denied it. At the same time, she asked another cousin, who had some contacts at the Vatican, to help Ariston win an annulment. Letters between Imelda's friends further underline the seriousness with which she regarded Ariston. She did not go to the Tacloban town fiesta on June 29, 1953, the most important day of the year in Leyte. "Well, Meldy is still here," a friend in Manila wrote. "She would not go to the fiesta because she is crazy about him even with the impediment. She would not like to leave him."

Soon after, Imelda wrote of Ariston to her father and asked for his blessing. She knew he would object, but she took the chance because she was determined to marry him. Vicente Orestes did not bother to reply; rather, he took the first flight to Manila and tried to talk her out of the marriage. His Old World values rejected even an annulment. He told his daughter that even if the previous marriage was annulled, she would remain only a mistress to Nakpil in his eyes.

Imelda returned to Tacloban in November 1953, torn between a recalcitrant father and a romance that seemed the fulfillment of her dreams. "Imelda said she misses somebody there," a friend wrote in a letter to Manila. "Somebody close to her heart. I think I agree with you about Meldy's being so in love. She's different now—there's love in her eyes when she talks about him." But whatever Imelda had told friends, l'affaire Nakpil was doomed. "My father was not only mad about the whole thing, he was furious," Imelda's youngest sister recalls. "The whole family was against the match. I knew that

Imelda would change her mind. With the whole family against it, I don't think she would have gone on with it."

It was not the first time that Imelda demonstrated her devotion to her family. Conchita recalls that at another time when she thought she had overheard a suitor discussing honeymoon plans and had run away to cry, Imelda assured her that she was not getting married and that if she ever did, Conchita would be among the first to know.

On December 10, 1953, Imelda returned to Manila with a troubled heart. She was not getting any younger and had it not been for the impediment, Ariston would have been everything she had wished for in a husband. She was adrift once more. The security and acceptance she had hankered for all her life were again out of her reach.

It was at this time that she met Ferdinand E. Marcos.

At the time Ferdinand and Imelda first crossed paths, he, too, was attempting to penetrate Manila society. But while Imelda followed the social route to acceptance, Marcos chose political power as his road to elite society. Even though he was a congressman and his father a former congressman, at the time, Marcos's name conjured images of neither influence nor wealth. In the 1950s politics was not, as a rule, the preoccupation of the Philippine aristocracy. That was left to the parvenus and the struggling classes. The wealthy, landed families had their men in politics to do the work for them. The not-so-rich feigned such behavior, while young talented men and women opted for more glamorous careers as executives or in family corporations. The hard core of Manila's aristocracy revolved around families with Spanish and Chinese ancestry or enormous wealth. The Romualdez name derived its prestige more from a combination of political, civic, and intellectual accomplishments than from wealth. However, the Romualdezes did have homes in respectable districts and comfortable incomes to support membership in Manila's social circles. Their children attended exclusive Catholic convents and spent their vacations in their summerhouse in Hong Kong. By Manila's standards, the Romualdezes and Nakpils were in, and the Marcoses were out.

Marcos had the will and tenacity to face this challenge, even if his attempts to climb the social ladder were sometimes clumsy. There is a story told of how he presented himself at the law offices of the late mayor of Manila, Arsenio Lacson, then a star politician. Marcos had come to apply for a job wearing an immaculate white sharkskin suit and shiny white shoes. The colorful mayor, who had himself set the pace for informal fashion, sent the aspiring Ilocano lawyer away for being improperly dressed for the job.

Marcos, like Imelda, was provincially bred. He was the eldest son of Mariano and Josefa Marcos, both schoolteachers from the barren northern province of Ilocos Norte, known for its hardy and frugal people. At the University of the Philippines, where Marcos was acknowledged to be a brilliant student, he could not mix with students from Manila's best social or political circles. He was grateful for the friendships of a few such schoolmates, however, some of whom he rewarded amply when he became President of the Philippines. The most famous of these was Roberto Benedicto, from a sugar-growing family in the south who would take charge of the sugar and communications monopoly for Marcos when he became dictator.

To Marcos Manila's social and political barriers were simply challenges that he eagerly faced with his greatest asset—ruthless ambition. From the little that is known of his family background (most of it from commissioned writers), it would seem that Marcos owed his obsessive ambition to a domineering mother who continually pushed him to excel. He was sent to the University of the Philippines at great cost, considering his family's meager financial resources. At this time the Marcos family suffered a financial and personal crisis, the resolution of which revealed much about Ferdinand's will to succeed. Marcos lost his scholarship money just when his father had lost a second congressional election against an arch political rival, Julio Nalundasan. Marcos went home to ask for money to continue his schooling, but was met with news of his father's defeat and the family's lack of funds. Three nights after the elections, Nalundasan was shot dead while brushing his teeth.

Marcos was charged with the murder. The trial revealed that the murder weapon had come from the university armory where Marcos was a national champion in small bore weapons. He was convicted in the lower courts but was acquitted in the Supreme Court after he defended himself and after the main witness's testimony was discredited and no further prosecution evidence was accepted. Justice José P. Laurel, who penned the decision and was said to have been similarly accused in his youth, wanted to give Marcos the same chance he had received.

Thus began Marcos's political career. The sensational murder trial gave him national publicity, a feat he would never have achieved as merely a brilliant student. The scandal drew Marcos to center stage and set him in pursuit of the highest office of the land. Marcos openly told friends that he sought the Presidency in order to "vindicate" his name. Herein lies the key to his political motivations. The drive toward political success would not clear his name. Despite the acquittal, those who followed the proceedings have never accepted Marcos's innocence. What Marcos wanted to demonstrate in his pursuit of the Presidency was that he could survive any odds, even a murder charge. In this he was a true child of the barren, bristling, dry land of Ilocos, which sometimes bred desperadoes for whom the only valued life is their own.

This was the man who proposed marriage to Imelda at their first meeting on the night of April 6, 1954. He knew nothing about her, except that she was beautiful and came from a powerful family. "It was love at first sight," Marcos later told eager reporters, and they believed him.

Nothing could have been more characteristic of the ambiance of Manila in the fifties, a time of American-imported moonlight and roses and Coca-Cola culture, than the Marcos-Romualdez courtship and marriage. It was, society editors sighed, so romantic. Typically, what caught the fancy and imagination of the public was not Marcos's political maneuver in marrying a Romualdez, but the romantic tale of how a dashing congressman courted and won the hand of the beautiful Miss Manila in eleven days.

The partnership that would pillage the Philippines for twenty years began when José Guevara, a congressional reporter, introduced Marcos to Imelda in the cafeteria of the Philippine Legislative Building on a balmy April evening. The beauteous Miss Manila had accompanied her cousin-in-law Paz to collect Danieling Romualdez, then the Speaker Pro Tempore of the House. Unprepared for the encounter, Imelda was dressed in a housedress and slippers. But as fate would have it, the Speaker sent word asking Paz and Imelda to wait for him in the cafeteria. Although Marcos had read of Imelda in the Miss Manila controversy, it was only then that he met her. He was immediately captivated by her beauty, but worried that the reporter's introduction would not be taken seriously by Imelda. He then asked Congressman Jacobo Gonzales to make a second introduction. When Imelda stood up, Marcos took note that he was half an inch taller than she and without further ado asked her to marry him. She was taken aback at his boldness and did not know whether he jested. The wily congressman was not her ideal man. She liked her men tall, rich, and aristocratic, with hands unsoiled by politics. Marcos, the short nouveau riche congressman, was none of these, while Nakpil, the scion of a distinguished family, was. Still, Imelda was eager for a secure marriage, and this made her vulnerable.

The next day Marcos sent her two roses, one fully spread, the other still a bud. It was, he said, an Ilocano's message of love—the bud represented his young love for her, and the fully spread rose stood for the love he hoped to develop if she so willed. After the roses came boxes of chocolates, gifts of books, and frequent telephone calls. Curiously, Guevara avers, Marcos did not see Imelda at all from the day he met her in the Legislative Building to the day before they drove together to the summer capital.

"Ferdinand visited her only once in Manila, during the entire eleven-day courtship, and that was the day before we left for Baguio," recalls the congressional reporter for the Manila *Times.*

Marcos's plan was to bring off a coup—courtship, proposal,

and marriage—by the end of the congressional recess for the Lenten holidays.

When he met her, Marcos had asked Imelda where she was spending the holidays. When Imelda replied that she was going up to Baguio, Guevara butted in, winked at Marcos, and said, "Well, then, come with us."

The congressman quickly took up the cue and pressed the invitation: "Yes, why don't you come along since we are also going up?" Marcos had just bought a shining white Plymouth, financed in part by illegal contributions he had received in return for his "sponsorship" of Chinese businessmen seeking valuable import licenses, in contravention of official government efforts to encourage sales of locally made goods. Even then Marcos was in the thick of political corruption.

Imelda initially turned down the offer, but Marcos persisted. At the end of that late-afternoon visit arrangements were made with the Speaker Pro Tempore's family that Imelda would ride with the congressman and the reporter she had just met. "I was a little surprised that she finally accepted," Guevara confessed. Her decision to ride up to Baguio did not gibe with a simple country girl's ways.

Guevara had been half-jesting about the trip to Baguio and told Marcos there was no way he could miss work at the newspaper. After much hemming and hawing, however, the willful congressman prevailed on him to join the party. The five-hour car trip to Baguio which followed, with Imelda seated between Guevara and Marcos, gave the would-be lovers their first chance to establish some rapport. "That five-hour trip set the tone of informality," Guevara has said. "Conversations between the two before this trip had still been strained and stiff. But I suppose after the five-hour trip, cooped up in a car, one can't help but be at least relaxed and friendly." To relieve tension, Guevara played his comic role and would teasingly hold Imelda's hand, an act which Marcos would object to by playfully hitting him on the head.

They took Imelda to the cottage of the Danieling Romualdezes on Congressional Hill and booked themselves a room at the Pines Hotel. The courtship—or what passed for the courtship—now began in earnest. Although not a Catholic, Marcos joined Imelda in observing the Lenten church rites. He played with Imelda's wards, the Romualdez children, and tried to please everyone. Marcos's strategy worked, and Imelda was besieged by a chorus of family members urging her to accept the congressman's offer. "What else do you want? He's rich, still young, a congressman as well! Accept him, Meldy."

But Imelda lent her family only half an anxious ear. She was still in love with Ariston Nakpil. On the night of Holy Thursday, when she was about to succumb to Marcos's offensive, Imelda placed a long-distance call to Ariston in Manila. The call was recorded at two o'clock in the morning. Nakpil remembers the call but says Imelda gave him no hint whatsoever that she was about to agree to marry Marcos. He sensed something was awry, however. Imelda went out with other men, and he knew that he could not and would not stop her from marrying someone else. But he expected her to be more forthright with him. Even then, more than a decade before she became co-dictator of the Philippines, Imelda could be ruthless.

The next day, Good Friday, Imelda slammed the door to an uncertain future with Nakpil and took fate into her own hands. She accepted Marcos's marriage proposal. "We were driving along Burnham Park," Guevara recalls. They were again seated as they had been on the drive up to Baguio, with Marcos at the wheel and Imelda seated between him and Guevara. Barely two days before that ride, Marcos had been certain he had convinced Imelda. He had gotten in touch with Judge Francisco Chanco, a former classmate at the University of the Philippines who lived in faraway Trinidad Valley, to ask him for a marriage license. The judge had initially refused, aware of the congressman's reputation. "The judge told Marcos that his career would be ruined, that he was quite satisfied with his success as a justice of the peace, and that he would not let any naughty congressman ruin it," recalls Guevara. But the persuasive congressman ultimately had his way. Marcos had the marriage documents in his pocket as he, Guevara, and Imelda drove around Burnham Park. With Guevara present, the setting could hardly be romantic, nor did the congressman pretend otherwise, for he presented the question quite bluntly, as if it were a business deal. Marcos, too, was engaged to a comely beauty, a Miss Carmen Ortega, who was also a beauty title holder, Miss Press Photography. It was well known that she was the lady in residence at his San Juan bungalow at the time of the eleven-day courtship, and their engagement had been announced in the newspapers only months before.

But the chance encounter with Imelda at the Congress cafeteria overrode other considerations or commitments he may have made. Marcos dissociated romance from the hard realities of politics and as far as he was concerned it was Imelda, the beauty with a name, who would fulfill the role of his wife in his political ambition. The night before he married Imelda, Guevara recalls, Marcos hardly slept. Not a voluble man, he nevertheless kept the congressional reporter awake, talking of his plans, of the Nalundasan murder and his drive to be President in order to "vindicate" his name. He also told Guevara that Imelda was lucky, because she would be the wife of the future President of the Philippines. He was that confident.

"Don't you want to be the First Lady of the Philippines someday?" joked Guevara to Imelda as they drove through the park the next day. Imelda laughed, unsure whether to take the matter seriously. After all, very few people marry on such a basis. But Marcos was serious. He followed up Guevara's "joke" and told Imelda he meant her to be his wife and would she please sign on the dotted line. He whipped the documents from his pocket. Imelda received the papers and nervously whispered to the reporter, "What is the name of the congressman? Is it Edralin or Marcos?"

"Finally I signed that marriage contract," Imelda recounted in a magazine interview later. "It's funny, but I didn't know we were already married. The next day, Holy Saturday, we went to Trinidad Valley to formalize the marriage before Judge Chanco. The judge had finally agreed to perform the ceremony, and the contract was in Ferdinand's pocket. I wired my father." Presumably, what Imelda meant was that the ceremony at the judge's home was merely a ritual. Marcos saw to that, with the signed marriage contract already in his pocket.

It was decided that church rites would be held later. Imelda was to return to Manila and live with the Danieling Romualdezes until arrangements could be made for the church wedding. That night a friend of Guevara's, Eugenio Baltao Jr., rang up their Pines Hotel room and was asked to be the second witness in the civil ceremony. The judge was still unconvinced that the marriage was genuine; he kept mumbling throughout the ceremony, while his wife gathered flowers from the garden to add a fragile ceremonial touch to the occasion.

After the rites the wedding party proceeded to the Pines Hotel for a small celebration. Guevara remembers there was an Igorot (a mountain Indian tribe) dance troupe performing at the supper club, and he whispered to Imelda that Marcos was an Igorot. Imelda turned pale. The joke reminded her how little she knew of the man she had just married. Marcos noticed her crestfallen look and reassured her before she could have second thoughts about the abrupt marriage. "Never mind how fast it happened," he said. "We have our whole lives to be happy together." Whereupon he proposed a toast. It was only later that Guevara told Marcos about the Igorot joke and that Imelda may have believed him.

The easy interpretation of the eleven-day courtship was that Imelda, a poor country girl, was no match for the predatory skills of a hard-boiled politician, determined to catch his prey. But there is another, equally compelling interpretation. If the famous Marcos coup-marriage was accomplished in eleven days, it was because Imelda did not resist it. She was a willing, even active, prey, determined to be caught. After all, she was in love and engaged to another man, and her acquiescence to Marcos's style of courtship, from a five-hour car ride on Ash

Wednesday to signing a marriage document on Good Friday, was not country-girl behavior. Like Marcos, she entered the marriage with cold calculations. Beneath the idyllic romance lurked two wounded figures from the past, both driven by the will to win power and acceptance. When Marcos stood in court at age twenty-two, accused of the murder of his father's political rival, Imelda at age nine was standing on the outside of her father's first family, consigned to live in a garage only a few steps from the glitter of Malacanang Palace. They had come together to erase their tragic pasts, but during that fateful spring of 1954 they simply showed the world a picture of a "perfect marriage" between a beautiful, talented woman and a hard-driving, brilliant man.

CHAPTER THREE

Imelda's Transformation

IN THE LITTLE HOUSE in Calle Real, Vicente Orestes and Conchita both awoke on Easter Sunday unaware that Imelda's marriage to a congressman was national news. "It was good I woke up early that morning," Imelda's youngest sister recalls. When she went out to buy bread, a neighbor told her that Imelda's marriage was "on the front page!" It was big news to a sleepy town in the rural Philippines, especially when it concerned Meldy, their very own Rose of Tacloban. But to Conchita, the news meant she had to move fast to make sure that her father did not see the newspaper before a telegram arrived. It would hurt him terribly if he saw the newspaper without having received any word from Imelda, for like most Filipino parents, he regarded his children's marriages as family affairs.

Luckily, the mailman soon came with the much-awaited telegram. "Its message," Conchita recalls, was, "one which asked for forgiveness and blessing. When I handed Papa the telegram, even without knowing its contents, he went inside his room and stayed there for a while before he came out again to show me the telegram."

He was misty-eyed and said that he was happy because at least "Imelda was not getting married to Ariston Nakpil." Still, he was sad to lose a daughter, the first one in his family to marry. "And besides," he said, "who is this Marcos, anyway? I do not know him." That whole day Conchita and Vicente Orestes ransacked the house, looking for articles in old magazines to learn all they could about Marcos. Luckily, he was featured as one of the year's outstanding congressmen in a magazine they had kept only because Danieling was also listed. That day Vicente Orestes read the article over and over again, to know better the man whom his daughter had decided to marry after only eleven days.

Indeed, the beautiful daughter had married an important man. The article said Marcos was a top-caliber student and had graduated *cum laude* from the College of Law of the University of the Philippines. He was also a war hero and a brilliant trial lawyer.

But there was much that Imelda's father would not learn about Marcos from the article or from any other public source of information. He would not know or understand why, with so much virtue and talent attributed to him, Marcos could never quite come to terms with himself. Throughout his public career he would be accused of all sorts of chicanery and machinations to portray a greater-than-life image of himself. Indeed, Marcos could never be content with what he was or what he had. It was a double-edged character flaw, which not a few observers would wrongly perceive as a source of strength. Marcos could not be just a brilliant student—he had to be the best. He could not be just a war hero—he had to be the most decorated hero ever. He could not be just a politician —he had to be President of the Philippines. Nor could he simply be President—he had to be dictator for life. Imelda had married an obsessively driven man.

On her return from Baguio, Imelda flashed an expensive ring for her friends, then mostly her own circle of provincial folk living in Manila. "He courted me with diamonds," she boasted. The engagement ring was encircled with eleven diamonds representing the eleven days of courtship. To Imelda, marriage to Marcos at that time meant no more than the end of material want. She looked forward to the peace and security of life as housewife to a rich man. But Marcos had other plans, beginning with their wedding.

Every detail in preparation for the church wedding was designed to mark his debut as a Presidential contender. His marriage to a Romualdez was played up by the society-page editors. Marriage to Imelda, with her glamorous name, gave Marcos an aura of success and a measure of acceptability to the Philippine aristocracy. Press releases played up Imelda's relationship to Danieling Romualdez, the Speaker Pro Tempore of the Senate, but her own father was only briefly noted. Almost nothing was said of her maternal origins.

Ramon Valera, the country's foremost couturier, whose clothes Imelda had once modeled but could not afford, was commissioned to do the wedding gown. Even Imelda was not allowed to see the design. Valera was simply instructed to create the best that money could buy for a rich congressman's bride. The couturier came up with a fabulous creation that was drooled over by the press. The gown was made of nylon tulle and white satin, with a wide skirt covered with leaves in nacre sequins, seed pearls, and rhinestones. The sleeves were also of satin and traced in chenille. The wisteria motif was repeated on the panels and the mitts, and a long satin train trailed at the back. A veil of illusion tulle was held in place by a small coronet with white feathers covering the ears and framing the face.

Marcos, unable to produce either a baptismal or a birth certificate, was baptized at the Lourdes Church twenty-four hours before the wedding, with the parish records keeper as his sponsor. His father was Aglipayan (the Independent Church of the Philippines, which broke away from Rome at the time of the revolution), but his mother was a Catholic.

On May 1, 1954, a thousand guests, mostly members of Congress, cabinet officials, and a sprinkling of notable society figures, crowded into the San Miguel Pro-Cathedral to witness the wedding. "We were there," Conchita said. "But the family stayed in the background. We knew it was more of a political wedding." Imelda carried her mother's prayerbook, given to Remedios at her own wedding. But to the society editors it was no more significant than such details as the wedding cake, depicting the Legislative Building, or the rope motif on the bridegroom's wedding ring. Only one other person could have reminded Imelda of the symbolic significance of Remedios's prayerbook—Estrella, the faithful helper —but she had no place at a wedding designed to destroy memories of the past.

Of the immediate members of her family, Imelda's stepsister, Remedios's arch enemy Lourdes, was the only one who did not attend. She was in the United States pursuing advanced medical studies. It was just as well. It is an unwritten law in Filipino families that the member with the greatest advantages is recognized as the head of the clan—just as Norberto was titular head even when the old man Daniel was still alive, because of his scholarly achievements, the important offices he held, and the relative prosperity he had achieved. Imelda's "substantial marriage" broke Lourdes's claim to leadership of the family. In time, the shift occasioned by Imelda's marriage would bring the once-lowly outsiders from the garage to power.

After the wedding the guests were treated to a sumptuous breakfast in the lavish setting of Malacanang Park, which was made available to the Marcoses by one of the hosts, then President Ramon Magsaysay. It pleased Marcos immensely that his wedding reception should be in the Presidential palace where he hoped he would one day be lord of the manor. What many of the guests did not know was that the manicured lawns of the park had once been the bamboo-covered land of the tubercular Daniel Romualdez of Pandacan and that such land had financed the education of his three sons in Manila, one of them Imelda's father. Decades ago the three boys, laughed at and scorned as provincial folk, had crossed this land several times each day on their way to school.

84

A sense of history was irrelevant to the bubbling politicians, engrossed in their personal fortunes and the machinations to advance them. The aspirations engendered by Filipino nationalists led by the intellectual Senator Claro M. Recto were drenched once more by the more urgent task of containing an advancing pro-Communist Hukbalahap Movement. The fifties saw the intensification of the cold war. In the Philippines the hero of the hour was the American-made former defense secretary turned President, Ramon Magsaysay, who had successfully repelled the Huks. His presence as host of the wedding reception was a score for the ambitious Marcos.

The conversations among the guests, however, were centered on solemn pronouncements condemning "turncoatism" as an evil to be expunged from the political scene, and a round of congratulations to the lucky groom, who belonged to the Liberal Party, for having bagged the niece of the Speaker Pro Tempore of the Nacionalista Party. After all, the incumbent President himself was a former Liberal, the defense secretary of the previous administration who won under the sponsorship of the Nacionalistas. And three decades before, Quezon, the master of political strategy, had laid down the maxim: "My loyalty to my party ends where my loyalty to my country begins." To Marcos, what could be more innocent than a wedding to herald the drop of his hat in the Presidential ring? It was also all too soon overlooked by the cunning politicians who had come to wish the couple well.

Vicente Orestes and Conchita, who remained on the sidelines of Imelda's political wedding, returned to Leyte to await the couple's return from their honeymoon, at which time Marcos would be properly introduced to the "Leyte folk." Vicente Orestes was glad to leave Manila. Imelda's wedding at the San Miguel Pro-Cathedral had brought him too close to the house in General Solano and its bitter memories. In that church he had attended the last rites for both of his late wives.

Moreover, the stage-managed presentation of Imelda as aristocratic heiress of the powerful Romualdez family not only embarrassed him; it presented him with a very real problem.

While society editors congratulated the congressman for stepping up the social ladder, Imelda's family was in a quandary about where they would billet the couple when they visited Tacloban. Orestes's remodeled Quonset hut without the most basic amenities was hardly up to the standards of a rising congressman. The town folk joined ranks to help solve the problem. It was finally arranged that the Marcoses would stay in a rich neighbor's house.

But Vicente Orestes had his little revenge on Marcos. He refuted the congressman's magnanimous estimate of his worth by giving him a guided tour of the Quonset hut in which Imelda grew up. "I was so ashamed when Papa had to show our primitive toilet," she later told friends.

The trip to Tacloban was a revelation to Marcos. Although he had known that Imelda was a poor relative of the Danieling Romualdezes in Manila, he had not known she was "that poor." After the civil rites in Baguio, he had immediately given her a thick envelope of cash for whatever she might need before the wedding, but he was not prepared for the Quonset hut in which she had grown up. Indeed, he knew little about her lack of sophistication. A friend who had come to visit the couple remembers how Imelda ran to greet her without putting on her shoes, a habit she carried from her provincial upbringing. Shoes were to be preserved from wear and tear and worn only on special occasions. She was halfway to the door when she realized Marcos was staring at her. He did not say a word. Imelda quickly returned and put on her shoes before greeting her friend. She was, as Nakpil aptly described her, "absolutely raw." To him, Imelda was herself, an honest country girl, and she had confided to him her bitterness about her rich relatives. Although of a prestigious family, he accepted her poverty and provincialism.

But to Marcos, who fell in love with Imelda's impressive family name, the Rose of Tacloban had a long way to go. He was the superior being, the master who would mold Imelda to his likeness and make her the patrician wife he wanted. He had married an aristocratic heiress, and she had to live up to that image.

Early in her marriage Imelda still retained the "goodness of heart" her mother had bequeathed to her. Upon her return to Leyte, she was worried about her father's health. He had grown thinner and now coughed and complained of frequent chest pains, but no one could persuade him to see a doctor. He feared surgery. Nevertheless, Imelda insisted that once she was settled in Marcos's home in San Juan she would send for Vicente Orestes so he could receive the best medical attention.

Nor did Imelda forget her original goal in moving to Manila. She summoned her brothers and sisters so they, too, could improve themselves in the city. Marcos helped her in this enterprise. At this time, Imelda remained close to the Reyeses, the couple to whom she owed so much. She eagerly told Marcos all about her foster parents, as she called them, and about how they had helped her win the Miss Manila contest. At her prodding, the newlyweds visited the couple's modest home in Sampaloc, where Imelda had slept many nights.

To the music teacher, Imelda and Marcos were like any newly married couple—romantic and solicitous of each other. But clearly, the congressman had the upper hand, with Imelda following his bidding. Marcos teased his new bride and told the Reyeses how childlike she was. "I gave her a bunch of keys, and even now she does not know which key belongs to which door," he said. At the end of the meal he had just enjoyed, Marcos told Imelda she should learn how to cook. That evening Imelda betrayed no hint of the future First Lady who would try systematically to erase all traces of her past, including her friendship with the Reyeses. It was a happy get-together that evening, and the Reyeses felt sure that their friendship with Imelda would last.

Marcos's reputation in knowledgeable political circles was that of a hustler. Although he carefully nurtured a scholarly and statesmanlike image, it was no secret that he sponsored avaricious Chinese businessmen in Congress, and he was known there as a wheeler-dealer. Moreover, as a representative of the Solid North, where money and violence ruled, his capacity for ruthlessness was well-known. He belonged to the league of lords from Ilocano fiefdoms, which controlled the so-called tobacco monopoly, the economic backbone of the region. His sprawling bungalow with its magnificent gardens in smart suburban San Juan on Ortega Street was a showcase of his success. Here he entertained both politicians and businessmen. A superstitious man, Marcos regarded his house as lucky and prohibited Imelda from making any changes in its appearance. Throughout his political career, the house served as Marcos's campaign headquarters.

Imelda was unprepared for her husband's posh life-style. Her beliefs and attitudes had been shaped by her simple life in Tacloban, by her father, and by the nuns at the Holy Infant Academy. If she was ambitious and coveted the good things in life, she had nevertheless been brought up to pursue these goals within a moral framework. Moreover, years at the bottom of the heap had taught her the virtues of meekness, humility, and resignation—virtues that were ill-suited to Marcos's ambitions. She was initially overwhelmed by the wealth of the Marcos household. There was money hidden all over the house, stacks of bills bundled up in sacks and piled like wastepaper in cabinets.

The former bank clerk now had to run a household that paid a cook several times more than her own former monthly salary. In the beginning Imelda was repelled by the waste and extravagance. Since she was not doing anything most of the time, she asked Marcos if she could cook instead and be paid for her work. Marcos was amused with the deal and played along with his wife's innocence. Late one night a man visited the house, and after some hours of huddled whispers, Marcos asked Imelda to give the man five thousand pesos. She later learned the man was one of Marcos's hundreds of political leaders, which explained why the house was always bulging with cash.

The next morning she told Marcos, "Gosh, I have such a hard time cooking. My nails are all broken, and I get only a hundred and twenty pesos a month. A man comes along from out of the blue and you give him five thousand pesos just like that."

Marcos laughed. "It's your fault. Who told you to work hard for only a hundred and twenty pesos?" Imelda told this story to a cousin to explain how she learned to live as the wife of a rich congressman. From then on, she never again felt guilty about money or what it could buy. Soon there were rumors in the political grapevine about the spendthrift Mrs. Marcos.

But Imelda's most pressing battles at this time concerned her internal conflicts regarding her roles as wife and daughter. Late in 1955 Imelda sent for her ailing father, who, Conchita wrote, was dying. The doctors had diagnosed his chest pains as advanced lung cancer. He spent the last days of his life in the Marcos home in Ortega, where Imelda gave him the attention and care of a devoted daughter.

The unsuccessful son of Doña Trinidad de Romualdez found solace in the peaceful home of his eldest daughter by Remedios Trinidad. But it was a bittersweet happiness. Nothing could wipe out the tragedy of the hell in the house in General Solano. To the end of his days, Vicente Orestes wished that the children from both his marriages would reconcile and make peace with one another. As in the past, Imelda had to give way to her father's wishes, to deny her bitterness in order to be accepted and to survive. Her repressed anger and sorrow came out in the form of sweetness and generosity. During Vicente Orestes's last days Imelda called Lourdes, then in the United States, to come home and help her dying father. Imelda did this to please Vicente Orestes.

Vicente Orestes's last words to Lourdes said everything about his willful romanticism. "I wish Remedios had seen the way you took care of her children." He died at one o'clock in the afternoon of September 30, 1955. His tired, lined face relaxed, and he was once more the handsome, aristocratic, and destructively romantic gentleman of his youth.

But despite Imelda's generosity and magnanimity, the children of Vicente Orestes's first marriage retained sole title to his properties. Had Imelda not married into wealth, she and her brothers and sisters would have remained as dispossessed as in the days when they lived in the garage. The only likely explanation for Vicente Orestes's oversight lay in a kind of profound carelessness based on the assumption that his second set of children would be able to fend for themselves or would be protected by Providence. It is an irony that he died in Imelda's home, for as Mrs. Marcos, Imelda would be driven to make up for the shortcomings and disappointments of her childhood.

To Marcos, who accepted Imelda and her family into the Ortega house, there remained the fulfillment of the role he wanted his bride to play in his pursuit of the Presidency of the Philippines. When Marcos lavished Imelda with gifts and money, it was because he expected she would become the political asset he had hoped for when he first decided to marry her. Contrary to claims made by image makers, Marcos did not transform Imelda into an accomplished wife at the outset of their marriage. Money could not buy the kind of personality change that Marcos demanded. Expensive clothes and diamonds could not hide the wounded, simple girl from Tacloban.

Moreover, despite her name and marriage to a congressman, she did not belong to that exclusive society of aristocratic women who traced their friendships to schooldays or to their parents' friendships. As far as Manila's top-drawer society was concerned, Imelda was an outsider. She soon discovered that winning beauty contests was far simpler than coping with well-bred, wealthy women. She felt out of place and lacked the confidence to overcome such social barriers, a talent she would later cultivate with success in international café society.

She held on to her old friends at this time and asked Adoración to come out on lonely Sunday afternoons when Marcos was on a political campaign. When she heard that an old friend from Tacloban had settled in Manila, she tracked down her address and had her called for by the chauffeur. This particular friend stayed with Imelda in the hospital when she gave birth to her first child, Imee. "She told me that Marcos presented her with a diamond, saying, 'For every girl one diamond, and for every boy two diamonds,'" the friend recalls.

But Marcos's solicitousness had a price. He kept pushing her to be other than what she was—to be sophisticated, well-read, a woman with worldly élan. He did not want a simple wife; if he had, he could have chosen any number of equally beautiful women for such a role. She was a Romualdez, an aristocrat, and most of all, a prized political asset.

For a time Imelda resisted Marcos's pressure to keep in step with his life-style. When she became First Lady, she often looked back to those first months of her marriage as a turning point in her life. The push to adopt a new, assertive, and self-confident persona completely overwhelmed her, and she escaped into excruciating and interminable migraine headaches.

Of this crucial phase in Imelda's marriage, Conchita, her sister, says, "There were times when she would just collapse and her feet would grow numb and cold. We would take her to Dr. Barcelona, who lived nearby." Like her grandmother, Imelda cracked under the pressure of difficult times. She suffered a nervous breakdown. But unlike Doña Trinidad, who had her rest cure by the sea, Imelda was sent to a psychiatric hospital in New York. Although the Marcoses have freely admitted she underwent psychiatric treatment, very little is known about what exactly precipitated her "nervous breakdown." Her publicists cavalierly dismissed the event by noting that Imelda recovered soon after a Jewish psychiatrist told her that the cure lay within her own will. According to Imelda's official biographer, the psychiatrist prescribed daily autosuggestion to convince her that she could change and become the wife Marcos wanted her to be. The thrust of the therapy seems to have centered on convincing Imelda that it was in her own best interest to resolve the conflict, as the success of her marriage depended on it.

In any event, Imelda returned from the psychiatric treatment in New York a new person. She began to cast away her inhibitions and uncertainties and expressed a willingness to try new things, to become more extroverted, resourceful, and adaptable. She became willing to meet and study the people who ran the government and the people who put them there, to further Marcos's career. All would have been well except that her new personality did not include acceptance of her past. One of the major casualties of Imelda's new personality was the sad little girl in General Solano. The change bode well for Marcos, but it would later carry devastating side effects for the people of the Philippines.

In 1960, after the birth of her youngest child, Irene, with little more than sheer determination Imelda dedicated herself to the task of becoming the exemplary politician's wife that Marcos wanted her to be. She made her debut at the Liberal Party convention of that year where she met Connie Manahan, one of the few senators' wives whose friendship she cultivated to get into the political "in crowd." Mrs. Manahan recalls, "Imelda was very simple, very unaffected. She wore conspicuous jewelry and expensive-looking clothes. But when she moved and talked, she quickly gave away her provincial background."

Social success continued to elude Imelda at that time. She was much too eager to please and became the subject of rather nasty gossip. It did not help that she declared rather naïvely that Marcos would run for the Presidency of the Philippines. Those who met her relate how she would refer to Marcos as "Marcos" when she talked about politics and "Ferdie" when she talked of him as her husband. One source of such gossip lay in Imelda's tendency to make dramatic entrances—a habit she would continue in more imperial days when her husband was dictator. But then she was only a congressman's wife, and such entrances were regarded as presumptuous, especially by envious women. "When she entered a room, she usually would pause at the door, and the women would nudge each other and raise their eyebrows to prepare for a collective snub," narrates Connie.

Among the senators' wives who resented Imelda's incursions into traditionally rich society was Lily Padilla, wife of

Senator Ambrosio Padilla who also had Presidential ambitions. The rivalry between the two women was another favorite topic of gossip about Imelda. Although it was said that the cause of the fights had to do with a contest as to who had most real jewelry, the deeper reason could have been that the young senator had once visited Leyte and urged Imelda to come to the city. Worse, the beauteous Rose of Tacloban did not hesitate to call on him once she was in Manila, to the consternation of Lily, who although a beauty herself, found the visit disconcerting. "She used to come to our house," a Padilla daughter narrates, "with her skirt held together by a safety pin. But we were kind to her." When Imelda was later featured as a blue-blooded aristocrat in *Life* magazine, she would accuse Lily of authoring an anonymous letter to the editor which refuted the claim of an upper-class background. Whatever the root of the animosity, stories of this quarrel illustrate Imelda's isolation in her first attempts to break into high society. She would continue this hopeless quest throughout her reign as First Lady, for Imelda the international jet-setter would never achieve true acceptance in Manila's high society.

Up to the time of the campaign for Senate Presidency, Imelda's so-called political prowess was provincial and crude. Marcos needed two votes to wrest the Senate Presidency in 1963: those of Senators Manuel Manahan and Raul Manglapus. Winning their votes was Imelda's first assignment, and she pursued it with characteristic tenacity and zeal. "Pacita Manglapus and myself were sometimes embarrassed by Imelda's solicitousness," Connie Manahan relates. "Once when she saw that we were standing at a party, she carried chairs by herself to offer to us." If the sight of a regal-looking woman carrying chairs to other women seemed awkward, it showed that Imelda would do anything to help Marcos become Senate President, a crucial step to the Presidency. Throughout that campaign Imelda wooed the two women, embarrassing them with gifts of food, and on one occasion by crying so profusely while visiting Connie in the hospital that the nurses wondered whether she was the mother or the sister of the patient. Imelda's ability to cry at will was another political talent she began to hone in this campaign.

To those who knew her then, Imelda was a puzzle. Obsequious and naïve at one moment, she could speak ruthlessly at the next. Friends remember how, on a campaign trip to Isabela, she warned some political recalcitrants by making a cutting gesture with her finger to her neck and saying sweetly, almost flirtatiously, "It is up to you." A transformation was taking place in her, but ever so subtly. Though Marcos taught her to play politics, her drive and ambition were her own. Master though he was, Marcos would ultimately fail to calculate the full consequences of his influence on her. Imelda's innate shrewdness and longtime familiarity with cruelty would one day be unlocked with power. Already the signs were evident. She began to boast about her gowns and jewelry to less affluent friends while depreciating their value to the truly rich. She would later expound a political philosophy based on the premise that the poor needed dreams and she fulfilled their wishes by being a star.

As a senator's wife, she told a woman reporter that she read a lot of books, on Asia, communism, and just about everything else. She spoke of how Marcos read so many books. "Ferdie finishes so many books; I usually lag behind in my reading, so I end up asking him a lot of questions." She presented the image of a devoted wife, collecting his speeches and newspaper clippings which she filed for easy reference.

It was then also that the her well-known extravagance had its beginnings. The jewelry collection of the comely senator's wife began to be talked about. Her jewels were portrayed as family heirlooms of the "rich" Romualdezes, as were the china and silver. These were things she was used to, society editors were told.

But even when she had vast amounts of money at her disposal, she always consulted Ferdie. For him she learned Ilocano, Tagalog, and Moro songs. She went with Marcos on grueling campaign trips, flattered by his declaration that he wanted to show off his beautiful wife to the electorate. Imelda

94

had played a supporting role in the Senate race, but the victory stemmed principally from Marcos's political cunning. In the Presidential campaign to follow, it would be Imelda—vote getter, mediator, actress, and star—who would clinch victory.

Marcos made hard bargains with the political influence he had achieved step by step since the Nalundasan murder. As early as 1959, incumbent President Diosdado Macapagal promised Marcos the official Liberal Party Presidential candidacy in 1965 in exchange for his support and that of the Ilocano bloc, the so-called Solid North. But, Marcos alleged, Macapagal had reneged on his promise and had failed to support Marcos in the 1963 contest for the Senate Presidency. Marcos was left out in the cold and had no choice but to resign his position as President of the Liberal Party. However, there was more to this decision than his wounded pride. Breaking away from the incumbent President and his party at a time when its popularity had ebbed made a lot of political sense at election time. Marcos knew he had a better chance of winning the upcoming Presidential election if he ran as the nominee of the opposition Nacionalista Party. The open breach and the ensuing publicity provided Marcos with the rationale to switch parties, but becoming the Nacionalista standard-bearer still seemed an impossible task.

At this time, Marcos put Imelda's powerful name to work again. Her name and family tie to Senate Speaker Pro Tempore and Nacionalista leader Danieling Romualdez provided Marcos with a bridge to the other side. In fact, Imelda's political stardom in the Presidential campaign of 1965 owed little to her name or relatives. Marcos's political aides agree that Imelda played a vital role in that campaign from the nomination struggle at the Nacionalist Party convention up to the eve of the November 1965 election—and they marvel at her grit and determination. "She was a perfect political partner," is how one aide summed up her role. This gibes with her declaration that she would do anything for Marcos. Indeed, Imelda had become, a sort of hybrid: part Marcos clone, but driven by the motives and needs of the child in Calle General Solano. She attended all the caucuses, participated in all the campaign plans, offered suggestions and criticism and argued over all the problems, but there could be no doubt that Imelda spoke and thought like Marcos. More important, her loyalty and obeisance to him was absolute. Thus as the campaign progressed, Marcos gave her greater and greater responsibilities.

But Imelda's drive and obsession to win owed nothing to Marcos. True, the woman who would help plunge the Philippines into its worst political crisis ever was compelled to be a powerful political figure because her rescue from obscurity—and her survival—depended on how well she fit Marcos's ambitions. But the deeper force driving the Marcos clone came from the nine-year-old child who wished to be part of the family in the Big House. It was the same child who would blossom as the Rose of Tacloban, only to become bitter at having been thrown out of the ancestral house in Gran Capitán, and the poor but beautiful Muse of Manila, snubbed by her rich relatives and unable to marry the scion of a prominent family.

Marcos might have been a brilliant tactician, but it was Imelda's fierce motivation that won him the nomination and, ultimately, the Presidency. There were 1,347 delegates to the convention, most of whose votes were already pledged to four other Nacionalista Presidential aspirants—Fernando Lopez, Arturo Tolentino, Gil Puyat, and Emmanuel Pelaez. Marcos's challenge was to sway these delegates to vote for a newcomer to whom they owed no political favors and who was not especially charismatic. Filipino party delegates, as with party delegates anywhere in the world, are a difficult and capricious lot. There was no single formula for winning their support. They ranged from arrogant provincial governors to simple farmers with a faithful following. To win the nomination, Marcos had to muster 60 percent of their votes. The only way to win involved tracking down all 1,347 delegates in their far-flung localities. Among the principal players in the Marcos camp, only Imelda had the stamina and single-mindedness such a campaign required.

"It was not an exaggeration to say that she used plane,

motorboat, banca, and literally crawled on hands and knees to reach each delegate who had a vote," a political aide recalls.

"I did not do it once but twice, in some cases even thrice over," Imelda said later of the grueling nomination campaign. Her politicking was a stunning performance that surprised even Marcos.

"I knew every delegate at that convention because I shook hands and talked with each and every one of them, visited them in their homes, knew their first and last names, the circumstances in their families. I had to attend weddings, baptisms, anniversary parties. Then the next time I came around, I had the new window, the new roof, or whatever was needed in each house. I had to say *compadre* to the right name and person, to show that my concern was not just faked," Imelda recalled to a newspaper reporter. Her style was neither brilliant nor original. But none of the other candidates' wives had bothered with such details. Imelda's uniqueness had to do with a past that fired her with the motivation to undertake such a task. The stoic face hid an obsession to vindicate the years when she had known only want and frustration.

During the long months before the Nacionalista Party convention, the Marcoses were mostly alone in their quest for the nomination. Imelda's new political role had by then become public knowledge and threatened many Nacionalista wives. They viewed her as an overachiever, a newcomer whose victory would upset the balance of power in their political enclave. On the day of the convention Imelda phoned a few of the Nacionalista women, hoping to be in their company when she attended the proceedings at the Manila Hotel. But her invitation was greeted with the tart reply of one wife who said, "We could all meet there."

To Marcos, it was not enough that Imelda had gone on the arduous campaign to meet and woo the 1,347 delegates. That was only one aspect of her role. Marcos had expressly instructed Imelda to be on the convention stage, looking her beautiful best.

When Imelda reached the Manila Hotel, she was a full hour

late, and not a single Nacionalista wife was in the lobby to meet her. Her heart sank. She had been brave enough to cross land and sea to reach the delegates, but once in the convention hall, she was intimidated. She thought of the new roofs she had given their battered houses and of the kind words she had spoken. Would her kindnesses matter to them now, when her success and ambition depended on their almighty votes? Despite their promises, she could not know whom they would finally choose as their 1965 Presidential candidate. It did not help that she had spent a week of sleepless nights or that in her rush to get to the hotel on time she had forgotten to eat breakfast.

She felt faint as she climbed the tortuous steps to the stage of the convention hall, walking slowly and waving her hand in acknowledgement of greetings. Her regal bearing hid the coil of torment, hunger, and fear within her. When she at last reached the stage, every seat was taken. Even the bodyguards and maids of the Nacionalista wives were seated. No one bothered to offer her a chair, so she stood awkwardly for what seemed an eternal thirty minutes. She could hear giggling and whispering—but she stood fast. "I did not care. Marcos said I was to be on that stage. Well, I was—who cares if I was standing or sitting," she said later to friends.

The fact was she was better off standing. In her conspicuous position all eyes were on her—the star of the show as Marcos had wanted. From the stage she searched for and waved at familiar faces. Later a seat was offered to her, which was placed at the only space available, at the center front, giving her the best vantage point, while the rest of the Nacionalista wives muttered behind.

"It was such an awkward position, but I didn't mind. If I'd stood up again, I would have collapsed," she said. "I could hear my stomach grumbling, but I kept saying to myself, 'Oh, my God, help me, help me survive my ordeal.' It was already two o'clock, but I held fast to my seat." She was offered a glass of milk and a sandwich by a kind soul, but instead of taking it she promptly offered it to the lady next to her, who accepted it, to her dismay. Imelda's stomach groaned, but what occupied her was the thought of Marcos, who was somewhere in the hundred and one rooms of the hotel, probably closeted with supporters, and that she was doing what he wanted her to do.

When the voting began, Imelda slipped out of the hall and went to the San Agustin Church in Intramuros. She had done everything within her power to convince the delegates that her husband could win the Presidency for the Nacionalista Party. There was nothing more to do but to wait and see whether they had believed her. But fear overwhelmed her. What if they lost?

Defeat seemed her constant fate. The church was closed. She went to the sacristy, in her resplendent gown, and asked the church helper to let her in through a side entrance.

Imelda later told a journalist that she lighted five candles for the five nominees, and said the following prayer: "Lord, these five candles stand for five men. They are all good. One of them will win. I pray for that one whoever he may be. But, Lord, may that one be Ferdie."

She knelt there alone for three hours, praying ardently. If Marcos won, she too could claim victory.

When she returned to the convention hall, the results of the first balloting showed that Marcos had garnered 541 votes and led the candidates. His closest rival, former Vice-President Emmanuel Pelaez, trailed Marcos with 381 votes. The Marcos lead was comfortable enough to coax a bandwagon switch in favor of either of the two leading candidates. The Pelaez camp made a bid to delay the second balloting for eleven hours while Marcos lieutenants insisted on a marathon voting to conserve party unity after the convention. At this point he was already confident that he could break the impasse and prevent a third balloting. A suggestion was made to reduce the required majority to 50 percent plus one.

Pelaez won his request for a stay of balloting until the next day, but this failed to stem the onrushing tide for Marcos. Long before the results of the second balloting were out, Pelaez acceded to Marcos's bid to reduce the required majority vote to 50 percent plus one. Marcos received 777 votes to

Pelaez's 444. It was an extraordinary political upset. The much-vaunted anti-Marcos alliance had failed to materialize. Delegates from around the country had switched their votes to Marcos.

When Marcos's victory was announced, Imelda had tears in her eyes. This time they were tears of happiness. As they fell, Imelda was filled with new reserves of energy for her next political mission.

The problem centered on who would be Marcos's vice-presidential running mate—a difficult problem, given the bitterness of the convention struggle. The Marcoses chose Fernando Lopez because of his following among hard-core Nacionalistas. The role of emissary to persuade Lopez first fell to Speaker José B. Laurel Jr. But he was unsuccessful. Former President Carlos P. Garcia was then asked to try, but he, too, failed. Lopez was adamant. He was old and tired and sick of politics. The Marcos boys racked their brains as to how to convince this senior political figure from one of the oldest and richest families of the land to run with Marcos.

Marcos finally suggested that Imelda mediate between him and Lopez. It would be the first of many mediating missions Imelda performed during their long political partnership.

Imelda proceeded on her mission with speed and cunning. First she sent a note to Lopez, requesting an appointment if he was not too tired or busy. She would call at his suite, she wrote. The lady's approach was disarming, and, gallant gentleman that he was, Lopez replied that he would talk with her in her suite. The strategy to get the enemy into her territory worked. In Imelda's lair Lopez's resistance would be considerably lower. Lopez arrived at her door with two of his sons. "Here I am—what is it you want from me?" he asked.

Imelda used her considerable theatrical talents to appeal to his sympathy. "You don't know how difficult it has been for me, for Marcos, working for his nomination to uphold the principles for which the Nacionalista Party stands, and now we are being abandoned," she said.

"I am very tired. I am already old. I do not wish to go through all these politics again," Lopez quickly replied.

But Imelda was just as quick with her next words. Like a tiger, she had watched his reactions very closely, waiting for the time to make her kill. After Marcos's triumph in the convention hall this man was all that stood in the way of the Presidency. "You say you are old and tired, but you allowed yourself to be put up for the Presidential candidate," she replied, wondering if she might offend him with this remark.

He was pensive, but showed no sign of anger. For a full five minutes he seemed immovable, then he shook his head and said, "No."

Imelda burst into tears. It is difficult to say how much of her reaction was theatrics and how much was real. For it is Imelda who tells this story, and relatives who have heard it describe the relish with which Imelda embroiders her facts. Yet she had used tears in the past, and there is no reason to doubt she would have used them now if she thought her prey was vulnerable.

Lopez was in a quandary. He held Imelda's hand and tried to comfort her, begging her not to cry. He had a heart condition, and it hurt him to see her cry. With claws about to grasp her victim, and still in tears, Imelda said, "Oh, you have a heart, so you will have kindness enough to be the Nacionalista vice-presidential candidate."

Lopez sincerely wanted her to stop crying so he could leave the room, but he was caught. "Well, what is it you want?" he asked. She quickly dried her tears and pulled out a document. "Sign." The document said Lopez accepted nomination as the Nacionalista vice-presidential candidate. Like her husband, Imelda would not leave anything to chance. Only a signed document could seal the agreement she sought. It was the trophy she had to bring back to Marcos, who in the meantime was concluding some hard bargaining with Lopez's brother, Don Eugenio, the moneybag of the Nacionalista Party and the acknowledged kingmaker of Philippine politics.

It was characteristic of their partnership that Marcos handled the nitty gritty of a political problem while Imelda lent it a human touch. In this instance, Imelda also gave the recalcitrant Lopez a gracious excuse to accept the nomination—for the sake of a woman in tears. Lopez's deal hurt many old-time Nacionalista colleagues, such as Eulogio Rodriguez, the grand old man of the party, whom Marcos had earlier dislodged as president of the Senate, and former Vice-President Emmanuel Pelaez, who had fought valiantly to exclude Marcos, the Ilocano turncoat.

To mend his political fences, Marcos personally called on these two men. Imelda, too, visited the vanquished gentlemen. These missions of Imelda, although regarded merely as a follow-up to Marcos's were the first steps in her ascendancy as a political figure in her own right. Imelda's effectiveness in the campaign of 1965 convinced Marcos that he could concede more and more responsibility to his wife. Imelda's transformation from pupil to political partner had begun.

This development did not escape avid political observers who became alarmed at Imelda's growing influence. In defense, a political aide publicly stated, "It would be false to assume that such political reconciliations were Imelda's doings. She merely moves in for the 'human touch,' which derives from a woman's warmth."

But even a seasoned politician such as former Vice-President Emmanuel Pelaez confirmed that Imelda made a formidable opponent. Despite the aide's words, Marcos had used Imelda as his shield in the deadly battles for power. For a while the woman with her sweet face and winning ways blurted the accusations of ruthlessness.

Imelda did not see herself as being used. Marcos and she were together in battle, and she would say again and again that they were a partnership. "When Marcos was east, I was west; when Marcos was south, I was north," she said.

Publicists, taking the cue from the Marcoses, described the 1965 campaign as the point at which Imelda blossomed into an accomplished political figure. Later Imelda would describe herself as "a butterfly breaking out of its cocoon," anteceding the foreign journalist who would one day dub her "the iron butterfly." No doubt, a change had taken place. At the time, no one knew how big the change had been, but it was accurate to say that the pupil was overtaking her master. Marcos was enamored of this new, dazzling figure, a concoction of the aristocrat he had wished-fulfilled to marry and the poor country girl underneath driven by a tragic childhood. But in the delirious rise to power, Imelda, the poor country girl, who provided the verve and determination to win, had no place. True, Marcos transformed her, but in the process he too was transformed, and she would in time come to make him believe she was an indomitable figure to be awed in return.

If political analysts had looked closely enough, they would have seen that Imelda, the much vaunted political asset who won the Presidency for Marcos in 1965, was still acting the role of the Rose of Tacloban, singing to the war-weary American soldiers who would provide steel mattings for her family's Quonset hut in Calle Real.

Flushed with her victories in the convention hall, she plunged into the Presidential campaign with Marcos, in her words, "reconciling warring factions," and "mending political fences." Together they brought key political voting blocs to their side—the sugar and tobacco bloc, the Iglesia in Kristo (a religious bloc), social groups such as the Federation of Women's Clubs, as well as pivotal labor groups. Always Imelda gave the impression that she was merely adding to Marcos's hard sell and shrewd diplomacy. But those who knew better were to concede that Marcos relied heavily on Imelda. Her stamina and remarkable memory for details enabled him to keep track of the political picture.

As in the previous campaign, Imelda never missed a chance to call on important supporters on their birthdays and anniversaries. While other candidates' wives were content merely to send gifts and cards, she would personally grace the affair and make the celebrant feel important. She took the trouble to find out what the celebrant would want as a gift and kept track of the dozens of small details that normally escaped the notice of busy politicians. She was, quite simply, indefatigable.

Imelda, the daughter of embattled Remedios and Vicente Orestes, liked bringing people together and was a popular matchmaker—a useful talent in factionalized Philippine politics. Nor was Imelda inhibited from attending parties without an invitation if she knew that the celebrant or an important guest at the party could help Marcos's campaign.

But her major contribution to the campaign lay in playing star to the barrio folk, the millions of apolitical, ordinary Filipinos who were drawn to Marcos's campaign by this beautiful woman with a beautiful voice. Political strategists plugged Imelda as the "most beautiful and youngest First Lady" the Philippines would ever have and made this promise the center of the Marcos campaign. Accordingly, Imelda always dressed to the hilt whether her audience was Manila's elite or the simple folk of the barrio, she was at all times an actress making a stage appearance. She wore elaborate rhinestone-studded *ternos,* the formal Philippine national dress, when she sang on wobbly makeshift stages in the provinces. Poor Filipinos living eventless days in the outbacks surged to get a glimpse of the spectacularly dressed star. Some travel-weary foreign journalists mistook Imelda's popularity for "charisma."

Backstage those who accompanied Imelda on the campaign trail were astonished at her stamina and endurance. She had to travel from barrio to barrio, snatching sleep only when fatigue overtook her, and often sleeping in her gown and full makeup while in transit to the next appearance. She seemed unaffected by cockroach-infested third-class hotels and by the potholed roads leading to godforsaken little towns.

Back in the city, Imelda would revert to being a lady of leisure, pursued now by the wives of rich industrialists and politicians whom she would later describe to foreign journalists as "friends from childhood" or "my ladies in waiting." In the local press they were known as the "Blue Ladies," a euphemism for the wives of men whose fortunes depended on making the right political connections at the right time. They offered Imelda the social acceptance she had always sought. Ever the student, Imelda learned the "ways of women of the world" from these women. They were not like her, guilt-ridden and inhibited. They moved with ease and confidence and enjoyed life without a shred of guilt. One of her teachers in worldliness described Imelda as an "oyster" which needs to be shocked open to reveal the pearl inside.

Imelda now complained that she saw less and less of Marcos, and that his disappearances had little to do with the campaign. She was, the lady said, frightfully moralistic and had to be taught the virtue of cool indifference. One of the things Imelda learned in those days was to accept that there would be other women in Marcos's life, especially as he grew in political stature and wealth.

Close to the end of the campaign, Imelda proved her new capacity for indifference. Copies of a photograph of her in the nude began to circulate around universities and nightclubs. She called a 3 A.M. meeting to discuss strategy. Although hurt by the smear tactic, Imelda appeared quite unruffled. She viewed the whole matter with detachment, took the picture— a collage of another woman's body with her face—and asked the dozen political aides she had assembled, "And what shall we do about this?" The embarrassed men fumbled for a suitable reply, but Imelda spared them from further embarrassment, shrugging her shoulders and saying, "Well, at least I hope that the body they supplied for my face is nice."

On November 2, 1965, Ferdinand Marcos was elected President of the Philippines. In the last lap of the campaign the Liberals had resuscitated the murder charges against Marcos. The son of the murdered man appeared on television to retell the old story and condemned the powers that allowed Marcos to run free, much less to aspire to the highest office of the land. But the macabre revival failed to deliver the technical knockout the Liberals had hoped. The 1965 election put Macapagal's Presidency on trial; the Nalundasan murder was an irrelevant issue to an electorate wowed by the Camelot couple and hopeful that Marcos would bring about Filipino independence at last. The obsessive country girl and her ambitious husband were on their way to Malacanang Palace to rule fifty-four million Filipinos.

CHAPTER FOUR

The Book

LORETO, IMELDA'S COUSIN, dismissed her fears of what Imelda might have meant when she told relatives after the state visit to America that she was now on "top of the world." These were, after all, the euphoric first days of the Marcos administration, and some intoxication from newly gained power was human and forgivable. Imelda's cousin, who is regarded by the clan as the custodian of the family's historical records, went back to her teaching and, like most Filipinos, waited for the fulfillment of the promise held out by the newly elected President and his First Lady.

At her first press conference, however, Imelda signaled nothing other than a productive First Ladyship. "My dream is to have a theater—a completely equipped auditorium where artists can find full expression of their talent. Something like Carnegie Hall, perhaps. But, of course, I shall ask the advice of experts and of the artists themselves as I do not presume to know everything about the subject. I have to push through the beautification project begun by Teodoro Valencia [a newspaper columnist who spearheaded the beautification of Manila's major park] and so ably implemented by my predecessor, Evangelina Macapagal. She deserves credit for that. My idea

about projects in general is not to disrupt but to provide
... some continuity, for instance of work that has already been
started."

The tone was faultless. If it was the work of her publicists,
Imelda successfully presented the image of a First Lady who
would not be content with merely serving as a decorative
appendage. She would accomplish things.

Moreover, she assured everyone that her work would complement Marcos's government program, an oblique reply to
growing public apprehension that she would overreach her
role as wife of the highest official of the land. The areas she
selected for her activities were culture and social welfare, both
traditionally accepted spheres for a First Lady. She was ever
quick to emphasize, however, that Marcos shared her aspirations for the people. Her deference to Marcos as her mentor
and senior partner was genuine, and gave a valuable clue to
the nature of their partnership, which she melodramatically
described in her official biography: ". . . while the President
governed, she would inspire. The President would build the
body; she would provide the soul. He would put up the house
and she would furnish it."

Her two-pronged program, she announced, would help
Filipinos who had been neglected—the artists and the handi-
capped. For culture, she unveiled projects that included construction of the Cultural Center, restoration of the old Spanish
cities of Intramuros and Fort Santiago and other historic sites.
Imelda would lead and encourage archaeological digs to give
Filipinos a greater sense of their past, and she proposed offering more public band concerts to make music accessible to
even the lowliest park stroller.

Her social welfare plan, if a bit less specific, was equally
ambitious. It called for an integrated program that would:
expand Welfareville, a crowded institution for juvenile delin-
quents; distribute Christmas groceries to the lucky poor invited to the palace; promote home gardens; and offer relief to
disaster victims. Other highlights included a project pom-
pously named "Save a Life in Every Barrio," and a seed distri-
bution program called "Share for Progress." Foreign

journalists were deeply impressed and took to describing Imelda as a cross between Eleanor Roosevelt and Jacqueline Kennedy.

But the public saw only part of the picture. On paper Imelda's ambitious projects could not be faulted. They looked good. The danger lay elsewhere and during those first years went almost totally undetected. To accusations that she was overmotivated, she replied, "Never mind, as long as your motives are good." It was easy to overlook the perversion of her plans in a struggling Third World country. The other part of the picture kept out of view concerned Imelda's quest for power and wealth. She set her own rules, and with Marcos's concurrence they created a powerful role for her in his government unprecedented in previous administrations. What began as innocuous blueprints for culture and social welfare would soon become instruments through which she would acquire a mind-boggling fortune.

Of all the edifices and monuments that Imelda built during Marcos's twenty-year rule, the Cultural Center stands out as the premier symbol of her relentless drive. It was also the first project she completed. She began the project with a small grant of seed money from the Philippine-American Cultural Foundation. The center, a magnificent architectural showpiece built on reclaimed land in Manila Bay, would eventually cost a staggering fifty million pesos. There were many explanations advanced as to why a project that began so humbly should end up costing millions of pesos. Imelda's defenders cited the cost of imported material, which rose nearly 40 percent from planning to completion. No one seemed to have considered scaling down the project to what the country could afford. On the contrary, Imelda openly boasted that she tapped every available source of funds to see her dream come true, ranging from private donations to government loans. When these were still not enough, she borrowed money from foreign sources. Imelda had been encouraged to look abroad for funds during the state visit to the United States in September 1966. President Johnson had "offered to help" the Philippines, using veterans' war damage funds. But Imelda turned this offer down, perhaps in a pique of conscience, and instead sought a twenty-eight-million dollar grant for research and educational purposes. Johnson, who called Marcos "his right arm in Asia," was eager to please and generously offered approval of the grant, provided half of it went to Mrs. Marcos. In this way Imelda discovered a seemingly limitless cornucopia of foreign loans available to her with only her government's guarantee. These loans would pave her way to great wealth for the next twenty years.

Although the ostentatious project was pure Imelda, Marcos clearly approved of the arrangements. For one thing, the whole affair was properly legalized, which is characteristic of Marcos. The loan was negotiated only after the justice secretary ruled that the Center was legally qualified to contract obligations and that the National Investment Development Corporation was empowered to guarantee the loan.

But Senator Benigno Aquino, whose meteoric rise in politics would later place him on a collision course with Marcos for the Presidency, attacked the expensive Cultural Center as ludicrous in an impoverished country such as the Philippines. In his memorable speech on the floor of Congress, Aquino did not condemn the idea of a Cultural Center but deplored its ostentation—and Imelda's determination to see it through at any cost. Aquino then threw down the gauntlet and said Imelda reminded him of Evita Perón, the wife of the Argentine dictator.

To the Marcoses, Aquino's attack on Imelda's flair and extravagance represented a major threat. Moreover, Aquino's innuendo suggesting that these qualities were traceable to an impoverished childhood similar to that of Evita Perón marked a foray onto sacred ground. Since Aquino represented the Philippine social elite to which the Marcoses aspired, the attack added insult to injury. The colorful, swashbuckling senator was a true blue blood; what's more, he was married to Corazón Cojuangco—heiress to a fabulous sugar fortune. The Cojuangcos represented the crème de la crème, at the top of Manila's Four Hundred. They were archetypes of Marcos's and Imelda's ambitions.

Aquino had lanced at a gaping wound, an act for which he would never be forgiven. Indeed, Aquino would pay dearly for his words in years to come. Despite letters which "flooded" newspaper editorial offices attacking Aquino for his lack of chivalry, the Evita Perón issue did not go away. People began to ask questions about the First Lady's past. Even as these questions surfaced, however, Imelda was moving to erase all evidence of her true history and to master her old defeat at the hands of her family.

After the Presidential inauguration of 1965, Imelda had laid wreaths on her father's and Speaker Danieling Romualdez's tombs. When asked why she did not lay a wreath on her mother's tomb, she was said to have merely shrugged. The public became increasingly curious about this reticence concerning her maternal origins. It was a well-circulated rumor that Imelda's mother was a mystery. No one seemed to know anything about her. The official biographical data that she was a beauty from Bulacan only heightened speculation that this was all Malacanang wanted the public to know about Remedios Trinidad. There were those who said Imelda was an illegitimate child, and still others who claimed that her mother was a servant or a market vendor. Only a few knew the truth, but they were actively discouraged from communicating this knowledge to anyone outside family circles.

As for laying a wreath on Remedios's tomb, this was not possible, because her remains had neither tomb nor marker. During the war her grave, like others at La Loma Cemetery, was emptied by Japanese soldiers, who used the graves as foxholes. The faithful Estrella had wanted to ask Imelda to put a marker on the spot where her mother's remains had once been. But the memory of Remedios, repressed from the day she died, had become even more irrelevant to the aristocratic image of the powerful First Lady of the Philippines.

Indeed, Imelda's triumphal return to her "ancestral house" in Tolosa (in reality Marcos's resort house) before a crowd of hundreds of common folk, showed how far she would go to erase her past. Estrella, who knew the real Imelda, was prohibited by strict security guards from attending the gala. "Imelda waved at me from the car, so I thought maybe I should see her and remind her to help me," she recalls.

Estrella was unaware that in Imelda's new life her wish would never be fulfilled. Any trace of the past that belied Imelda's aristocratic image was unwelcome. That same year Imelda invited her cousins Loreto and Carmen (both sisters of Norberto Romualdez Jr.) to lunch at Malacanang, where she announced her brother Benjamin's plan to run as governor of Leyte on the Nacionalista ticket. It would be in the interest of Norberto Jr. the incumbent governor and a Liberal, not to run for reelection. "It will be useless for him to fight Benjamin, who will be backed by the Nacionalista Party," she said. "Benjamin will have the money and the entire machinery of the party in power. How can Norberto fight that?"

Loreto felt the same vague unease that she had experienced when Imelda had boasted to her family of her trip to America. The woman before her was no longer her sweet provincial cousin. She was the First Lady and her message was clear: She would use any means to take over the leadership of Leyte. Imelda asked her cousins to convince Norberto Jr. to come to the palace so she could personally announce to him her take-over of the political supremacy of the Romualdez family.

"I don't think he will come just like that," Loreto replied.

"Then fetch him. Tomorrow morning I'll dispatch a plane for your use just to fetch him," Imelda commanded.

Early the next morning, at the appointed time and place, an Air Force plane arrived to transport Norberto to Manila, by order of the First Lady. Although Norberto consented to come to Manila, he refused to go to Malacanang. He wisely told his sisters that if Imelda wanted to discuss the leadership of Leyte, she should come see him at his home in suburban Manila. Two hours later, Imelda arrived in a show of official force, accompanied by an entourage of security men and screaming sirens. She had come as First Lady, not as poor cousin Imelda.

"She talked tough," Loreto recalls. "Imelda said in no uncertain terms that if Norberto ran for reelection he would only suffer devastating defeat." Loreto recalls Imelda saying, "Benjamin will run. With the backing of power and money, how can you fight him? Besides, Norberto, you have to be practical. I'll use every available means to ensure Benjamin's victory. The whole weight of Malacanang will bear down on you."

But Norberto was unmoved. He understood Imelda's threat, but he was not prepared to relinquish the political leadership of Leyte to her bullying tactics. He knew that she had the power and the money to carry out her threat and that it would be foolhardy to challenge her. But more than that, the governorship was useless if the party in power was not on his side. His father's motto was, "Leyte above self," and he would follow that precept if Imelda asked him more graciously. But Norberto realized that she wanted more than the mere governorship of Leyte. She was bent on revenge, on bringing him to his knees to recognize her new status. This he refused to do.

Imelda left Norberto's house in a huff. The following week she called for Father Almendra, a priest from Tacloban who was a protégé of the governor. She sought his help in convincing her cousin to withdraw from the race. The poor priest, who had never been near anything as grand as Malacanang, was properly initiated before he entered Imelda's inner sanctum. He was led down labyrinthine passageways and through innumerable doors before he was left to wait in a darkened hallway for further instructions.

The young priest was awed and breathless when Imelda suddenly appeared in a lounging costume and led him to her boudoir. He would never forget the sight of her, brushing her hair as she asked him to sit on a divan just a few paces from her. He had known her during her impoverished days in Tacloban and could not make out why she put on such a show. What was she up to? Despite the drama, Imelda talked casually, and they proceeded to discuss the question of Norberto's recalcitrance. But she had the priest by the neck. To him, the most important part of Imelda's message was left unsaid: She was the sweet Rose of Tacloban no longer. He stammered his advice, that she should change her approach, and noted that Norberto would rather run and be defeated than be pushed to the wall without a fight. The priest prayed his answers would mollify Imelda and that she would release him from her clutches shortly.

The next time Imelda went to see Norberto, she put on the sorrowful act that had worked so well with Vice-President Fernando Lopez. She came teary-eyed, remorseful, and pleading. "I come not as a First Lady," she said, "but as a humble cousin, a Romualdez. Please try to understand why I am doing this. I do not want to fight my own blood. I'm tired of Romualdezes fighting Romualdezes." Imelda performed the old ritual, and Norberto Jr. this time capitulated. Proud as he was, he had sense, and Imelda had put her ultimatum in acceptable terms at last. But this victory over her past would not be enough to assuage Imelda's enduring bitterness about her second-class childhood.

Despite her money and power, Imelda remained deeply insecure about her status with friends and relatives who had once known she was poor. No longer did she swallow the hurt; now she went into paroxysms of anger when figures from the past failed to pay adequate homage to her new stature. Such was Imelda's reaction to Adoración, the music teacher whom Imelda had described only a few years earlier as "like a mother" to her. Their falling-out began when Imelda invited the music teacher to Malacanang to discuss a cultural project. Adoración had been unable to make the appointment because she had a lesson scheduled for that day. Imelda, however, had expected her to drop everything for an invitation to the Palace. "I had a class when she wanted me to come, so I merely asked for another date, not knowing that this would make her so angry," Adoración recalls. She was never again asked to Malacanang. The message passed to Adoración implied that ambassadors, senators, governors, and industrialists would queue to see the First Lady. A music teacher could hardly do less.

But perhaps the biggest blow to Imelda's carefully shaped

image came in the form of a book. The unauthorized biography (as opposed to Imelda's official biography, which was being kept under wraps until the opportune moment arrived for Imelda to announce her bid for the Presidency) told the true story of Imelda's youth.

The project to write her story was first suggested to me by my husband in 1966 and was prompted by the unprecedented publicity accorded a Filipino President and his First Lady on a state visit to the United States. *The New York Times* had featured Imelda on its front and inside pages. Perhaps it was her youth, or her beauty, or her candid remarks, but she was very good copy. At that time I rejected the idea because I thought then that if she was good copy, she owed it to good publicity agents. I did not think that there was any worthwhile story to tell. I reluctantly undertook research on what I thought would be a harmless enterprise, a straightforward biography. I sought as many people who knew her before she became the First Lady and discovered in the course of time that there was a controversial story behind the story and one which the Marcoses would not accept. But despite their attempts to squelch the book, it made public at last the truth about Imelda's poverty-stricken childhood.

The most invaluable source for the book was Imelda's cousin Loreto. To her, my project was a god-send. It seemed to her in those days that Imelda presented a confused figure. In an unguarded moment she had once told Loreto, "You don't know me. Nobody really knows me. How can anyone know me?" Once Imelda had invited her to Malacanang and shown her a makeup palette with forty brushes. "Look," she said, "how I will transform myself." Whereupon, Imelda showed Loreto the secrets of cosmetic makeup.

What concerned Loreto most, however, was Imelda's acquiescence to the suppression of the truth about her mother. To Loreto, this was a serious offense, and whenever possible she badgered Imelda and her press assistants to let the world know about Remedios Trinidad. But Imelda would not listen. The enemy was anything that reminded her that she had once been poor and had lived with her mother in the family garage.

To Loreto, the book thus offered a chance to reverse the harmful effects of Imelda's break with the past, and for that reason Loreto opened the Romualdez family memoirs and albums to me. Through the book, she hoped Imelda would give her mother the honor she deserved. Loreto believed that the loss of the aristocratic image Marcos demanded Imelda have was a small price to pay for the truth. But Loreto understood the risk she was taking. She understood that Imelda's ambition was rooted in the inferiority complex she had developed through years as a poor relation of the rich Romualdezes. If Imelda could be made to face and understand that past, Loreto thought, she would be better equipped to handle her role as First Lady. She would also be made to see in perspective that she owed her name to the successes of the senior Norberto Romualdez and that her vindictiveness against that branch of the family was ill-placed. It was a gamble, with only a slim chance for success. Loreto took the risk.

The book was published under the title *The Untold Story of Imelda Marcos* in 1970, well over a year after it was written. Marcos and Imelda had tried unsuccessfully during that year to stop it from reaching the bookstores. But the book escaped their clutches and became a cause célèbre in the first year of Marcos's second term.

From the date of its publication, Imelda's projects were viewed by the public with reservation, if not outright suspicion. Loreto's documented story of the evolution of the Romualdez clan, Imelda's tragic childhood as vividly told by Estrella, and Adoración's narrative of her impoverished first days in Manila, just a year before she became Mrs. Marcos, brought home the truth of Aquino's prophecy that the First Lady was a potential despot, an Evita Perón, in power. This was explosive stuff in an election year.

Indeed, those who knew Marcos well knew that once in power he would not voluntarily give it up, no matter what the public learned about him or his wife. By 1969, in fact, he was already preparing four different scenarios in order to stay in power at the end of his second term. These were: reelection for a third term; running Imelda as the Presidential candidate;

changing the structure of government from republican to parliamentarian with himself as prime minister; or declaring martial law and setting himself up as dictator. Thus, when the rumor mills buzzed about Imelda's probable Presidential candidacy, there was no doubt that this was Malacanang-inspired. Minister of Labor Blas F. Ople, who doubled as chief propagandist of the Marcoses, carried with him his portfolio of what he called "long-term plans" on how to stay in power. An aide of his outlined the order of succession: First, Marcos would seek reelection, then Imelda would take over, and finally they would establish a "People's Republic." Given Marcos's secret plan, his furious war to discredit *The Untold Story* made a lot of sense.

In classic succession, the Marcoses attempted to stop the book, first by offering to purchase the rights outright. As an aide put it to me, "The people in Malacanang want the rights to the book, lock, stock, and barrel. Forget that you ever wrote the book. What's wrong with that?" Failing the bribery attempt, Palace agents conducted a systematic campaign to harass me and smear my reputation, posting goons at the gate of my house, compiling dossiers on me, and making telephone threats. There is little doubt that Marcos was the mastermind of these tactics, for they closely follow his brand of thinking: If you cannot buy your enemies, destroy them. What he missed in the *Untold Story* episode was that the book belonged to documented Romualdez history; attacking the author's credibility could not affect the truth. The Marcoses went a step further, printing pirated copies of the book. A columnist theorized that the Marcoses intended to plant the pirated edition in the headquarters of the opposing party, in an attempt to destroy my credibility. The Marcoses could then charge that the book was political propaganda. I responded by postponing publication of the book until after the 1969 elections.

Following Marcos's election to a second term, he and Imelda assumed that the book was dead. Thus, when *The Untold Story of Imelda Marcos* appeared in 1970, the Marcoses were shocked. The public rushed to the bookstores and within weeks bought thousands of copies of the book. A press war then ensued between me and the Marcoses. Imelda, ignoring reams of copy released by Malacanang in previous years on her "aristocratic origins," denied she was ashamed of her one-time poverty. In any case, she asked, "What was wrong with being poor?"

Simultaneous to this publicity blitz, the Marcoses began lining up the sources for the book in preparation for a libel suit. The press was divided between Marcos partisans who tried to defend Imelda by championing her poverty and Marcos critics who felt vindicated in their repeated warnings that a dangerous element lurked behind Imelda's "good deeds." To close friends, Imelda claimed she did not mind if Filipinos knew about her poverty. What worried her, she said, was what her "gang" would say. When pressed as to who this gang included, she said, "Lyndon B. Johnson, Queen Sirikit, Indira Gandhi, David Rockefeller . . ." with tears in her eyes.

Out of the public eye the Marcoses worked behind the scenes to destroy the book. At the same time that the press war raged, Imelda met privately with Loreto, Adoración, and Estrella, the three primary sources of the book, and tried to persuade them to retract their testimonies. Adoración, the rebuffed music teacher, was called to Malacanang. After an exchange of niceties which avoided the issue of their lost friendship, Imelda peremptorily handed her an affidavit retracting all she had told me. "You must help me put down that book," Imelda said to her. Adoración recalls that although the interview was between her and Imelda, Marcos hovered in the background, and when Imelda gave her the affidavit, he briefly came forward with a look of disapproval on his face. Whereupon Imelda retracted the affidavit and returned to pleasantries. Marcos, the shrewd tactician, knew Adoración could not be bought.

But to Estrella, unable to make ends meet ever since she met Imelda in the Escolta in 1953, the call to Malacanang was long-awaited. Idyllic Leyte and the shore towns to which she and her family had returned offered no future to her ten children who, she was determined, should learn to read and write, as she had not. Estrella needed money. To her, the day when she was snatched from my car and forcibly brought to the Palace was a dream come true. She had, after all, been turned away from the gates of Imelda's rest house in Ulot, Leyte. "I could not believe that I was actually being brought to Malacanang. I was a bit afraid because I was between two men armed with guns, and they were speaking on walkie-talkies. I could hear the name of the man who was giving orders, a Colonel Ver, who would be later promoted to General by Marcos. There was a car behind and a car in front, and several more joined us at various corners as we neared the Palace," she recalls.

Estrella felt elated and hopeful that the fulfillment of Remedios's promise was at hand. She was escorted down the grand stairs, past the huge ballroom for state receptions and into the First Family's private quarters. There in a semicircle of luxurious sofas sat Imelda and her brothers and sisters. Curiously, in that awesome moment Estrella lost all her fears. This might be Malacanang and Imelda might be First Lady, but to Estrella she would always be Meldy, the little crying girl she had so often held in her arms. That memory was Estrella's strength, and she held fast.

To her surprise, Imelda and her brothers and sisters encouraged her to talk about their mother. They were hungry for more details than she had already told in the book. "It was three o'clock in the morning when we broke up. By then we were in tears," Estrella says. She too recalls that although Marcos did not join in the conversation, he kept watch, coming in and going out of the room. Just before Estrella was sent away, Imelda left the room for a while, and when she returned with Marcos, he said, "That is your own family's business." There was a ring of disdain to his words, Estrella said. The tears that had flowed briefly from Imelda's eyes during their hours-long storytelling were wiped dry and she was upright once more, almost imperious, the "sentimentality" gone.

Marcos's suppressive influence on Imelda is corroborated

by the publishers of the pirated edition of the book. During their call on Malacanang, they described how Imelda sat quietly while the President ranted about the book, saying it was written to harm the First Lady. He read passages from it aloud, and when he came to the description of Imelda's life in the garage, he was beside himself with rage. It implied, he said, that his wife and First Lady of the land had been conceived on top of potato boxes. He would not listen to arguments that the book was no more than a Cinderella story. Aristocratic Imelda was his creature, and the book had torn his fiction to pieces.

Estrella and her husband, Siloy, were promised a pension of three hundred pesos per month and were told to bring their children to Manila. The elder ones would be given jobs and the younger ones could continue with their studies. It was the long-overdue payment of wages, and Estrella received it gratefully. The question of a retraction was not raised at that time. But Estrella and her family would remain under guard until further instructions. She was also barred from communicating with me or any member of the press. The newspaper battle on the book was still on, and the threat of a libel suit persisted. That was in September 1970. It would be four months before Estrella was able to break away and contact me to reveal what happened the night she was brought to Malacanang. Characteristically, Imelda tailored her tactics once again in order to force Loreto to retract her contributions to the book.

In the years since the elder Norberto's death, Imelda had reversed positions with her cousin Loreto. Although she remained a distinguished member of Manila society, Loreto had neither the wealth nor the power of Imelda. Loreto, a music teacher, lived in a modest bungalow not far from Marcos's own "lucky" house in San Juan. Imelda had frequently visited this house in her early days in Manila, but could no longer be expected to visit there now that she was First Lady.

Playing on Loreto's vulnerability, however, Imelda did not call Loreto to Malacanang. She went unannounced to Loreto's little house, mindful that this would soften Loreto's resistance when she brought out the question of retracting her part in

The Untold Story. Imelda started by asking Loreto if she had any pending loans with any of government institutions. When Loreto replied that she had, Imelda quickly shifted the conversation to the question of the book. She made the startling statement that the book had destroyed her marriage. Contrary to press reports, it was Marcos who was most affected by the revelations of her past. According to Loreto, Imelda said he could not accept what the book seemed to confirm—that she was not a virgin when he married her. He was devastated by the thought that he had been fooled.

Loreto protested that this was hardly the most significant aspect of the book and that he was not lily-white himself. Moreover, after more than sixteen years of marriage and three children, it could hardly matter if she was a virgin or not when she married him. But Imelda was inconsolable. She said that Marcos would never believe her now and added that there were even "operations in Japan" to simulate virginity. Loreto could not make out the relevance of the latter statement. The only part of the book having to do with Imelda's virginity relates to the weekends she had spent with former beau Ariston Nakpil. He, too, would be interviewed by Marcos men and asked to retract his allegations—with an implied threat that it would be in the interest of his children's safety to do so. What Imelda tried to convey to Loreto was that Marcos was devastated that he had been "had." If he was the supreme macho (which is prized in Philippine culture), then he had been shortchanged. Nakpil refused to retract and told them it was impossible for him to do so because Imelda's rendezvous with him in their Batangas farm was known by a number of people and it would make him ridiculous if he denied it.

Loreto believes that the virginity issue was merely a smoke-screen; what truly galled Marcos and Imelda was that the book caught them "lying in public." It was the shot that cracked their carefully constructed public image. Loreto's assessment of Imelda's anger about the book was correct. It had nothing to do with virginity. It had to do with how Imelda perceived her political worth to Marcos. It became apparent that the

Remedios Trinidad, Imelda's mother, on the day of her marriage to Vicente Orestes.

Vicente Orestes, Imelda's father.

Imelda, age 7, at her First Holy Communion.

Remedios Trinidad at the convent, prior to her marriage to Vicente Orestes.

Imelda as a teenager in Leyte. This photo, one of Ferdinand Marcos's favorites, was found in his study after the Marcoses fled the palace.

Above: The photo Imelda submitted to the Miss Manila contest in 1953.

Left: Imelda—the Rose of Tacloban —at age 18.

Imelda and Ferdinand at the time of their wedding in 1954.

Above: Imelda campaigning for Ferdinand prior to the 1965 Presidential elections.

Left: Imelda and Lady Bird Johnson attend an opening at the Metropolitan Opera during the Marcoses' state visit to the U.S. in 1966.

A painting of the "Filipino Royal Family" commissioned by Imelda.

Imelda on the campaign trail in the Philippines.

In New York City with friends.

Right: A rare picture of a casual Imelda.

Below: Dancing with Brooke Shields.

At a party in her New York City townhouse.

Imelda, pianist Van Cliburn, George Hamilton, and guests in the
New York townhouse.

At the United Nations.

With Peter O'Toole at the Manila Film Festival in 1982.

With Fidel Castro.

Inside Malacanang Palace.

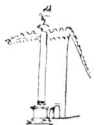

Salvatore Ferragamo
Firenze

Mrs. Gliceria R. Tantoco
Rustan Commercial Corporation
P. O. Box 7167
Airmail Division Mia
Pasay City - Philippines
=====================

September 30, 1980

Dear Mrs. Tantoco,
thank you very much for your letter of August 30 which has just arrived.

I am pleased to enclose a few sketches of our new shoes for Spring-Summer 1981 and the colour swatches per each style.

As a policy we do not make special orders but, as an exception, we will be glad to produce the styles Mrs. Marcos will select.

I would like to inform you that this will take approximately 8 weeks and I recommend that you let us know the exact size and width Mrs. Marcos wears.

The trip of my brother Leonardo to the Philippines has not been scheduled yet but as soon as it is, I will let you know.

Hoping to hear from you in the near future, I send all best personal regards.

Sincerely yours,

Ferruccio Ferragamo

Original letter from Salvatore Ferragamo, "Shoemaker of Dreams," regarding Imelda's shoe order from him. She commissioned many of her 3,000-plus pairs of shoes from him.

May 1, 1972

Dearest Ferdinand,

For 18 years I've loved you,
And after this a whole eternity.
    Our life was filled with joys
and madness.
    Showered thru with success
and sadness.
    Our love has transcended human
passions,
    The splendor of heaven it has
known
    So what Today can I give you
once more, a love faithful,
loyal and true!
        Happy Anniversary darling!
        Imelda

An anniversary letter to Ferdinand from Imelda in 1972.

Imelda and Ferdinand at their silver wedding anniversary in 1979.

Irene and Imee Marcos in 1979.

Ralph Cowan with his "royal portraits" of President and Nancy Reagan, Imelda and Ferdinand Marcos.

Another Cowan portrait of Imelda.

Marcoses, despite their vaunted political astuteness, felt they had to reject anything that contradicted Imelda's aristocratic image. The falsification of Imelda's life story was not just a question of personal vanity, but an essential piece of Marcos's political identity, along with his fake war medals. Marcos's perception of himself as the greatest President of the Philippines included the notion of his marriage into Philippine aristocracy. To accept the book would mean abandoning the image he had projected for himself. From here on, it would be difficult for Imelda to continue playing the role of the "coveted rich and aristocratic lady he had married." Marcos, the impoverished youth, had always dreamed of marrying his way to the top, and the book had brought his dream crushing down. Imelda did, in fact, suffer diminished worth in Marcos's eyes this time.

But an event that soon followed the book scandal provided Imelda with ample ammunition of her own to counteract Marcos's rejection. Not long after Imelda's visit to Loreto, a voluptuous American B-movie star named Dovie Beams would reveal her affair with "Fred." She produced tapes and held hour-long press conferences on a story that led straight to Malacanang. There were sighs, breathless half-minute pauses, and, most titillating of all, singing while it all happened. The voice, Marcos watchers avowed, sounded uncomfortably reminiscent of the President's baritone vowing to lead the country to greatness. Miss Beams told of escapades arranged by a colonel who acted like a guardian, always on the lookout for prying eyes or the storming in of a betrayed wife. On one occasion he seems to have slipped, and the offended lady barged into the room screaming a litany of epithets unworthy of an aristocratic lady of impeccable breeding. But the lady made it clear to the horrified starlet that it was not the affair with her husband that offended her. Dovie and Fred could by all means enjoy themselves, for all she cared. But did Miss Beams need to make it so public? The scorned wife was even grateful to her, the American actress alleged, for fulfilling a role she was unable to play for her husband. Miss Beams spoke of Fred's gratitude to her. She had been told he was the most powerful man in the Philippines, and she was thrilled to have him in her arms. He had spoken of his undying love for her because she had overcome his years of impotence.

The press could hardly believe Miss Beams outrageous revelations. Equally puzzling was why Malacanang was so anxious to remove Miss Beams from the local scene or why Marcos's publicists had tried so desperately to suppress her press conference about Fred.

Miss Beams said she came to the Philippines in 1968 to do a film with USV Arts, a local film group. At that time she was told vaguely that it would be a war film, but on arrival in Manila she was told it would be entitled *Maharlika,* which by coincidence was Marcos's *nom de guerre.* In the beginning she was in contact with persons she referred to only as Messrs X, Y, and Z. It soon became evident that these gentlemen had set up her meeting with "Fred," to whom they all seemed to defer. On the night she and "Fred" first met, there was an exchange of pleasantries, and she heard the men refer to her as "Big Eyes." She soon found herself alone with "Fred." The meeting place was a high-walled and heavily guarded house in Green Hills, a posh suburban subdivision. On their second date again she was left alone with "Fred." On that occasion, she said, he kissed her tenderly on the neck. But nothing was discussed about the film, and she began to be alarmed.

She claims that she and a friend tried to find out just whom they were to deal with regarding the film. They were advised of a certain Mr. Marson and that they were to wait until he was available. The next day a plane took Miss Beams to Baguio, the summer capital, but she found it strange that the plane's marking read "President of the Philippines." She was brought to a palatial house, where she met "Fred" once more. In bed, he finally revealed his true identity. She would not have believed him had he not showed her the grand house and the many guards who saluted them as they passed by. The affair began in earnest, but "Fred" warned her, "It must be a personal thing between us." She was not to speak of it to anyone.

The story then becomes unbelievable. Miss Beams claimed the affair developed smoothly. "Fred" was very kind and gentle, and they spent many ecstatic moments together. He gave her a Volkswagen van to serve as her dressing room during the filming of *Maharlika,* as well as a Mercedes-Benz for traveling around the country. Then the bombshell: She claimed that "Fred" wanted her to have his baby as a lasting remembrance of his undying love for her. He claimed that he would never forget how she had saved him from the nervous breakdown he would have suffered because of his inability to make love to Mrs. "Fred" for the last two years.

But the love affair suddenly ended. By coincidence it ended at about the time Imelda returned from a trip to London and the United States. Miss Beams was served with a deportation order by the immigration commissioner, who accused her of being a professional strip-tease artist and an undesirable alien. Filming on *Maharlika* was abruptly stopped and the payments due her not paid.

It was then that Miss Beams decided to reveal all about "Fred" and who she thought he really was. It was a scandal that puzzled everyone. Why did a B-movie actress trying to collect back pay merit the mobilization and wrath of the entire Philippine government? The answer would come many years later, buried among the papers left by the Marcoses when they fled Malacanang.

Among the papers found in Imelda's bedroom was a dossier on Dovie Beams that described her as "in the habit of dropping names of important persons as being close to her or having had bedroom relations with her." The dossier went on to list some of Miss Beams's alleged boyfriends, including "President John F. Kennedy and his brother, Ted Kennedy; Canadian Prime Minister Trudeau; the present Prime Minister of West Germany; the President of France; Howard Hughes; as well as all of the most prominent producers, directors, and actors in Hollywood." The dossier concludes that "Most, if not all, of these statements are mere hallucinations. . . ." Ergo, too, Miss Beams's relationship with Marcos, if the dossier or Imelda is to be believed. The same envelope held nude pictures of Miss Beams, including one where her most private parts had been furiously scribbled over with a pen.

Imelda was deeply hurt and humiliated by Miss Beams's revelations of her affair with Marcos, but what hurt most were Miss Beams's allegations about the state of their marriage. There was no marriage between Marcos and Imelda, Miss Beams charged, only a political partnership. This charge joined the rumors then circulating in Manila which said Imelda had sought medical help abroad about a disease which the foreign press dubbed "virginitis." Whether the two were connected remained mere speculation, but it took a very long time to rid Manila's rumor mills of talk on *l'affaire* "Fred."

Whatever the doubts about Miss Beams's revelations, there was no doubt about the nature of the storm that visited Malacanang. Something had torn in the First Couple's relationship.

"Imelda had caught him philandering, and that weakened his hold over her," said insiders. Marcos had been cast as a bumbling Casanova, with his lovemaking allegedly taped by a mere second-rate American actress, who claimed she had indubitable proof that her lover, "Fred," was none other than the President of the Philippines. To Imelda, who had so carefully nurtured the image of a perfect marriage—and her image of Marcos as a superhero—his public humiliation was unforgivable. Marcos had squandered his side of the partnership, and now the scales of power tipped in Imelda's favor.

Henceforth, the Marcoses ruled separate but equal empires even as they continued to appear devoted to one another in public. The fallout from the Dovie Beams affair gave Imelda the leverage to acquire more power.

Surprisingly with scandal after scandal, Marcos did not go under. Any other incumbent President should have gone down in the election of 1969. But Marcos was not any other President. Power to him was survival, the shield against rejection, and he must keep it at any cost—or perish.

The Filipino electorate in 1969 was not geared for this kind of challenge. Although they were willing to concede that the incumbent President was more clever and more shrewd than the run-of-the-mill politician, they were not up to his dynastic ambition and the stratagems he would employ to keep himself in power.

In the meantime Marcos's political strategy for his second term was to portray himself as a nationalist, no matter how corrupt, and to connect his opponent with the imperialist Americans. It was a potent formula. While Marcos would continue to concede to American demands, he would nevertheless successfully portray himself as a nationalist. Marcos had expert political advice when he echoed the nationalist aspirations of the thousands of Filipinos who had taken to the streets that year to proclaim war on America's continuing domination of the Philippines. The protests had spilled into the streets, the churches, and the schools. Marcos's opponent fell further and further behind. Despite his formidable accusations of Marcos's corruption, the only true issue was which of the two candidates represented the people's nationalist vision. Osmena, Marcos's opponent, entered the trap laid out for him. It is said that an American public relations firm played no small part in the stratagem.

As for the Filipino electorate, they paid the price of their nationalist aspirations, albeit reluctantly, to return Marcos for another four-year term, the first Philippine President ever to achieve it. The desire to break away from American domination, which Filipinos perceived rightly or wrongly as the cause of the backwardness and poverty in their country, was so paramount that it temporarily overrode all doubts about the danger in giving Marcos a second term. Those who had gone to see him inaugurated in Luneta for the second time spoke of the gloom and distress that they might have voted for their own doom. In voting for Marcos again, the Philippine people had taken political hemlock and only waited for the outcome that was certain to follow.

CHAPTER FIVE

"The Richest Woman in the World"

ON THE WAY to the funeral of Soviet President Leonid Brezh-nev in 1982, Imelda and about fifty of her friends took a commercial airline to Dharan from Manila. At the same time, a government-run Philippine Airlines 727 was pulled out of regular service, dislodging hundreds of paying passengers. It flew empty to rendezvous with the First Lady's party for a one-month journey to Moscow, London, Rome, and New York. The plane even had its own special crew of trusted men and women. But back in the Philippines, the government-controlled press told only of Imelda's exemplary austerity and of the diplomatic success she was bringing her country. In the Philippines no questions were raised concerning the size of the First Lady's diplomatic entourage, nor were there questions as to why an official trip to a state funeral in Moscow should include shopping and partying in London, Rome, and New York. For this information, one referred to the pages of *Hola, Harpers Bazaar, Queen, Oui, Paris Match,* and *Town and Country*—Western magazines which chronicled the doings of the titled, the rich, and the powerful. This was Imelda's fabulous double life as First Lady and co-dictator of the

Philippines after her husband's declaration of martial law in 1972.

Indeed, martial law provided Marcos and Imelda with almost magical powers and opened the way to the fortune that would soon make Imelda "the richest woman in the world." Under martial law the Marcoses could control the press and jail their political enemies. It provided Marcos with absolute political control and freed Imelda from the constraints of public opinion, allowing her to play out freely her deepest fantasies of power and social acceptance.

With U.S. support, the Marcos regime would collect billions of dollars in international bank loans to finance "development." This money would not only support Imelda's extravagant pet projects but would also find its way into her personal bank accounts. As co-dictator, Imelda would take responsibility for Philippine diplomatic efforts. She would make more than fifty international junkets in less than a decade, ostensibly to discuss pressing world problems with dozens of heads of state.

In fact, these trips would provide Imelda with a global stage on which to attempt once and for all to erase the true story of her past which the book had so painfully recalled. To accomplish this, she relentlessly pursued the international jet set, surrounding herself with admiring men, and spending unheard-of sums of money in a futile attempt to fill the emptiness inside her. The more she denied the truth of the book, the deeper she plunged into Marcos's political act. Her identity depended on his success, and she would go to any lengths to maintain his power.

Imelda's revulsion toward her own family's poverty began to assume irrational proportions. Her public pronouncements on behalf of the poor camouflaged the aversion and contempt she felt for their helplessness, for it mirrored her own worst fears. To close friends and relatives she spoke of her past as something she wished had never been. Had she accepted her past, Imelda might have been the symbol of the people's aspirations and so could have become a legitimate successor to

Marcos. Instead, the Marcoses devised self-destructive machinations and fantasies which in the end left them easy prey to the power of the truth.

By Marcos's second term, Imelda's extravagance had become the focus of the people's discontent. The public no longer believed her earlier avowals that she was merely an active First Lady. She also was on the way to becoming the second most powerful person in the country, without ever having been elected, however, her chances of winning a Presidential election were slim. Thus, with Marcos barred from running for a third term, Imelda's growing unpopularity became one of the factors leading him to declare martial law.

Long before Imelda's extravagance reached its zenith, in fact, the Filipino people clearly disapproved of her as a Presidential candidate. Despite the crowds which still came to hear her sing, an American corporation's 1969 survey of 1,000 Filipino respondents revealed that 83 percent rejected Imelda as a Presidential candidate. The survey also revealed that 80 percent of the people rejected the notion that Marcos would be justified in imposing martial law in order to stop the threat of "invasion, insurrection, or rebellion." But at this time few Filipinos pursued the meaning of this survey to its logical conclusion. The Marcoses did. By 1969 they knew they were finished in traditional politics: Martial law began to emerge as their only option for staying in power.

At this time Imelda remained a consummate actress. But every now and then occasions arose when she revealed her true character. One such occasion occurred when the wife of a newspaper publisher accompanied Imelda on one of her campaign sorties. The publisher's wife later told friends of her shock when Imelda quickly closed her car window as they drove past a street lined with barefoot, waving provincial Filipinos. "Smile, smile at the fools," Imelda had said. "That is all they want." Imelda then flashed her sweetest smile to the surging crowd. On a state visit to the United States more than a decade later, Mrs. Marcos would outline more of this philosophy to the readers of *Newsweek* magazine. "Yes, the Filipinos are living in slums and hovels. But what counts is the human spirit, and the Filipinos are smiling. They smile because they are a little healthy, a little educated, and a little loved. And for me the real index of this country is the smiles of the people, not the economic index."

But if Imelda managed to hide her contempt for the poor for a time, a 1971 scandal exposed her true ambitions and pushed Marcos even further toward declaring martial law. The William Hickey column of London's *Daily Express* reported Imelda's purchase of a $325,000 penthouse in the fashionable Kensington neighborhood. The story was picked up by the wire services and became a major scandal in Manila. At the same time, the Philippine press revived rumors of Marcos's plan to run Imelda for President. Marcos denied the English reports. He attacked Filipino opposition leaders for trying to track down the Marcoses's "hidden wealth," even then suspected to run to millions of dollars. The penthouse purchase, he said, was no more true than previous gossip which linked him to other real estate purchases in the United States. "It looks like the mud slinging is starting very early," he said, in an oblique reference to his wife's Presidential candidacy in 1973. Imelda made a separate denial of the purchase, as well as of her Presidential aspirations. So did the Philippine ambassador to the Court of St. James, Mr. Jaime Zobel, who would later be an able defender of Marcos's martial law.

Without a proven link to Marcos, the penthouse scandal eventually died down. Had the enterprising reporter who broke the story pursued the details of the property purchase, the public would have learned that the property was bought in the name of Laurel Limited, a company registered in Britain's tax-free Isle of Man, and was leased to a Benjamin Trinidad of Leyte (Imelda's favorite brother, using their maternal name). The property was paid for by the Philippine Sugar Commission. This modus operandi would be used by the Marcoses again and again to purchase properties around the world.

But the real scandal of the penthouse episode lay not in the revelation that Marcos had purchased foreign property beyond his means as a public official. The more serious revelation, not known at the time, concerned the fact that Imelda herself had requested that William Hickey write a column about her daughter Imee. The penthouse purchase and the write-up in the society column which chronicled the doings of the internationally rich was Imelda's scheme for a more permanent stake in international café society. She had even commissioned a free-lance photographer to photograph herself and Imee in the newly purchased flat.

While Marcos belittled the *Express* report as mere gossip, Imelda flattered the reporter by saying, "If there is any column in which I would like to appear, it would be the William Hickey column." What was true was that even before the declaration of martial law in 1972, Imelda had embarked on a project that had little to do with the social and economic welfare of Filipinos. This project was for her to be accepted in international high society as a charter member. She loved the company of the rich, the famous, and the powerful of the world. For the once-shy lass from an impoverished province in the Philippines, this was heady stuff that she could flaunt before Philippine high society. None of Manila's Four Hundred, after all, had penetrated the exclusive social circles of the international super-rich.

Dragging her daughter Imee in tow, Imelda stepped onto the world stage and aggressively sought to hobnob with the likes of Prince Rainier and Princess Grace of Monaco, the Begum Aga Khan, Prince Bertil of Sweden, and a host of other European blue bloods and American industrialists. She called the world's Beautiful People her "gang." Her periodic rendezvous with them was a way of denying her past. Despite the book, Imelda wanted the world to know she was accepted in its most exclusive society. In the coming years she would expend unimaginable energy reminiscent of the campaign of 1965 to achieve this goal, and to win back her "lost esteem."

Not satisfied with being merely an occasional guest at the

parties of the Beautiful People as First Lady of the Philippines, Imelda expected Imee to solidify her social position through a successful marriage, either to an industrial fortune like Agnelli of Fiat or to a member of European royalty, such as Prince Charles. After all, in her own time she had moved up in Philippine society this way. Imee would have unlimited money and power as well as Imelda's prowess behind her. The only thing she lacked was physical beauty. Although she said she loved her daughter dearly, Imelda fretted to friends that she could not understand why Imee had not inherited her good looks. Friends spoke of how the younger Ms. Marcos often suffered from cruel public comparisons to her beautiful mother, and how this may have contributed to her rebelliousness years later. Still, Imelda was not discouraged. There were many ways to concoct attention in the society pages.

On behalf of Imee, Imelda befriended matchmakers and hostesses connected to Europe's social elite. The wife of a Philippine ambassador tells how Imelda inveigled an invitation for Imee to an exclusive weekend party given by Mrs. March, the Marabella circuit's society hostess par excellence, the first time Imelda ever met her. Imee spent a summer with the Marches and met an Agnelli son, but no romance developed. Imelda would often tell friends how disappointed she was that Imee was not as beautiful as she was; good looks could have made things much easier for Imee.

As for Imelda, when she heard that a Greek with vague connections to the Philippines was a personal friend of Princess Margaret, she unashamedly offered him the post of ambassador to the Court of St. James. Soon it was being whispered that the First Lady of the Philippines was trading anything from loans to ambassadorships in return for coveted dinner invitations!

Not long after the London penthouse imbroglio, an even more explosive exposé hit the Marcos administration. The Marcoses had attempted to bribe members of the Constitutional Convention to amend the Constitution to allow Marcos to stay in power. Eduardo Quintero, an aging delegate from

Imelda's home province, produced envelopes which he said contained cash payments Imelda had given to a number of delegates. In exchange, Quintero charged, the delegates were expected to vote in favor of changing the Presidential system of government to a parliamentary system. This would enable Marcos to become prime minister, thus circumventing the constitutional hindrance to a third term. The delegates were also expected to block a pending resolution that would bar past and present Presidents and their relatives from running in future Presidential elections.

But Marcos was adept at playing to public sympathy. To sidestep the scandal, Marcos made the surprising announcement that Imelda was pregnant. How could Filipinos take sides with an old man against a pregnant woman? The First Lady's scandalous attempt to bend the will of the Constitutional Convention to the Marcoses's ambition was lost in the ensuing confusion. Indeed, behind the political skirmishes Marcos was secretly putting the finishing touches to Oplan Sagittarius, the code name for his declaration of martial law. Malacanang soon announced that Imelda had had a miscarriage due to pressure from political events. As for Mr. Quintero's recalcitrance, Marcos reminded him that his efforts were in vain, for the Constitutional Convention's will would be nullified under martial law. Moreover, Marcos warned him, he could "arrest any man."

Filipinos were not cowed by Marcos's threats. Nor were they taken in by his attempt to destroy Quintero's credibility. The old man was acclaimed a hero in the feverish weeks that preceded martial law. In fact, Quintero's revelations ignited renewed nationalism in the Philippines. Ordinary citizens, nuns, priests, and professionals joined with students and political activists to cheer Quintero's revelations and to boo Marcos's supporters. Although a futile show of patriotism then, these Filipinos anteceded the millions who would block Marcos's tanks in February 1986 in the final showdown of his dictatorship.

In 1969 the respected American journalist and Philippine

observer Robert Shaplen had predicted the movement of the early 1970s: "While watching this election, I had the feeling, for the first time in the two and a half decades I have been visiting the islands, that the Philippines may at last be on the verge of real change, including an end to, or at least alteration of, their post-colonial relationship with the United States, which has been profitable for a privileged few but has done little for national pride."

What incensed Filipinos most about Marcos was not his failure to solve the economic and social hardships of the country. Other Philippine Presidents, too, had failed to turn the economy around. The people's anger stemmed from the perception that Marcos had betrayed his country—and would use force against the very people he had sworn to serve—in order to maintain power. Despite his questionable reputation, Filipinos in 1965 and again in 1969 had hoped Marcos would fulfill his promise to steer the country away from the shadow of U.S. imperialism. But Marcos had not only continued the Philippine's dependence on the United States, he had also traded on his country's honor to stay in power. Even as he declared that relations with America had to be "reappraised" and changed, Marcos was laying the groundwork to reaffirm the former colonizer's "special rights."

The country's economic hardships were real enough, but the vigor of the rising protest against Marcos had its roots in the destruction of the Filipino dream. Whatever else was said, 1899 was immutable and lurked in the nation's collective psyche. Filipinos, rightly or wrongly, blamed the country's neocolonial relationship to the United States for the huge gap between the rich and the poor. To nationalists, the Laurel-Langley treaty of 1955 had merely reinforced the position of the elites, unbroken from the Spanish regime. The small number of families who had once enjoyed the patronage of the Spanish crown had formed economic alliances with American business and divided the spoils as if the poor, or indeed the rest of the nation, did not exist.

The most onerous aspect of this treaty was that it allowed

Americans equal rights to Filipinos in the exploitation of local resources, the operation of public utilities, and in scores of other business enterprises. In exchange, privileged Filipinos were given tariff exemptions in the United States on exports of sugar, tobacco, and other products. Although both governments were poised to end these "special relations," a number of American business leaders based in Manila balked at any change that could endanger their businesses and landholdings. These American interests soon suffered another blow, which set them even more firmly against the rising nationalist movement—and even closer to Marcos.

On August 17, 1972, the Philippine Supreme Court, in a landmark decision on the "Parity Amendment" to the 1935 constitution, declared that American citizens and business enterprises could no longer acquire or own private agricultural lands in the Philippines, except in cases of hereditary succession. It also ruled that all other rights acquired by American parties would expire on July 3, 1974. Suddenly Filipino nationalism appeared to threaten not only American businessmen, but U.S. foreign policy as well. In such an atmosphere, American policy makers despaired of negotiating a new trade treaty and military base agreement.

This was the juncture in Philippine history when Marcos's personal ambitions gibed with American interests. Marcos would have found it difficult to impose dictatorship in the Philippines without some tacit approval from Washington. There is evidence that such approval was sought and received. Rather than face up to the inevitability of Filipino national independence, some American policy makers saw the sponsorship of a corrupt Filipino leader as an easy way out, or at least as a delaying tactic.

Everywhere in the country, from Manila's fashionable drawing rooms to barbershops and corner stores, Filipinos began talking of the ominous threat of martial law. Politicians, civic organizations, students, and the press kept up a relentless siege of protest to keep Marcos at bay. It was a magnificent last stand that led even the late Senator Benigno Aquino to believe that Filipinos would riot in the streets sooner than allow the loss of their freedoms. Aquino was correct, but it would take Filipinos another fourteen years to reach this point.

That August, when the monsoon season should have passed, the Philippines were hit by a violent typhoon that devastated the country's rice granary. Rain fell for thirty days and thirty nights, killing hundreds and destroying crops worth millions. To superstitious Filipinos, the catastrophe was God's punishment for the excesses of Marcos's government. Marcos saw otherwise, saying, "I guess the only thing left to do is to pray." He did not allude to the people's prayers for their country.

The entire morning of September 23, 1972, the Philippines were out of touch with the world. A radio behavior report issued by the British Broadcasting Corporation noted that Philippine radio stations could not be monitored that day. Broadcasts finally resumed at 13:08 Philippine time. Listeners were asked to stand by for a national address by President Marcos. It was to be the long-feared declaration of martial law.

Letters written at this time told of the apprehension and disbelief among Filipinos when martial law was declared. Music was played in the meantime. By 19:15 Marcos was on the air live. In exactly twenty-nine minutes, Marcos ended twenty-six years of democracy in the Philippines. Filipinos had to recall the time of the Japanese invasion to match the anxiety that now pervaded the country. But this time the enemy was one among themselves. Music continued to play, intermittently interrupted by the announcement. The few people who ventured out of their houses remember the eerie atmosphere of deserted streets and empty newspaper stands.

By the time Marcos went on the air to declare martial law, the operation Oplan Sagittarius was completed. Every newspaper except one owned by a Marcos crony was padlocked and placed under military guard. Six of the city's major television stations and nine radio stations were shut. Only one radio and one TV station, both linked to Marcos, were left free to operate. Hundreds of opposition leaders, among them Benigno Aquino, José W. Diokno, Ramon Mitra, and journalists Max

Soliven, Amando Doronila, and Joaquin Roces were arrested before dawn. Enrique Voltaire Garcia, a prominent oppositionist in the Constitutional Convention who suffered from leukemia, was arrested at three o'clock in the morning. His widow recalls that the arresting officer would not listen to her pleas to wait until morning to move the seriously ill man. The officer replied, "We can't wait, we have many more to arrest." Later in the week Garcia would succumb, and his wife would search a long time to locate his body in a military hospital. The list of arrestees also included twenty-two other oppositionists, thirty-one Hukbalahap leaders, and a smattering of Marcos men for propaganda purposes. Among the latter, Roquito Alban, a notorious Marcos man reputed to have his own private army, would be freed soon after.

Filipinos were prohibited from leaving the country. A travel ban was imposed, and sky marshals were ordered on board all domestic flights. Schools were closed for a week. A midnight-to-four-A.M. curfew was announced. The death penalty was imposed for the illegal possession of firearms. Public demonstrations, rallies, and strikes were banned, and military commanders in the provinces were ordered to assume local government powers.

A stunned nation listened to Marcos defend martial law as the only way to stop the threat of insurrection posed by the Communist Party of the Philippines and the New People's Army. In reality, these groups controlled no more than 1,000 armed regulars, 10,000 part-time supporters, and 100,000 sympathizers in a country of more than 40 million people. Marcos also described a state of anarchy and lawlessness in the country and said that he, the commander in chief of the armed forces, was empowered by the constitution to "protect the state." The "state of anarchy" he referred to, in fact consisted of no more than a few bombings of public lavatories prior to the declaration of martial law. These bombings could hardly be described as the work of rebels determined to overthrow a government.

The Filipino people's apprehension that they had a leader

who would betray their country's independence was soon confirmed. Among the first to praise Marcos's action was the American Chamber of Commerce. It was also learned that U.S. Ambassador Henry Byroade was informed of the plan when he lunched with Marcos the day before martial law was announced. Although there were scattered criticisms, much of the Western press downplayed the declaration of martial law in a country modeled after the American democratic system. Portents of an evil dictatorship were largely ignored. Instead, many reporters fell over one another to describe the "chaos and disorder" that preceded martial law, and speculated that perhaps this was what the Filipino people wanted after all. No more was said of the discontent and protest of a people determined to take fate into their own hands. Indeed, with the boot on their necks, most Filipinos opted to allow Marcos to play out his strategy.

From the heap of her countrymen's shattered dreams rose Imelda, the flamboyant other half of the new dictatorship. After months of secretly pursuing her ambition to be "the richest woman in the world," Imelda was poised to pursue her goals without further regard for public or world opinion.

A few weeks before martial law was declared, a dying man had been brought to the Veterans Memorial Hospital in suburban Manila. He was a frail figure in late middle-age, with a face that mirrored pain from a massive brain tumor. Although his manner was aristocratic, he did not look wealthy. His wife and children crowded in the little room where he waited for the end to come. He called his wife to come closer and whispered his last wish. The man was Norberto Romualdez Jr., the former governor of Leyte, and Imelda's nemesis. Before his death in pitiful circumstances, he asked his wife, Rosa, to bury him in Leyte where he had served as governor before Imelda forced him out. It would be his last card in the continuing saga of the Romualdez family rivalry.

The hapless widow to whom he had entrusted this task lacked even the money to pay the huge sixty-thousand-pesos hospital bill to claim his body, let alone to pay for transporting him to Leyte. There had been no money since he'd become ill a long time before, and Imelda's promises that he would be given an honorable job in exchange for giving up the governorship were never fulfilled. In fact, he had been given an obscure clerical job in Manila and was forced to leave his big family behind in Leyte to make ends meet. With Filipinos, as with most Orientals, a dying man's wish cannot be denied. Norberto's wife had no one she could turn to but Imelda and Benjamin. After all, the widow reasoned, if Imelda could dispatch a plane to bring Norberto to Manila, she could as easily provide the plane that would take his body home. She also hoped to get a loan from Imelda to cover the hospital bill. She felt that a loan from Imelda would be small compensation for what her husband had given up. Severed from Leyte, Norberto had become increasingly despondent; before his death he was all but a broken man.

Rosa thought that Imelda would consider the sacrifice he had made, but her pleas were met with only scorn and venom. "Why does he need to be buried in Leyte? He is nobody in Leyte. What is wrong with Manila? Bury him here, in any corner" was Imelda's reply. Times had changed their fortunes, and Imelda was bent on exacting her last ounce of revenge.

Norberto's widow took the humiliation, hopeful that Imelda would at least accede to her request for a loan so she could claim her husband's body. This, too, was denied with a torrent of insults. Faced with Imelda's intransigence, Rosa begged and borrowed from friends until she had twenty thousand pesos and pleaded with the hospital to release Norberto's body on part payment. His last wish still remained: to be buried in Leyte. In desperation Norberto's widow sought an unlikely benefactor—Senator Benigno Aquino, chairman of the Liberal Party, to which her husband had belonged, and the Marcoses' mortal enemy. Although surprised that Rosa was unable to get Imelda's help, Aquino generously offered his personal plane.

On the day of the funeral, officials and townsfolk in Leyte prepared a hero's welcome for their former governor, much to the consternation of Imelda's brother Benjamin, the incumbent governor. Benjamin, in fact, had tried desperately to keep the crowds away by making false radio broadcasts as to the funeral schedule. When Imelda learned that Aquino would frustrate her last act of revenge against her cousin, she became fearful that he would use the incident as political propaganda. Accordingly, she quickly informed her cousin's widow that she and the President would preside over Norberto's funeral services. The widow was stopped from boarding the plane, but she curtly refused Imelda's belated attempts to honor her husband. Thus was Norberto Romualdez Jr. buried under the blazing sun of Leyte, as his father had been —all through the intercession of the hated Benigno Aquino Jr.

Four years later Imelda would call her cousins to Malacanang to recall Norberto's death and funeral. To Loreto's surprise, Imelda was in tears and asked them why they hated her so. Unable to understand what she meant by posing now as the offended party, Loreto pressed her to explain. Imelda replied, "They"—referring to Norberto's wife, Rosa, and her children —"were willing to run over me, just so the plane could take off." This was Imelda's astonishing version of the day Norberto was returned to be buried in Leyte.

But her brother Benjamin was more candid. Through the Romualdez grapevine the family learned why he and Imelda would not help Norberto's widow: "They, too, must suffer the way we have suffered."

In the days following the declaration of martial law, Imelda receded from public view. It was even rumored that she was abroad when martial law was declared. Marcos, the consummate tactician, had rightly calculated that her presence would only exacerbate the people's antipathy following the succession of scandals that implicated her. He bided his time before returning his principal character to the limelight.

On December 7, 1972, an assassin tried to kill Imelda Marcos. The event took place on live television as the First Lady distributed prizes to winners of the National Beautification and Cleanliness contest. Imelda successfully parried the keen blade of a bolo knife the assassin wielded. Although she suffered some slash wounds and broken nails, she was on the whole unharmed, as soldiers gunned down the would-be assassin. Her heroic survival, captured in front-page pictures with her husband at her side, provided the counterpoint to the other major story of the day—the arrest of the sons of three powerful families, one of whom Marcos owed a political debt. Among those arrested was Eugenio Lopez Jr., son of Eugenio Lopez Sr., the kingmaker who was Marcos's chief ally in the 1965 and 1969 Presidential elections. If he broke a cardinal rule of Filipino mores—gratitude—Marcos could excuse his action by citing the assassination attempt on his wife. In a stroke he met the demands of political exigency without offending Filipino ideals.

Had this fortuitous event simply fallen into his lap, or was it another display of Marcos's political prowess? Whatever the truth, Imelda once again played the role of consummate political partner and very nearly sacrificed her life to prove her worth. She would, in time, collect on Marcos's debt to her. Over time the relationship between creator and creature, master and pupil, had progressively blurred. Their partnership exhibited chameleonlike qualities that intrigued and fascinated Marcos watchers unable to determine who was master and who was follower. The partners had become one in purpose. As Marcos's successor to the throne, Imelda occupied an equal place in his regime. The assassination attempt sealed Imelda's claim to half of the empire.

On January 16, 1973, Imelda, her arm still bandaged, occupied a prominent place among world leaders as the official Philippine representative to the inauguration of American President Richard Nixon. It was the first of a score of highly personalized diplomatic missions Imelda would undertake during the next decade. After the inauguration she and a twenty-one-member party flew to London. Wearing a leopard-skin coat and with two hundred suitcases, Imelda was greeted at the airport by her dear friend, world-famous ballerina Margot Fonteyn. William Hickey once again paid Imelda the attention she so craved, asking why Madame Marcos should need to book a suite at Claridge's when she had her penthouse at the Duchess of Bedford Walk. Rather than take offense at the imputation that she was an extravagant woman, Imelda was pleased to be mentioned in the same breath as Jacqueline and Christina Onassis, both reputed to have permanently reserved suites at Claridge's. This was the publicity she coveted, and martial law meant this news would never reach Manila.

The British press also carried a small news item about Madame Marcos's party exceeding the allowable weight and being trapped in an elevator at the penthouse. Other bits of gossip followed. Harrods was said to be de rigueur for this moneyed group from the impoverished Philippines, and Fortnum & Mason had received orders for smoked salmon, roast turkey with chestnut stuffing, and cases of Dom Pérignon for a dinner party. And of course there was talk of the night at the exclusive Annabel's for dusk-till-dawn dancing with the likes of actor John Mills and his daughter Hayley, an evening designed by Imelda and arranged for by the Philippine ambassador.

But the trip had to have a "serious side" to it, and a thirty-minute audience with Prime Minister Edward Heath was included in the agenda. The audience lasted two hours and was immediately beamed to the Manila press as a diplomatic feat. Prime Minister Heath, an ascetic bachelor who valued his time, it was trumpeted, had extended Imelda's thirty-minute appointment to two hours! There were no press releases describing how Mr. Heath viewed his charming visitor. "Goodness, the woman could talk," he was overheard to remark by foreign office wags after the grueling "top-level" interview.

There were many other missions to follow, all of them "triumphs and successes." Imelda's trips abroad, which were ridiculed as mere junkets in the pre-martial-law Philippine press, now assumed a new dimension. They were henceforth described as diplomatic breakthroughs of an ambassador plenipotentiary the likes of which the world had never seen: beautiful, daring, talented Imelda—the Kissinger of the East. With Marcos's absolute powers of arrest, the press never questioned whether such missions might not be accomplished more economically through normal diplomatic channels. Embassies were now relegated to halfway houses kept in perpetual readiness for the call of the globe-trotting First Lady and her entourage. If there was oil to be bought from Iran, a telex inquiry was not sufficient; Imelda had to call personally on the Shah in Tehran. When there was a suggestion of forming a sugar cartel with Cuba, Imelda quickly took the opportunity to fly to Cuba and meet Fidel Castro. En route she collected daughters Irene and Imee to complete a diplomatic entourage of fifty, and she included a shopping trip to New York in the itinerary.

Such whims had the full approval of Marcos. It satisfied a marital arrangement then that gave space for both of them to live their own private lives. The book and the Dovie Beams scandal had hurt the marriage, friends said, but the distance had paradoxically reinforced their working relationship as ruling partners of the Philippines. Imelda had at last, it seemed, achieved the detachment and sophistication that separated emotional needs from political necessity. She was a woman of the world par excellence.

Away from the Philippines and Malacanang Palace, Imelda relived a fantasy of youth, surrounding herself with handsome male escorts. Her favorite in this coterie of handsome men was Hollywood actor George Hamilton, whom she met in the early 1980s. Both deny having anything but a "platonic" relationship. This could well have been true. After all, if Imelda had medical problems like the "virginitis" described by *Newsweek*, the issue of sex could be avoided. Moreover, she always had a retinue of security guards. But other well-placed sources aver that Imelda and George Hamilton had a very special friendship. How else to explain the sweetness of their tête-à-têtes? Imelda's schedule from a 1983 rendezvous with the actor read, "Breakfast with G. Hamilton, lunch with G. Hamilton, shopping with G. Hamilton, disco with G. Hamilton, midnight snack at the gazebo with G. Hamilton, and back to Makiki Heights with G. Hamilton."

And what of Marcos? As Imelda once told a reporter, Marcos approved of the friendship. "Oh, the President, he is a very sweet man," Imelda said. "He knows very well it's nothing. My dear, what would be terrible is if you were hiding something—then that would be really bad. In fact, last night it was a disaster because right in front of the President, poor George, I pulled him to the dance floor because first of all we dance so beautifully together. I like dancing with people who are perfect dancers, and he's neither too tall nor too short, too fat nor too thin—you know I am tall. It was so much fun. . . ." Friends, however, say, that the real fun took place at disco parties held in the darkness of her Manhattan penthouse on 66th Street. These parties sometimes lasted till five in the morning.

After the Marcoses fled in 1986, George and Imelda's relationship came under a different sort of scrutiny when it became apparent that there might be questionable money-laundering involved. *Star* magazine reported that Hamilton bought a $1.2 million house in Beverly Hills in 1982. The house was said to have been bought by Imelda and refurbished by Filipino architect George Ramos. The property attracted attention only when the Hollywood actor used it as collateral for a five-year $4 million loan from Calno Holdings NV, a Netherlands Antilles firm. The deal seemed straightforward enough until the press learned the identity of the men behind Calno. Diosdado Ordonez, who negotiated the loan on behalf of Calno Holdings, was an employee of Antonio Floirendo, a crony of the Marcoses and fondly called the "Banana King" by George's mother, Ann Hamilton. A few weeks after the collapse of the Marcos regime, George sold the property to Adnan Khashoggi, another friend of Marcos and Imelda, for $6 million. There is more to it than meets the eye, and people are conjecturing that with that kind of money perhaps there was really something more to *l'affaire* Georgie. One of Imelda's friends adds, "I did notice how the dancing partners continued to hold hands even when the music was over."

Another Imelda favorite was pianist Van Cliburn. Their love of music originally brought them together, and Imelda makes much of how they met at the clinic of a famous American doctor who specialized in the care and treatment of hands. This was in 1973, when her hands were lacerated during the assassination attempt. After that first encounter, according to Imelda's stories to friends, Van Cliburn invited her to the Metropolitan Opera. Imelda had worn an ostrich cape for the occasion, and a few feathers fell from the cape as they descended the carpeted stairs. The famous pianist picked up the feathers and tucked them carefully into his pocket. "Oh, just leave them there—don't bother to pick them up," Imelda said. But Van Cliburn allegedly replied, "Madame, those feathers are precious. Anything that touches your body is beautiful."

She thought the world of Van Cliburn and had hour-long telephone conversations with him mostly on sweet nothings, as would a love-struck teenager. On one occasion, a musical prodigy played at the piano for him over the telephone when Imelda wanted his opinion on her talent. No wonder Malacanang's phone bill paid by the people amounted to millions of pesos. Van Cliburn also received some reward for his friendship with Madame. When the Kildia Bee O'Bryan Cliburn Foundation, a trust fund, was founded in April 1982, Antonio Floirendo was one of the founding directors along with Van Cliburn, his mother, Nancy Hanks, Clement Stone, Robert Reid, and Frank Miner.

A joke circulating around Manila asked, "What happens if death takes the chief from our midst?" Answer: "Then the President would have to run the whole thing himself."

Indeed, for a time some American policy makers agreed with Marcos that Imelda could be an acceptable successor who could carry on with the help of able technocrats. It was a well-known rumor that Imelda had admirers in Washington who favored a future combination rule between her and United Nations Deputy Secretary General Rafael Salas, a disaffected former Marcos cabinet minister and an able administrator.

The Duke and Duchess of Gloucester were in Manila in 1975, when Imelda was named the first governor of Metro Manila, a territory encompassing four cities and thirteen towns. The position put her powers and resources second only to those of the President. Just as the whole country was under one man's rule, its premier city was put under one woman's rule, with mayors acting merely as her "action officers." The stage was set for Imelda's succession to the Presidency should Marcos die or be incapacitated.

At the time, Marcos denied he was grooming his wife as his successor. More than a decade later the world would finally learn of Marcos's handwritten order, entitled Presidential Decree Number 731, and dated June 7, 1975. The decree read:

> By the virtue of the powers vested in me by the Constitution of the Philippines as President of the Republic, I, Ferdinand E. Marcos, hereby decree that Presidential Number 100, dated January 17, 1975, on the Presidential Succession shall be amended so that the Commission succeeding me in the exercise of powers and duties as President in the event of my death or permanent incapacity shall be composed of the following: Chairman, Mrs. Imelda R. Marcos; and members, the Secretary of National Defense; the Executive Secretary; the Secretary of Foreign Affairs; the Secretary of Finance; the Secretary of Industry; the Secretary of Local Government and Community Development.

Marcos's passion for power and his dynastic ambition underpinned the question of succession. It was his obsession to live on in the person of Imelda. Despite their marital differences and her personal inadequacies, she was his only hope for immortality. After her, his power would pass on to his children and his children's children. But Imelda's flamboyance and seemingly assertive will blurred the picture, and not a few journalists, Filipinos and foreigners alike, branded her the world's most ambitious woman. The title had merit insofar as Imelda had to emulate Marcos's ambition and drive in order to protect her secure position in his reign. But to say that her ambition rivaled Marcos's would miss the true nature of the relationship between these two strong-willed rulers. If Imelda sought political power, it was in response to Marcos's vision of himself. To her, what mattered was access to resources and wealth, through which she sought the happiness and acceptance she had been denied as a child. She could not understand that these were not commodities that could be bought and sold.

Between 1974 and 1985 Imelda flew from one end of the globe to the other. Each trip was a superproduction involving one and sometimes two planeloads of cabinet ministers, press, and friends, and hundreds of thousands of dollars in expenses for first-class hotels and limousines. Marcos, his cabinet ministers, and the entire Manila diplomatic corps were obliged to be on hand for Imelda's every arrival and departure to lend her trips the official seal. But like her politicking, Imelda's diplomacy was a personal crusade, disjointed from reality. She was simply out to prove that she was good, better than anyone else—the most talented Filipino to conduct the foreign affairs of the country. Whatever Imelda's diplomatic skills, she was undeniably beautiful. That was always a factor in Marcos's or Imelda's calculations. No man or woman could be immune to the power of that attribute, Imelda claims. And indeed, she has repeatedly proved its effectiveness. She told relatives that Marcos was sending her to meet a group of bankers in New York because she could accomplish feats beyond the skills of any foreign affairs minister or ambassador. Heads of state, in her scheme of things, were reduced to bosom friends or constituents whom she could win to her side by a panoply of persuasive charms and expensive gifts. As she was later to say in a no-holds-barred interview with a group of Filipino women journalists: "I don't think at this point, and this is a little immodest but it is true—there is probably no First Lady, not even a head of state in any part of the world who has been to all the corridors of power, has been a friend to all the major superpowers like the First Lady. I can go to Li Xianian (chairman of China's People's Consultative Committee), Hu Yaobang, Deng Hsiao Ping (chairman of the Communist Party of China), Chernenko (Soviet Union), Khadaffy (Libya), Fahd, anybody. I can go to any one of them. And all I have to do is, if I see that the country is in trouble, I'll get my little bag and say: 'Huwag naman. (Please don't.)' And I don't need to be President. I don't have to be anything—I'll do it because I love this country. This is my country. It's the only country I will seek for its survival."

She was unable to accept the notion that diplomacy has limited power to influence a country's foreign policy and that such diplomacy must ultimately rest on facts. During her diplomatic spree she ordered Filipino ambassadors around the world to refurbish their chanceries, spending thousands so "these Westerners cannot look down on us." She moved the Philippine ambassador's residence in Paris to elegant Avenue Foch, cheek by jowl with the rich Arab and Western embassies, at the height of the oil crisis, when every other country was tightening its purse strings. The move took place despite the fact that there was no foreseeable increase in trade or cultural relations between the two countries. The change could not have looked more insensitive or inopportune than when hundreds of hapless Filipino women who had fled the civil wars in Lebanon and Iran faced deportation in France. The women, some of whom were teachers and professionals, had been forced to work as domestic help in rich Arab households owing to high unemployment at home. The wars in the Middle East had caught them unawares. Typically, the Philippine embassy washed its hands of this problem, concerned as it was with Imelda's priorities.

Even the much-heralded opening of diplomatic ties with China was credited to Imelda's special friendship with the late Mao Tse-Tung, who was said to have been charmed by her schoolgirl approach. She supposedly gave him a daughterly buss on the cheeks which enchanted him. Little was said of the obvious fact that the Chinese used the Marcos visit in its own public relations campaign to offset the political gains of the Soviet Union.

Perhaps Imelda's most notorious junket after the declaration of martial law was her trip to Katmandu in March 1975 to attend the coronation and wedding of King Birendra Bir Bikram Shad Dev. She was entertaining her "gang," which included bosom friend Christina Ford, Dr. and Mrs. Christiaan Barnard, and Gina Lollobrigida in Malacanang Palace. Instead of ending the party when it was time to go to Katmandu, Imelda had the capricious idea of taking the entire party of forty to the coronation—including six hairdressers—without much thought to protocol or expense.

Acting like a heady medieval potentate, she commandeered four planes and flew to Katmandu as if to a party around the block. One plane carried her own food, just in case Nepalese cuisine failed to please her guests' palates. The trip was scandalous, but the only criticism in the Western press was confined to gossip columns—merely adding to Imelda's mystique in international café society. A former classmate of King Shad Dev at Eton recalls the rest of the guests' dismay when Imelda walked straight up to the King upon her arrival at the reception, ignoring the line of protocol, which included the King's mother. During the rest of the festivities the First Lady of the Philippines kept close to Prince Charles, who was, as usual, the focus of TV cameras throughout the event. Back at home, newspaper headlines read: "First Lady Scores in 'Quiet Diplomacy.' " Her diplomatic feat was to invite Prince Charles to visit Manila. Others wondered whether this was not the reason why she brought her "gang" in the first place—to impress British royalty.

Above all, what preoccupied Imelda was that no one should ever belittle her, not even the future king of England. The venue and the dramatis personae might have changed, but it was still the beauteous Imelda of Leyte battling for her place in the sun. Bedecked with fabulous jewelry and haute couture from Paris and Rome, she set out to conquer the world. After each trip when the proper press conferences had been done with, Imelda would call close friends and tell them the stories behind the stories, and particularly how she had beguiled and seduced these so-called world leaders.

When she visited King Hassan of Morocco, she recalled to friends, Imelda did not think the trip would be anything special. But he was so fascinated with her that the routine audience took two hours, and at the end of it, she claims, the monarch removed his royal cape and gave it to her. It was the first time he had ever given it to anyone outside the Royal family, as the cape symbolized the protection and friendship of the king. King Hassan was so enamored of her that he even followed her to New York and playfully reached her hotel room incognito, wearing tight jeans, after an arduous hike up a narrow fire escape!

And Fidel Castro! For all that socialistic macho, this ruler was putty in her fingers. Only a day into her visit, he discarded his security guards, and they drove alone to Los Pintos, his project to help Cuba's poor. After Imelda briefed Castro on her own projects for the poor of the Philippines, he said admiringly, "My lady, what is there that you cannot do?"

The press witnessed another such admiring interlude. It reported on a formal dinner wherein Castro and Imelda sat across the table from each other. Now and then the impetuous Cuban leader would be caught casting long, intent glances at Imelda and finally, reports said, he was unable to control himself and exclaimed, "Ah, this is a different kind of diplomacy!"

Imelda was even the beguiling diplomat in the spartan tent of the redoubtable Muammar Khaddafy, who strikes terror in the hearts of millions. Khaddafy's heart could only melt for this woman of the East, so resolutely on the side of peace for her Muslim brothers. And it was said that the puritanical Khaddafy was so entranced with Imelda's spirituality that he insisted on giving her lessons on the Koran between negotiations. Their longest meeting lasted a full six hours, leading the opposition to charge that she had flirted with Khaddafy to win his consent to the Tripoli Agreement. On her return home she was given a heroine's welcome, and no less than Carlos Romulo, Mr. United Nations himself, praised her for virtually saving the country from what could have been a disastrous fratricidal war. "I do not believe one can find a better example of personal diplomacy in recent times," opined Mr. Romulo.

The Tripoli Agreement ended the bitter war in the south between the rebel Muslims and Marcos's army, but only for a time. Marcos would soon renege on his part of the agreement, and war would recommence.

Following this coup, some of Imelda's adoring fans wrote the Nobel Prize committee recommending her for the 1978 peace prize for her valor. Presumably the valor referred to her many hours with Khaddafy, whom *Newsweek* had called "the most dangerous man in the world"!

But despite her successes, Imelda remained haunted. Nothing satisfied her. Her official duties completed, she became obsessed with shopping, throwing away millions of dollars without thought to her country's languishing economy. Those who accompanied her on such shopping sprees describe her buying habits. "If she liked something, whether it was chocolates, silk blouses, the finest leather bags or shoes, she would buy ten dozen, and when she was not sure whether she liked something, only five dozen," says a former friend and frequent guest at Imelda's parties. She would ransack department stores, floor by floor, section by section, with her party of courtiers and hangers-on in tow. It was not uncommon for her to run up bills of hundreds of thousands of dollars before she was through shopping at Harrods in London, Bloomingdale's in New York, Takashimaya in Tokyo, or at Liberty House in Honolulu. Other favorite haunts included Bond Street, the Rue Faubourg San Honoré, and the Via Condotti. And, when necessary, Imelda had the world brought to her: Harry Winston, Balestra, Mila Schoen, Valentino, Hanae Mori, Gucci— they all either called on her in Malacanang or sent their representatives with clothing, diamonds, or even sketches for the latest styles of summer shoes.

One of her favorites was the shoe firm Salvatore Ferragamo, whose sons, Ferrucio and Leonardo, continued the spirit of their father, self-styled shoemaker of "dreams"—handcrafted, classical designs for the rich and the famous. Although luminaries such as Greta Garbo, Gloria Swanson, and Paulette Goddard trooped to Florence to seek out the master of shoes who wrote "there was no limit in beauty, and no saturation in design," his sons broke away from tradition and brought their shoes to Imelda's doorstep, even making special designs for her.

But such were her dreams that the more she bought, the more she craved. Satisfaction eluded her. If Imelda was circumspect about showing off her fabulous jewelry collection in her own country, she did not hesitate to exhibit them to her gang, the "Beautiful People" of international café society. After all, there were those among them who would envy her cache of goodies.

Imelda is said to have invited an impoverished Russian princess, a reliable standby of the Roman jet set, to her suite at the Hotel Excelsior in order to show off her collection of jewelry. The pieces were all carefully labeled in padded leather cases not unlike the treasure chests avidly sought by medieval pirates. "It was like a page from 'A Thousand and One Nights,'" the princess is said to have exclaimed. Imelda then coaxed her to touch the jewelry, whereupon the princess became indignant. She would later tell friends that Imelda did not simply wish to show off her jewelry, but to gloat at others' envy of it. The humiliated princess did not understand that Imelda's vindictive edge stemmed from her deep-seated insecurity.

For a time Imelda was satisfied with expensive jewelry of the type worn by multimillionaire's wives—pieces costing hundreds of thousands of dollars from such world-renowned jewelers as Bulgari, Bucellati, and Harry Winston. But soon even these pieces failed to impress her. It was soon said that she was in the market only for "historical jewelry."

In this quest, Imelda learned of the Idol's Eye—the biggest diamond in the world—from her jewelers in New York. The diamond was originally identified in 1607, when the East India Company seized the stone from Persian Prince Rahab in payment for his debts. It disappeared for three hundred years and was rediscovered in 1906 as the eye of a sacred idol in the Temple of Benghazi. After being stolen by a messenger and sold to a Paris pawnshop, it was purchased by a Spanish grandee and remained in his London safe-deposit vault for several years. The Idol's Eye was later acquired by Harry Winston, the New York City gem dealer, who sold it to a Mrs. Stanton in 1947 for $675,000. In 1962 it was sold at auction to a Chicago gem dealer for $375,000. Imelda ultimately paid a cool $5.5 million dollars for this gem, and is rumored to own it still.

At this time of Imelda's heady diplomatic and shopping triumphs, Senator Benigno Aquino, the hated benefactor of Norberto Romualdez Jr., and the country's most celebrated political prisoner, went on a hunger strike in a desperate protest against Marcos's attempts to try him in a military court on charges of murder and subversion. The man who would most certainly have defeated Marcos at the polls in 1973 had martial law not been declared lost forty pounds on his hunger strike. He symbolized the resistance against martial law, but at that time, only his quiet and unassuming wife, Corazón, his mother, and a few friends were by his side. There seemed to be a conspiracy of silence among the people he had championed, the people he said would rather riot than lose their freedom. When questioned about Aquino's fast by a bold friend, Imelda was unforgiving. "That criminal! How many times were we—Ferdie and I—the targets of his assassination attempts! There have been bombs found all over the place! Bombs placed everywhere! Besides, I don't believe that criminal is really starving!"

As partner and would-be successor to Marcos, Imelda had demanded carte blanche to buy her way to happiness. This carte blanche was the Philippine treasury. A series of memorandums found after the revolution instructed the president of the Philippine National Bank to disburse funds to Imelda from an "intelligence account." This was how Marcos manipulated and juggled public funds to provide his wife with her pocket money. But the woman who would soon be named "the richest woman in the world" demanded a lot more than small change. Keeping up with the Joneses, in this case European royalty and the like, involved millions and millions of dollars. She had to contend with the industrial fortunes and crown estates of the Onassises, the Rockefellers, and the royal families of the world.

Her personal wealth, which was valued at $250 million just a year after the declaration of martial law, would rise to $350 million in 1975 and to $1.6 billion by the end of their rule. An undetermined amount of that wealth would come from huge development loans sponsored by the World Bank and the International Monetary Fund. The care and maintenance of these crucial loans, as well as of the bankers themselves, would fall to Imelda.

In December 1975 an article in *Cosmopolitan* named Imelda "one of the ten richest women in the world." She had joined the company of Elizabeth II of England, Dina Merrill, Christina Onassis, Barbara Hutton, Juliana of the Netherlands, The Begum Aga Khan, Doris Duke, Madeleine Dassault, and the Duchess of Alba. To Imelda, the *Cosmopolitan* article was her much-awaited entry into the exclusive international sisterhood she had worked so hard to join. The author of the article had done Imelda the singular favor of making it impossible for the "right people" to ignore her self-created status. Although she was seventh in the list of countable wealth, the reporter wrote, "There is nothing plain or unassuming, I hasten to point out, about Imelda Marcos, wife of the Philippines President, who spends prodigious sums of money and is rumored to be the richest woman in the world, bar none." Richard Baker went on to describe Imelda as the debutante of the year the year she arrived in Manila, and noted that she was born on the same day of the same year as Jacqueline Kennedy. He described her family as comfortable, but by no means dripping with wealth, and said Imelda had been educated in private schools and had studied music, dance, and voice.

Questions might be asked regarding the source for the reporter's article. Indeed, far from infuriating Imelda, it pleased her immensely. Whatever the source, the reporter had made no mention of the less-than-glamorous origin of Imelda's enormous wealth.

Incredibly, the article evoked no public outrage over the fact that among the ten richest women in the world Imelda alone came from an impoverished country with a per capita income of barely $200 year. At the time that the *Cosmopolitan* article appeared, it was estimated that 30 percent of Filipinos could barely afford basic necessities such as food, shelter, clothing, and medicine. Six and a half million Filipinos lived in dilapidated houses, and six million out-of-school youths in rural areas could not find work. The article occasioned a small furor from the Filipino opposition in America, but on the whole it aroused little interest and had no effect whatsoever on the Marcos dictatorship. America called the tune, and it was still very much on the Marcoses' side. The fabulous Imelda was on top of the world—rich, daring, inimitable. She was regarded more as a curiosity than as someone deserving condemnation.

But Imelda's excesses were not limited to shopping. At home, too, she dreamed of glamorous projects that would bring her further glory even as they bled the national treasury. Indeed, Imelda discovered the wonderful world of international bank loans in her search to fund her projects. These loans would flow to the Philippines for more than a decade, plunging the economy further into debt even as the Marcoses diverted millions of dollars to their personal assets.

She craved the attention of the world with the fervor of the child long ago who had so craved the attention of her self-absorbed parents. She was driven to do something truly unique now to win the attention she had failed to receive then —no cost was too high to reach this goal.

Following the 1965 Cultural Center, her first project, she built in dizzying succession the gleaming Population, Nutrition, and Heart Centers, the grandiose National Arts Center and Folk Arts theater, the Convention Center, as well as fourteen luxury hotels amidst a sea of slums and poverty. In those days Imelda hardly slept, and people who worked closely with her recall how she would sometimes call them in the middle of the night to check on the progress of construction. Sometimes she would even make pre-dawn visits to the sites. It was a bizarre obsession, as if she were in a race with fate to seize her moment of glory, or perhaps as if she were driven by the fearful memory of losing a roof over her head.

With uncanny wit, Filipinos dubbed this building obsession her "edifice complex." Yet as she built one mighty monument after another, there remained one building she could not face —a building she saw each time she left the Palace. Just around the block from Malacanang stood the Romualdez house on General Solano, and the garage to which she and her mother had been banished.

Before martial law was declared, Imelda had approached the building's owners about buying the property. They had offered it to Imelda at the ridiculously low price of a hundred fifty thousand pesos, mindful of the memories it carried for her. But curiously, she turned down the offer, saying it was too expensive. Not very long afterward, without much ado and with martial law in force, the house was torn down. Not a brick of it remains. Instead, Imelda bought the grandest and most historic mansion on General Solano, the Goldenberg Mansion, in which she housed the Marcos Foundation, rumored to be the catch-all for their fabulous wealth.

It was Imelda's dream house, with a magnificent staircase and a huge reception hall with doors opening to a sweeping veranda. Imelda furnished this mansion with a mixture of the finest Philippine and French period pieces. Antique procelain vases were scattered everywhere. When entertaining foreign guests in this mansion, described by a friend as Imelda's version of Marie Antoinette's Petit Trianon, Imelda referred to the house as the place where she had spent her childhood.

When Imelda spruced up the city for the annual International Monetary Fund–World Bank conference in October 1976, 60,000 squatters' shacks of tin and cardboard, not very different from the shack she had once called home, were removed so as not to offend her banker guests. Along the Del Pan Bridge, some twenty squatters were first told to whitewash and beautify their houses for the visiting bankers. But the next day, in an apparent change of mind, she had the houses bulldozed to get rid of the "eyesore" once and for all.

Among the houses leveled to the ground was that of Estrella, the faithful helper of Remedios Trinidad. After the book scandal she had remained under then-Colonel Fabian Ver's custody. She was first brought to a safehouse in Manila, but subsequently moved to Imelda's "White House" in Tacloban, Leyte. There she slept under guard at night, and during the day was escorted to the rural bank, owned by Imelda's brother in the next town, where she performed janitorial duties for a paltry wage. "It was not a pension. I worked for it," recalls Estrella.

When martial law was declared, she was freed to fend for herself. She returned to live with her family in the barrio of San Joaquin until a severe typhoon brought the house down. Without home or money, she was once more forced to seek work in Manila. In this way Estrella ended up living in the slums of the bayshore area. Following her forced resettlement to make way for Imelda's bankers, Estrella lived out the rest of the martial law years in Sapang Palay, a resettlement zone which she described as a godforsaken place. Slum dwellers were thrown here each time Imelda went on a "beautification" binge in Manila. A Malacanang propagandist called these settlements "country estates." During the rainy season the land was a sea of mud, and in the summer the soil became as hard as rock under the merciless sun.

During this period Estrella sought Imelda's help one final time. Her husband, Siloy, the only other witness to the Romualdez misfortune in General Solano, had fallen ill. Estrella would not have gone to Imelda had she not been so desperate. Like Norberto's widow, she had been driven to seek help because of the gravity of her need and the vastness of Imelda's wealth. "A few hundred pesos would have been nothing to her at all," Estrella says. She was also prodded by the memory of that evening in the Palace when Imelda had talked to her sympathetically, and she hoped that this powerful woman's heart still held a tender spot for her.

Her only access to Imelda was through her younger brother Armando, who had lived with Estrella and Siloy for a few years. He had developed a fondness for them, and when Imelda's father decided to return his family to Leyte, Vicente Orestes asked them to keep the young Armando awhile in the city. That was how close the couple was to the family, yet even Armando had changed. He who used to speak kindly to Estrella had become rude and peremptory, and she wondered whether it had to do with the book. Her appeal to Imelda was quickly turned down, and she was told that she had been helped "enough."

Siloy died soon after for lack of adequate medical attention. Estrella was told by other Romualdezes that Imelda said she had helped her enough, and that "she had been given a house and a pension" after the book debacle. Although Estrella is dismayed at the lie, she is not bitter. Today, in her sixties, she still works as a servant—this time, she says without rancor, "with a really rich family in suburban San Juan"—within walking distance of both Marcos's "lucky" house and Loreto's modest musician's bungalow.

But forgotten promises and sad childhoods do not enter into the shrewd calculations of international bankers. Their goal was to finance Third World development programs with first world money. They had chosen Manila as the venue for their annual convention for the symbolic value of lenders bringing money halfway around the world. The IMF–World Bank conference in Manila signaled their commitment to making the Philippines a pilot project in "technocratic" modernization. The bankers believed that given an infusion of funds and U.S.-trained technocrats, as well as his absolute powers under martial law, Marcos could bring about a prosperous modern economy in his country. Despite their good intentions, the bankers' plan ignored the personalities of the principal political players they would be financing—Marcos and Imelda.

Backed by Washington's foreign policy, the World Bank and international commercial banks proceeded with a massive lending program. From a meager $165.1 million in 1974, World Bank assistance to the Philippines ballooned to $13.6 billion in 1983. Before martial law, the country was thirtieth among the league of borrowers of the Bank's funds; by 1980 it ranked eight-highest among 113 Third World countries.

But Imelda had other plans, and the World Bank unwittingly made them possible. With the influx of thousands of country folk in search of jobs in Manila, there arose the danger of popular discontent developing within the Philippine capital. The Bank was concerned about these teeming masses of poor people who could serve as fodder for political rabble-rousers, and proposed the establishment of a centralized metropolitan Manila government. The bank offered technical assistance as well as financing for this plan.

The Bankers had assumed that technocrats would be given charge of this project. They were considerably dismayed, then, when Imelda arrived in Washington in 1975 as governor of a newly constituted Metro Manila, which made up of the country's most prosperous region. The reorganization had destroyed the last checks to an already too-powerful Malacanang. Marcos had also appointed Imelda Minister of Human Settlements, a specially created department with such wide-ranging powers as to constitute a government within the government. What had been speculation for years was finally reality: Imelda was truly equal partner in the Marcos dictatorship. Even more disconcerting, Imelda soon unveiled her vision of her great new city—a megalopolis arising from megalomania—which would rival the great cities of the world.

It would be a financial center, with hotels and restaurants, an embassy row, theaters, and all the other luxuries befitting a prosperous city. "This city," she said without batting an eyelash, "would extend south and east of its present boundaries, as far south as Tagaytay City incorporating the Cavite and Laguna and as far east as the Pacific Ocean coast, by the borders of undeveloped Quezon Province." She was unfazed by the foothills of the Sierra Madre mountains, fifty miles east of Manila, because she wanted to rule the only city in the world that would have access to two great bodies of water—"the Manila Bay port receiving ships sailing in from the China Sea, and the Infanta port directly receiving ships coming from the Pacific."

And how did the poor figure in this magnificent scheme? To Imelda, they were to be shunted aside, hidden, banished from sight. Thus was the World Bank's ambitious development strategy in the Philippines shattered.

But even as bankers faced the mounting evidence that lending to the government in Manila was like passing water through a sieve, American businessmen in the Philippines had few complaints about the way the Marcoses were running the country. They spoke glowingly of how expertly long-range plans were being formulated, and how a country with 87 percent literacy was fast becoming an extension of the American market. They were also pleased that labor there was not only cheap, but strikes were prohibited by Marcos's decree. Although there was some concern at the growing debt, there were bankers as late as 1979 who remained unmoved. One official from a major American bank reported that year, "Our portfolio is very good. The jumbo loans are going into the right places. You might not agree one hundred percent but we don't think the money is being squandered." Another banker, though less effusive, was just as confident and said that his group would continue lending to the Marcos regime on favorable terms because "these people have been very skillful at managing their debt."

In another time and another country, bankers learned that

Bank Omran was the Shah's personal bank and the vehicle for his family's multimillion-dollar fortune. But the banks had not only continued to lend money to the Shah; they had also facilitated the transfer of government and oil company funds from Tehran to Switzerland and New York for the purchase of houses in Manhattan, Beverly Hills, Acapulco, Switzerland, and Great Britain. This precedent notwithstanding, they did exactly the same thing in the Philippines. One banker argued limply, "There's always a temptation to hold on too long— you don't want to bow out in case you were wrong."

In any case, there was money to be made, and the edict had been passed in the banking world that "a country can never go bankrupt." Moreover, the good housekeeping seal from the American State Department was firmly pinned on the Marcos regime. How could banks, whose business it was to seek the odd profit, think less?

Between 1978 and 1982 the Marcos regime borrowed a staggering $13.7 billion for various programs, among them a scheme to alleviate the lot of Manila's slum dwellers. From their drawing boards and armchair theories, bankers returned home convinced that the woman who had entertained them so lavishly could also be relied on to dispense responsibly millions of dollars to build roads, install water mains, and create other facilities in the city's teeming slums. Such was the bankers' faith in Imelda. She was a darling, and bankers jostled to join the lenders' queue. One bank even provided a reputedly unlimited expense account to one of its executives who happened to be her "bosom friend." Thus was the cornucopia of funds, or in Congressman Stephen Solarz's words, an American Express gold card, created for Imelda Marcos, richest woman in the world and First Lady of one of the poorest countries.

CHAPTER SIX

Sacrifice the "Queen"

By 1980 Imelda was indeed "on top of the world," as she had said to brother Benjamin, more than thirteen years ago when she accompanied Marcos on their first state visit to America. During those thirteen years she would return again and again to savor this "top of the world" view from the thirty-seventh floor of the Waldorf Towers, where she occupied the $1,700-a-day Royal Suite. Amid the splendor and luxury of Baccarat crystal chandeliers and French antique furniture, Imelda held court in this renowned suite that had been originally designed for Queen Elizabeth II of England in 1957. Normally, the Queen and the Duke of Edinburgh would have occupied the Waldorf's Presidential Suite, but King Faisal of Saudi Arabia fell ill and had to extend his stay. A suite comparable in elegance, decorated with antiques and period furniture, was hastily prepared for the royal couple. Although it was the first and last time the Queen used it, since then it came to be known as the Royal Suite. Thus was a "special room at the top" created inadvertently for Imelda, First Lady of the Philippines, with as much style as English royalty.

When Imelda came, even normally sedate Waldorf Towers

was thrown into a dither. For Madame traveled always with an entourage—perhaps a hundred, sometimes fifty security guards, cabinet members, friends, and hangers-on. She was the other half of the Philippine Government and exhibited her power by the amount of luggage she carried: two hundred pieces for a short stay and eight hundred for a state visit. On arrival day they spilled out of the Tower's smallish lobby up to the corner of Park Avenue. But the hotel's staff were on their toes, for Madame Philippines, as some of them called her, was also Lady Bountiful and within minutes order would be restored. Not only would her luggage be in place in the Royal Suite; bottles of Dom Pérignon would be cooled to the right temperature, and Madame's favorite flowers, red roses, would adorn the mantelpieces when she stepped out of the special elevator to 37R. Both the Waldorf and Imelda take pride in this successful custom, and publicity leaflets issued by the hotel unabashedly say, "The Royal Suite has been home to concert pianist Van Cliburn and Imelda Marcos, as well as a host of international travelers."

Her trips to New York were always deemed official by Marcos and made at the expense of the government even if they often combined the pleasures of shopping on Fifth Avenue, party hopping with her jet-setting friends, and making speeches on a new world order at the United Nations Assembly.

But the December visit of 1980 was especially important to her. She had come to see Benigno Aquino, her husband's arch political rival.

Although Aquino had survived the forty-day fast which he undertook five years earlier in a desperate bid to force Marcos to try him in a civilian court, his heart was battered. One May morning, after daily exercises in the cell that had been his home for nearly seven years, the celebrated prisoner collapsed. Military doctors who examined him diagnosed a severe heart condition and advised that he needed immediate bypass surgery. After much thought Marcos and Imelda allowed him to go to the United States for the operation. The medical reports assured them that Aquino in the United States would be a harmless invalid who would be unable to launch any campaign against the Marcos regime. This was the course of action the Marcoses preferred to taking the risk that he might die while in their hands. Above all, his release (said to have been conducted on the advice of President Carter) was trumpeted as a "humanitarian" gesture. But first Aquino had to sign a pact to return to the Philippines after his operation and to refrain while in the United States from making public statements criticizing the political situation in his country.

After his successful triple bypass operation at the Baylor Medical Center in Texas, the irrepressible Aquino was back on his political feet, giving speeches against Marcos in America and elsewhere. "A pact with the devil is no pact at all," he said in August 1980, and warned Marcos of the "gathering storm." Within days of that speech a revolutionary group calling itself the April 6th Liberation Movement bombed nine buildings in Manila, in what was described as the beginning of a destabilization campaign. The group represented an alliance of socially concerned priests, students, and professionals, loosely known as social democrats. Defense Minister Ponce Enrile later described this group as "more dangerous" than the Communists because they had access to "money, talent, and leadership, and because they were more acceptable to Filipinos because of their religious orientation." The Movement leaders believed that the key to ousting Marcos lay in destabilizing Manila. By selective bombing without loss of lives, they hoped to discourage continuing investment and support for Marcos from the foreign sources that had kept the Marcos dictatorship alive.

To the Marcoses only Aquino could have been behind such a group, along with other political exiles in America, such as Steve Psinakis, a Greek married to Presy Lopez, whose family had once been Marcos allies but had now turned bitter enemies; former Constitutional Convention delegate Heherson Alvarez; and former Senator Raul Manglapus. Under the guise of "negotiations," Imelda was dispatched by Marcos to find out just what Aquino was about and to remind him of Marcos's power.

This was Imelda's forte. A supreme actress, she was to deliver her threat using only charm and femininity. The majestic Royal Suite of the Waldorf Towers with its spotless carpets provided the proper setting in which to intimidate humbled Filipino exiles, once men of influence and power, who in years past would have ignored the Rose of Tacloban. While her main task was to find out exactly what Aquino and company were about, she would not miss the opportunity to gloat over their change of fortune.

But the oppositionists approached the meeting with their perceptions of the present while Imelda thought only of the past. What dominated her thinking were the years when she was a nobody; even in 1980 she was obsessed in proving that she would fight tooth and nail to stay on top. Steve Psinakis later wrote a book, *Between Two Terrorists,* about the six-hour meeting with Imelda and the bitterness the opposition felt when the negotiations failed. But Psinakis had missed the real point of Imelda's visit. From the moment Aquino entered the Royal Suite, the negotiations went nowhere. Imelda had not come to negotiate, nor had she asked them to negotiate; she had come to show them what power was all about. It was a pity that neither Remedios Trinidad nor Vicente Orestes could be there to see her glory.

Imelda had wanted to see Aquino first and separately from the other exiles. This was how he described their meeting to Psinakis: "Number one," he said, "it was a good friendly meeting. Number two, she did almost all the talking for more than four hours. I just let her talk. I didn't want to argue at this point. Number three, she tried to appear confident and impress me with her contacts with Reagan. I understand Reagan and Bush were also staying at the Waldorf, and she met with them. She told me they spent more time with her than with West German Chancellor Helmut Schmidt. Number four, you won't believe this, but she gave a dinner for Nixon in her suite last Sunday and she videotaped the whole affair.

She showed me the program. Nixon couldn't praise her enough. He referred to Imelda as 'the Angel from Asia' who came to him when he was down and out. Nixon said there's nothing he wouldn't do to support the Marcos government. Imelda claimed that Nixon is back in the Reagan camp with lots of influence. Lots of big shots at her party: bankers, oil people, et cetera. Number five, she told me that you and I have sent assassination teams to Manila to knock off some of her people. She said if we do, they'll do the same to us and no one will come out ahead. She told me we should put a stop to that. Number six, she sounded confident that the Reagan administration will go after us here, especially you. They have evidence, she says, on your activities. That's it in a nutshell."

Aquino wisely did not argue with Imelda. That was left for Psinakis to do. In his meeting with Imelda the Greek turned "Filipino rebel" would speak of the Filipino patriots and their fight for freedom and dignity—and of the inevitability of violent revolution if reforms did not begin soon. But these were wasted words. To Imelda, Psinakis was an ideal audience, one who reacted in the name of virtues such as "truth and goodness and freedom and justice." But neither Aquino, who kept silent in gratitude to Imelda for allowing him to have heart surgery in the United States, nor Psinakis, who seized this opportunity to speak on behalf of the opposition, fathomed Imelda's message. Amid all her chatter, Imelda had only one message to deliver—the message of power.

"Steve, the President has decided to lift martial law next month," were Imelda's opening words. "He is very sincere about it, and he has already made an announcement. You know, last week I met with President-elect Reagan and Mr. Bush; they both expressed their friendship and support for the Philippines and for the President. They realize what an important ally we are to the United States and how important our country is to the security of the U.S. interests in the region. Reagan is quite different from Carter. I told Reagan—please, Steve, keep this to yourself—that the President plans to lift martial law next month and Reagan told me not to act hastily.

He said the stability and security of our country is vital to the United States and we should not rush into any changes that might affect the stability of the Philippines. He practically told me not to lift martial law yet, but the President has made up his mind. He will do it next month."

Imelda went on to analyze the results of the American elections, how Americans had swung to the right, and how they realized that all their problems were caused by liberals. "Carter liked to lecture us and interfere with our internal affairs. Not so Reagan. American people now understand the need for a strong U.S. President. Reagan will support his true allies, not lecture them," she said to the attentive Psinakis.

Despite the clarity of Imelda's message, the idealistic Greek left the appointment hoping that Imelda had listened to his warnings about the looming Filipino revolution. He could not see that Imelda's monologues were defensive acts to shield herself from anything that might threaten the image she had cultivated for so long. But just as Psinakis was leaving, Imelda stopped to tell him about the Nixon reception and her video-tape to prove that she had persuaded a former American President to dance a Filipino fandango. She was a little girl once more, nudging for attention—but this time wearing the mask of the imperious First Lady. The deeper point she wanted to convey was that she was not just First Lady of the Philippines, she was a personal friend to American Presidents. They were a "gang"—a gang of rich and powerful people, and Imelda, once of a garage in General Solano, was at the center of it all. There could be no success greater than this.

The poise and dignity of the woman who had delivered the message of power earlier was shed, and with tiresome cadence she talked about her successes, anxious that he would come away convinced she was good, if not special. Imelda eagerly listed her diplomatic exploits to Psinakis, prattling on and on about various world leaders and her recent oil refinery agreement with Mexican President Lopez Portillo. "We agreed to undertake a joint venture of a huge refinery in Manila with a capacity of three hundred thousand barrels a day, larger than our total present needs. We plan to export the excess to neighboring countries. I went home very excited and told the President and my people. I guess the press headlined the story and the Saudis learned about it. You know, the Arabs are nice people, but sometimes they act like immature babies. Can you imagine? The Saudis felt slighted because my deal with Mexico was so big. . . ."

When Imelda returned to Manila from her "negotiations" at the Waldorf, the controlled press ran headlines proclaiming, "No more bombings in Manila." To the opposition at home, especially its more radical elements, Aquino appeared to play the bumbling appeaser who was always available to Imelda for "negotiations." In later years, however, Aquino's stance of taking every opportunity to negotiate a peaceful solution would be vindicated against the "purer" stand of misguided Marxists and the power tactics of Imelda Marcos.

Thus when Aquino slumped back to his Harvard quarters after Imelda's Waldorf triumph, he had unknowingly taken a giant step. In the shadows, where fate was decided, Aquino was ahead in the race to the finish line. But at that time, besieged by an American administration that had taken Marcos's side, he brooded on the futility of his cause. He talked to friends across the Atlantic and toyed with the idea of moving to West Germany or to France.

As Imelda had predicted, Marcos lifted martial law on January 17, 1981, but only on paper. He still retained his powers of arrest without recourse to judicial proceedings and reserved the right to overrule the national assembly by decree. The whole production was a farce, or as the Filipino opposition put it, a "cruel deception." But it satisfied American policy makers for it met the demands of "stability." It was a cosmetic concession to democracy and diffused growing criticism of human rights violations by the Marcos regime. To complete the operation toward "normalization," Marcos also unveiled a new constitution, conducted a plebiscite, and held Presidential elections, all stage-managed to suit his purpose of continuing absolute rule. The elections were filled with scenes of voters being dragged to polling booths by armed men in a Presidential contest that had been boycotted by the opposition.

But no matter. Elections were held in June 1981, and farcical though they were, they mightily pleased Marcos's most important guest, U.S. Vice President George Bush. Bush's inaugural toast to Marcos was simple and direct: "We love you, sir, we love your adherence to democratic principles and democratic processes, and we will not leave you in isolation." Most major American newspapers responded to this love song with indignation and editorializing against the Bush "faux pas." Confronted again in Washington, D.C., the Vice President told journalists it was no "faux pas"; he meant every word he said.

Bush's words deepened the gloom among Filipino oppositionists in America. Earlier, Reagan had dispatched newly appointed Secretary of State Alexander Haig to Manila to assure Marcos that the U.S. government would help the Philippines fight "terrorism" and would cooperate in prosecuting U.S.-based Filipino rebels. An extradition treaty between the two countries was prepared, and the F.B.I. soon visited the homes of opposition leaders to demonstrate the seriousness of the American government's war on "terrorism." With Reagan's warm endorsement for Marcos, Aquino's position as exile in freedom-loving America became increasingly tenuous. From Manila, pro-Marcos columnists taunted Aquino to leave America and speculated that he would resume exile in Europe, where he might be more welcome. But Aquino stayed on in the United States. In the face of an impossible situation, he refused to lose faith. He closed his eyes and ears to friends' pleas for his safety and to their argument that Marcos, with Reagan's full backing, was more impervious than ever to the democratic impulse.

At this time rumors abounded as to Marcos's health. The problem had to do with his kidneys, but no one outside the Palace knew the actual diagnosis. Television cameras and news photos showed the President's face bloated one day and taut and drawn the next. "Steroids," the press said. But Marcos laughed at them. "I'm as healthy as a bull and challenge anyone to fisticuffs to prove it."

Whatever Marcos's health problems, it was generally accepted that his dynasty would continue uninterruptedly, led first by Imelda and later by their children and their grandchildren. Of the three Marcos children Imee, the eldest, was most favored to succeed. She was said to be a female Marcos: strong, brilliant, and resolute. Unfortunately, to Imelda's way of thinking, these leadership qualities could not make up for Imee's plain looks. Imelda, whose power stemmed directly from her beauty, could not conceive of a woman leader who did not rely on tears and soft looks.

The tensions between Imee and her beauteous mother continued. Imee first sought a career in the theater. She had developed friends who believed she had the makings of a great actress. This dream was soon rebuffed by both Marcos and Imelda, who considered acting unworthy of the daughter of the "greatest President of the Philippines."

Imee was sent to England during those early years of her adolescence, where she pined away in a convent school in Mayfield, Sussex, and wrote to her friends about how she hated it. She seldom wrote home and, brilliant though she was, she told friends how delighted she was to flunk most of her subjects. From a long distance she coaxed friends to talk to her mother or father about allowing her to pursue acting, which she seemed to have wanted passionately. But apparently nothing came out of these delicate third-party negotiations. Instead Imee would in slow stages be made to abandon her love for the theater.

Like her mother before her, Imelda attempted to teach Imee the importance of self-sacrifice for the sake of "greater things." In Imee's case it was to be heir to the family dynasty, or as Imelda would say, "for a life dedicated to the people." Imee subsequently studied at Princeton, where she fell in love with Michael Colopy, a personal aide to New York Governor Hugh Carey. Friends say the affair was serious and that marriage was discussed, but the relationship ended in June 1979. Colopy had told friends he was constantly harassed by security guards, and at one point he told Marcos he was dating his daughter, not the government. Toward the end he concluded he faced great physical danger if he pressed his suit on Imee.

This was how zealously the Marcoses protected their children. The children were treated as sacred extensions of the parents, particularly Imee, who would be the first to succeed her mother to power. As for the only boy, Ferdinand Jr., although unhappy with his lack of freedom, he coasted along. After all, his every whim and wish was granted, despite warnings from a stern, candid English headmaster who wrote that he would be ill-equipped for the rigors of serious academic work if he never learned the meaning of the word "no." Younger daughter Irene, the family pet, was the most obedient of the children and did not seem to mind living in the shadow of her parents' ambitions.

But rebellious Imee was different. When the opportunity arose again for Marcos's eldest daughter to follow her instincts, she would do so secretly. She met her future husband, Tomas Manotoc, a tall, dark, and handsome sportsman recently divorced from the beauteous former Miss International, Aurora Pijuan, one summer while visiting Manila. Friends say it was Imee who fell head over heels in love with Manotoc on their first meeting in an antique shop in the romantic mountain city of Baguio, the site of her own parents' brief courtship earlier. It was she who pursued him. Although he was not fabulously wealthy, Manotoc belonged to an old, landed Filipino family. Inevitably, this meant he had relatives who opposed Marcos, most of them the "oligarchs" whom Marcos claimed to have dispossessed by his revolution from the top. When Imee secretly married Manotoc in Arlington, Virginia, the newspapers would make much of his relatives' opposition. But this was not the Marcoses' significant objection to Manotoc. Nor did they totally oppose his being a divorced man, although this presented a grave drawback. Put simply, Manotoc was not up to the Marcoses' standards for Imee—nor was any man except one whose throne or fortune superseded their own. Sadly, there were few such bachelors. Anything less represented a regression and therefore a threat to Marcos and Imelda's ever-expanding empire. Given their attitude, Imee's December 4, 1981 marriage to Manotoc could only bring catastrophe.

Imee could not have chosen a worse time to have married beneath her. For this was the time of doubt and failing light for the sick Marcos and the aging Imelda. When Imee presented Manotoc to Imelda as her husband, Imelda was on her top-of-the-world act and it was rumored that she and her associates were buying up the choicest commercial properties in Manhattan, including the spectacular Crown Building on Fifth Avenue.

How could Imee have done such a thing? How could she have betrayed her own parents and everything they had worked so hard to achieve? It did not help when Imee told her mother that the Agnellis of the Fiat fortune in Rome, Imelda's social friends, would help secure an annulment with their contacts in the Vatican. It was an uncanny déjà vu, but Imelda would not remember that she, too, had knocked on doors in despair for an annulment that would have allowed her to marry Ariston Nakpil. She would have been the last to imagine that the past could impinge on the present. As Imelda told her in between tears and recriminations, Imee had everything she had ever wished for—her own mansion in New Jersey, the best schools, jewelry, gowns, travel, anything, anything that money could buy. Where had she as a mother gone wrong, that this should happen to her? Even as she reached for the stars, her talented daughter and heiress to the throne was concocting a plot that could bring down the entire kingdom. As Manotoc later told his family, Imelda was beside herself with anger, and the newlyweds just stood and listened to her rant and rave. In any case, Imee was told she still had her father to contend with.

Imee's rebellious marriage gave Aquino his opening. Not long after Aquino's meeting with Imelda, a series of events would weaken Marcos's hold on power. The first such event was, ironically, outside of politics. An intimate family problem, in fact, would begin to reverse the parabola of the regime's invincibility. From that time on, the Marcos regime would decline rapidly. Political analysts had always predicted that the only possible threat to the Marcos regime would come from an "enemy" within its ranks, but never did anyone suggest it would come from such close ranks. They had ignored the personal factor; above all, the Marcoses were human beings unraveling their fates.

Published accounts said that Imee and Manotoc decided not to return home after their secret marriage. They would go it alone, with or without the Marcoses' approval. When Imelda had quieted, Imee called her father, who convinced her to return home. Further, reports said, he assured his daughter that they would be safer at home and that he would handle Imelda. But close relatives deny the implication that Imelda, raving and ranting though she may have been, would physically harm her own daughter or, for that matter, Imee's new husband. So why was such a story spread around? No one really knows. Imelda had often told relatives that it was a favorite game in Malacanang to begin a rumor and to see what form it would ultimately take. This official rumor mill operates again and again, and significantly, would operate on at least one more crucial occasion before the regime's final debacle.

But rumors aside, what did happen was that Marcos failed in his assurance to his daughter. On December 29, just two weeks after he and Imee arrived in Manila, Manotoc disappeared. The newlyweds had seen Marcos and had told friends that he had received his new son-in-law "kindly." The Marcoses betrayed not a hint of displeasure and only ventured to suggest that their new son-in-law should perhaps think about taking up something a bit more useful than sports, such as "economics." Manotoc's credentials may not have been up to Marcos's standards, but if Imee had married the divorced sportsman without seeking her parents' approval beforehand, she was merely following an irresistible impulse shaped in generations before her. She was fated to marry him.

As a relative said, the handsome and romantic Manotoc was very like—even a "reincarnation" of—Vicente Orestes. Manotoc shared Orestes's birth date and his gentle and unambitious nature. Manotoc was not aggressive and ruthless like Marcos; on the contrary, he most resembled Imelda's dear friends George Hamilton and Van Cliburn, and her first love, Ariston Nakpil. The latter had died earlier that year, and Imelda had attended his funeral. She was said to have generously given fifty thousand pesos to his widow and to have left his children with the mysterious statement, "Your father was the only man who treated me like a lady." Nakpil, friends say, was a true romantic. On his deathbed he requested that Brahms concertos be played until he died.

Imee had married a man after Imelda's heart—someone Imelda herself would have chosen had she been born rich, a relative said. With her daughter's marriage, Imelda mourned her lost youth.

Manotoc's parents had warned him that pursuing the courtship of the President's daughter would mean trouble. He was ready to give up after Imee's security guards, during one of their outings, punched holes in the tires of his car and warned him to stay away from Imee. Manotoc was downcast, but the strong-willed granddaughter of Trinidad Romualdez told him she could handle her parents and he dutifully followed. She peremptorily turned her full fury on the bodyguards and told them then and there to return the tires to their original condition.

But Imee had not reckoned that Manotoc would be kidnapped—abducted from a suburban restaurant—by her father. They had eaten there following Marcos's advice that they should be seen in public to be accepted. Nor did Imee foresee that the Manotocs would tell the world in press interviews that "President Marcos was behind the abduction of their son." At no time did they accuse Imelda of this crime, as some journalists were later cleverly manipulated to write. More knowledgeable people held that such violence was more in keeping with Marcos's past actions.

Even before the Manotocs received a ransom note, Marcos

called them to say that their son had been kidnapped and that they would receive a ransom note soon. The kidnappers were strongly suspected to be the New People's Army, but the Manotocs were not to contact the press or the police.

Marcos then issued a press statement denying he had anything to do with the kidnapping. To Manotoc's bewildered parents, what it all meant was that their son's life was in danger, if not already lost. While the press war between the two families burned, Marcos issued forty arrest warrants against opposition leaders in the United States, in an apparent effort to divert public attention from the family "problem." But the public's curiosity had already been aroused. Imelda even took center stage. She was the perfect decoy. To everyone's surprise, she offered to resign if Manotoc was killed. Wearing no makeup and with hair unkempt, an obviously distraught First Lady talked with a correspondent for one of the major international news agencies about her son-in-law, whom she called a "son of a bitch." What was Manotoc's fate compared to that of fifty-four million Filipinos who would be imperiled by this scandal? "Bring him back alive. I want him alive," she had screamed to the correspondent between uncontrollable sobs until aides came and rescued him. He was asked not to report anything of what he heard or saw.

Meanwhile Imee did some maneuvering of her own. She called her new in-laws and requested her husband's divorce papers and their marriage certificate, then held by Manotoc's lawyers. This move stopped any further telephone calls from Malacanang to the Manotocs. After more than forty-two suspenseful days, Manotoc reappeared, telling a story that no one believed, corroborating Marcos's charges that the New People's Army had kidnapped him. He even asked the President's forgiveness for any innuendos that might have cast aspersions on his good name. But Manotoc's own father, asked if he, too, had changed his belief that the Marcoses were behind the kidnapping, said, "I think it is hard to change the facts."

Many observers were surprised at Imee's calm demeanor throughout the kidnapping episode. She was relaxed, even radiant, they said, even while she refused to answer any questions from the press. And while many had speculated then that Imee would ultimately accede to her father's wishes, she would in the end bring Marcos around to accept her husband. In exchange, she took on her role as heir apparent with special assiduity. The family had at last resolved its crisis, but grave political damage had been done. To all and sundry, what saved Manotoc was the publicity of his marriage to Imee and the fact that neither the New People's Army nor any other opposition group would have had the slightest interest in the handsome sportsman. Millions of Filipinos would remember this episode for the pattern of violence and retribution that resulted when Marcos and Imelda's will was not heeded.

Very shortly thereafter, Imelda took her daughter's marriage in stride, telling reporters, "I have come to love him, too. Of course, you love those whom your children love." She thus quickly put a stop to any further intrusion into the family's affairs.

But far from losing her bravado, Imelda plunged into preparations for two major events lined up for 1982—the first Manila International Film Festival and the second state visit to America. Both would engage her in a frenzy of activity and spending that would sink the Marcos regime and the country even further into debt. The Manila International Film Festival (MIFF) was Imelda's version of a Hollywood superproduction; as one adoring fan described it, Imelda's chance to be Cecil B. DeMille. A special multimillion-dollar building rivaling the Parthenon was erected just for the show. Owing to a tight schedule, 8,000 men worked around the clock to get the building done. Imelda was calculating a feat that would make world headlines. She would accomplish the impossible: to build a massive structure like the Parthenon and inaugurate a film festival that would rival the one in Cannes. It would be a world event.

In the midst of construction, a wall collapsed, burying workers in mud and debris. Malacanang released a statement that seven workers had died and that their families would be compensated. But the public could not be mollified—there had been many more bereaved families, some of whom lived in shanties in the shadow of the imposing structure. There was a clamor to stop the construction to find out just how many had died. Private investigations by human rights groups placed the number of dead and missing workers at anywhere from thirty-five to a hundred and fifty men.

But the truth would never be known. Imelda would not listen to suggestions that the construction be stopped until all the bodies of the dead were unearthed and properly accounted for. To this day, there are still murmurings that the Parthenon-like Manila Film Center is a mausoleum for the workers who lie buried beneath its gleaming marble floor.

The show did go on, and Imelda accomplished the incredible feat she had set her sights on. The building was finished in record time. There were criticisms and some cancellations from international film stars, notably the French group led by Jeanne Moreau, but Imelda was unfazed. She was at the center of a spectacular event which she had only dreamed of in her youth: she would be the star among stars, and remote Hollywood figures whose names she had merely known in autograph books and third-hand movie magazines would pay her homage.

But the apple of her eye was the dashing George Hamilton, who, it is said, had suggested this project to her in the first place. They were a perfect couple in the whirl of dizzying balls and dinner dances. Those who attended the festival spoke of Imelda's radiance in youthful, ruffled gowns and spectacular jewelry. On one occasion Imelda changed gowns and accessories within the space of thirty minutes. She entered at one side of the huge lobby wearing one gown with all the accessories, to the applause of the audience, and returned from another side with a complete change of wardrobe, down to the last detail of matching shoes. A few jewelry fanciers noticed that she wore the multimillion-dollar marquise diamond earrings that matched a pendant reputed to have once belonged to Elizabeth Taylor. It is said that the difficult match for the earrings was obtained by buying one from the Shahbanu of Iran and the only other in the world from the wife of a Swiss industrialist. Imelda looked spectacular in the photographs taken at this event.

What the photographs did not show was the battle that raged within the beautiful body. The resplendently gowned and bejeweled figure was under a strict regimen of anti-aging tablets and antibiotics to cope with a recurring internal infection. This inner life was detailed in medical logbooks listing the First Lady's every activity and every meal in an effort to discover what was ailing her. Was it the dysentery she had had when she was eight years old? Was it the chicken pox when she was thirty-three? Her medical history was scrupulously noted, and every relevant test was carried out to determine the cause. She sought the best medical advice and care at home and abroad, but none of this advice suggested that her ill health signaled the coming of old age, and that it might be time to relinquish her leading role on the world stage.

As the opposition and the Western press had predicted, the film festival was of dubious artistic value, and the receipts it collected in no way offset the reported $4 million cost of the festival. A few film contracts followed the event, but most local movie producers were of the opinion that these could have been won with less expense and sensation. The festival had squandered millions to entertain foreign movie stars— costs that had hardly anything to do with selling Filipino films. In the end, locals and visitors agreed that the show had been all about Imelda and her need to be a star. It was a wild throw of the dice, and one that further crippled the ailing Philippine economy.

There were criticisms, even a belated warning, from the World Bank that things were not looking good for Manila. A huge $2 billion deficit in the balance of payments was recorded for that year. Its effect on the hungry poor of the Philippines was devastating. The purchasing power of the peso was half what it used to be, and wages had not risen anywhere close to matching the costs. Even more ominous as the year ended was the fact that the poor began fighting back. The repressive measures of the Marcos regime were simply unable to cope with the burgeoning economic debacle. For the first time, slum dwellers formed barricades and lobbying groups to defend their territory from Imelda's "beautification" offensives. Imelda's dream of Manila as a Shangri-la stretching from the Pacific Ocean to the China Sea was no closer to fulfillment in 1982 than when she had first envisioned it in 1975. Marcos had joined her in the campaign to wipe out the squatters, describing them as "more criminal than the murderers and forgers that we have fought, because they even blackmail, coerce, and intimidate those in power." In a Freudian slip at this time, he called the squatters a potentially greater threat to the economy than those "engaged in mulcting big financial institutions," and as such worthy of arrest. Imelda's abhorrence of the poor had created in her a blind spot. Poverty was an experience she had expunged from memory; she thus viewed slums and the poor as ugly things to be bulldozed and swept out of sight. Unlike Evita Perón, to whom she was often compared, Imelda failed to win public support for her political ambitions. Imelda was afraid of the poor. Her forays into poor man's territory were half-hour photography sessions with selected individuals for a handshake or the granting of some favor.

But neither the World Bank report nor the emboldened slum dwellers really mattered to Imelda or her ailing husband. They had Washington behind them. Their personal friend Ronald Reagan was in power. For years Imelda had tried to get an invitation to the White House, first from President Nixon, then from Presidents Ford and Carter, but always U.S. advisers had vetoed the idea—a state visit by the Marcoses would unnecessarily expose any administration. However, Reagan was unconvinced by his advisers. The Marcos–Reagan friendship dated from the time when Reagan was a struggling governor propped up by his wealthy California friends. When the Reagans visited Manila in 1969, Marcos and Imelda had laid out the red carpet and made their visit unforgettable. The

Marcoses had not known then that the California governor would become President of the United States of America.

It was another coup of Imelda's personal diplomacy. Friends spoke of the euphoria in Malacanang on Reagan's victory and the subsequent White House signals that an invitation would be forthcoming before the end of 1982. When the invitation finally arrived, Imelda was said to have assembled her court of fawning society matrons and industrialists' wives and told them that there would no longer be problems with the White House, which had been more troublesome under President Carter. The Marcoses had, she said, bought Reagan through a $10 million contribution to his campaign fund. Ten million dollars' worth of hundred-dollar bills were supposedly taken to Mexico City, where the money was laundered and subsequently deposited in a Houston bank in which Vice-President George Bush had an interest. From there, it was turned over to the Reagan campaign fund. A more unlikely version of this illegal contribution came from a group of Filipino expatriate bankers, who said the contribution totaled $67 million. Both stories have been dismissed by the White House as preposterous. But it remains nevertheless true that Reagan had a special friendship with the Marcoses that puzzles many political watchers. Through the years Imelda gave Nancy Reagan many gifts, including a sequined black velvet gown and a red silk strapless gown worth $10,000. Among the notes left in the Palace, there is also an entry for a $5,000 bracelet for the American First Lady. But by the time Imelda had told friends about it, the bracelet's supposed cost had risen to $2 million and was allegedly bought from Cartier.

In any case, the Marcoses were beside themselves with joy when it was announced that Reagan had won the election even before they knew what the White House policy would be with the new administration. A state visit to Washington at the time of their falling political fortune could not have been more opportune. It was indeed a kind turn. Imelda, ever the gracious friend, was already thinking of how she could reciprocate. The idea of a special gift occupied her.

But for the moment she had only to think of how best to make use of the trip to shore up their political image. Marcos, who had not been feeling well, left most of the trip preparations to her and her brother Benjamin, who was the ambassador to Washington. Like his sister, Benjamin's diplomacy rested primarily on a crude understanding of human nature. Both sister and brother were fond of saying that "everyone has a price," and both showered world leaders with all sorts of gifts. At one time, the ambassador, wishing to make friends, had sent gifts of "adobo" (the Philippine national dish of pork and chicken in vinegar marinade) to his neighbors on Diplomatic Row, earning himself the sobriquet "the adobo ambassador."

For this trip to end all trips, the budget would be a massive $30 million. The preparations had all the characteristics of an Imelda blitzkreig, reminiscent of her 1965 campaign to win Marcos the Presidency. To win, one must leave no stone unturned. The goal was to project America's support of the Marcoses to Filipinos at home, who had become increasingly disillusioned about their imperious reign. The Marcoses hoped this message of power would reverse their decline. Live television coverage would be crucial. The Marcoses, in fact, would saturate Manila with images of a successful state visit, with thousands of bused-in American-Filipinos as the supporting cast, lining the streets and cheering Marcos and Imelda. Viewers would see Marcos holding his own, not sick at all, delivering stately speeches and being warmly welcomed by the most powerful man in the world. And Imelda would appear supremely beautiful, still young, groomed to outdo even fashion-conscious former actress Nancy Reagan. It was to be a replay of the 1966 state visit sixteen years earlier, when Imelda had dazzled staid Washington and New York with her beauty.

But this time there would have to be a little cheating. Instead of the spontaneous welcome of those first days of the Marcos rule, the crowds would have to be brought to the demonstration. As for enthusiasm, the indefatigable "adobo" ambassador months earlier had flown Filipino entertainers to the United States and had instructed consular officials to fete the scattered Filipino communities across America in order to gain "their support" in preparation for the state visit. Oppositionists, on the other hand, would be isolated and intimidated.

But when the demonstration actually took place, the message beamed to Filipinos at home was far from triumphant. Although the crowds of American-Filipinos were dutifully present, they showed no sign of enthusiasm. They waved their flags limply and often appeared bored with Marcos's speeches and Imelda's singing. Many left carrying their doggie bags of free food even before the receptions were over. Most of those interviewed candidly said they came for the free ride to Washington and for the free food.

As for Imelda, she was no longer the babe in the woods who had gaped at American wealth sixteen years earlier. She was now as rich as if not richer than most of America's royalty—the Fords, the Whitneys, the Rockefellers, the Du Ponts. She could match their wealth, dollar for dollar. She even had her own fabulous collection of paintings bought from New York art dealers and said to be worth at least $20 million. The paintings, which Imelda claimed were intended for Philippine museums, included the "Madonna and Child" by Fra Filippo Lippi, El Greco's "Coronation of the Virgin," François Boucher's "Apotheosis of Aeneas," and Francisco de Zurbaran's "David and Goliath." She was an important client of both the Hammer Galleries and the Knoedler Gallery. Receipts examined by *The New York Times* when the Marcos regime fell showed she had bought seventy-seven paintings from Hammer for $4.61 million. Twelve of the works, including the Lippi, were dispatched on a private plane to Manila. Give or take a few duds, Imelda possessed some very precious paintings indeed, paintings to put her in league with American supermillionaire collectors. Parrying questions about her wealth, she told reporters, "I must confess that once upon a time his family and my family were oligarchs. But we are reformed oligarchs. The Romualdez family has been in office for many years, and thank God there is a family that is willing to serve the country. Thank God they know how to make money. Otherwise, if Marcos did not have money before, what experience would he have to make his country prosper? The United States is ashamed that it is rich. Why should we be ashamed? We have some gifted members of the family. Good. They want to serve the people. Wonderful."

She fooled no one. The press wanted answers to an Amnesty International report that described widespread torture, political arrests, and murders committed by the Marcos government. They also pressed her on reports of a multimillion-dollar hideaway the Marcoses had reportedly bought in Center Moriches, Long Island. Through an offshore company in the Antilles, the Marcoses had purchased the eight-acre Lindenmere Hotel property for $1 million and had spared no expense to refurbish it into a luxurious retreat complete with swimming pool, gazebo, and staff house. At the end of the renovation the value of the property was upped to $19 million. When the journalists failed to get answers to these questions, they ignored Imelda completely. She was no longer the star or the good copy she once had been.

Reagan's voice soared above the din of protest and anger outside the White House as he performed impressive military ceremonies with Marcos on the South Lawn. Echoing his Vice President's earlier controversial praise, he called Marcos a "respected voice for reason and moderation in international forums."

Not everyone agreed. Five American congressmen wrote the President in protest: "The visit does not have the character of a 'normal courtesy' accorded a foreign chief of state. Rather, it marks the culmination of a process of 'normalization' with a repressive ally. Over the last year and a half the Reagan administration has thrown its support fully behind Marcos, in spite of the latter's well-known and documented violations of human rights. This administration has even gone so far as declaring that these abuses are imaginary, as did Vice President Bush when he lauded Marcos last year as an 'adherent to democratic rights and processes.' " The authors were Representatives Ted Weiss of New York, Bob Edgar of Pennsylvania, Walter Fauntroy of Washington D.C., and Ron Dellums and Fortney Stark of California.

They were joined by other colleagues in Congress who asked Marcos some difficult questions. No matter that Marcos had brought along some former political opponents to prove that they had "even joined my government." Nor did it impress the congressmen that he claimed to have imposed martial law only after consulting with the legislature. To charges of corruption, Marcos replied, "You must mistake us for another nation. If any public official engages in corruption, he will land in jail." He said the Amnesty International report was written without even a visit to the Philippines. The group countered that Amnesty International had conducted seventeen days of investigations in the Philippines in November 1981. Marcos was lying, just as he had for most of his political career. But it wouldn't work anymore. For all his brilliance, he had not learned the elementary lesson that all things come to an end, including the lying and the fooling and the strong-arm tactics. And to compound the problem, he persisted in grooming Imelda as his successor. But when House leaders asked if Mrs. Marcos would succeed him to the Presidency, he answered that after his last election his supporters had urged him to appoint Mrs. Marcos Prime Minister. "But the First Lady and I stood our ground. Now, is that the action of anyone who is preparing to create a dynasty?"

He studiously ignored an earlier statement he had made to Seth Mydans of *The New York Times* before flying to Washington: "She wants to step down the moment I step down because, you know, we are a little tired about this whole thing. But there are certain obligations that you cannot disregard. One of them is that even if I am not here she will symbolize the cooperation of the Marcos followers with the new leadership, and that may be crucial."

In America, however, he denied engineering his own succession and made a veiled reference to the consequences should no appropriate person be found. "Unless I can train my successors to protect the liberties and the freedom that we have established," he said, "any failure on our part will end up with the Communist Party taking over the Philippines and the elimination of American influence in the country."

Despite his assurances to Congress, Marcos had already submitted the formula for succession to his New Society Party. A committee of ten trusted aides with Imelda as chairman was to serve as government in case of his disability or death.

Even though Marcos denied Imelda was his successor, she was present at all the crucial talks that took place during the nine-day U.S. visit, including the wide-ranging talks between Marcos and Reagan on political, military, and economic issues. The military bases agreement, which was up for review in 1984, was on the top of their agenda. Imelda's schedule also included meetings at both the Import and Export Bank and at the World Bank. Sometimes Marcos would disappear and Imelda would take over his schedule, even if that included high-level discussions with Cabinet officials. This doused any American hopes of influencing Marcos on who or what should succeed him. American policy makers now feared a dynasty with the unpopular Imelda at the helm and had planned to voice their concerns strongly to Marcos. But they never had the chance. He had brought his successor with him.

CHAPTER SEVEN

Flight of the Steel Butterfly

AMONG THE SMALL CROWD gathered outside the Waldorf to protest the Marcoses' White House visit was the man most Filipinos would have preferred as their President. Ninoy Aquino was a sorry figure, out in the cold, while his nemeses were being toasted by America's most important business moguls and industrialists. It was a deplorable travesty. In democratic times Aquino was a bustling, robust figure—a man who had matched Marcos in daring and courage and who had often ridiculed "the comic President from the Ilocos" in the halls of the Philippine Congress. He was the upper-class politician with a social conscience, a magnetic crowd-getter. Most of all, he had the confidence of a man born to a distinguished line of patriots. His grandfather, General Servillano Aquino, had fought both the Spanish and American wars, and his father, Senator Benigno Aquino Sr., was Speaker of the Assembly and a Cabinet Minister. On that cold day, however, Ninoy Aquino was just another protester held back by New York police—a true exile in a country that stood for freedom and democracy.

At the rally Aquino called Marcos "a tyrant destroying the

civil liberties of the people." He charged that the external debt of the Philippines was more than $18 billion, of which at least 10 percent "has gone to line the pockets of the Marcos family and their cronies." Except for a few Democratic congressmen and a few sections of the press, America was not listening.

At that time both the Foreign Relations Committee of the Senate and the House supported the Reagan administration's position on Marcos—it was good for America to support him, no matter what charges his own people leveled against him. Although Marcos had made a show of nonchalance when interviewed before his departure for the United States, saying that he had no intention of asking for anything from Reagan, he had "privately" asked the President to reopen negotiations on U.S. military bases in the Philippines. It was agreed that formal negotiations for a new rental agreement would take place in April of 1983. Marcos wanted more money and Reagan wanted to keep his bases. This was a foreign policy matter that needed no further enunciation. While the last military bases agreement had taken years to negotiate under President Carter, the new agreement was thrashed out in days. America agreed to raise the base rental fee from the $500 million in aid paid out between 1979 and 1984, to $900 million for the next five years.

But despite this foreign policy "victory," the state visit to the United States had failed to quiet growing discontent with the Marcos regime at home. The trip had only added to the shame of the Filipino people. Paid crowds which included Cambodians were made to line the streets of New York and Washington, D.C., to welcome Marcos and to highlight the small number of intimidated oppositionists. More than seven hundred people, including two hundred members of the Philippine press corps, had accompanied the Marcoses at government expense.

From across the miles, Filipinos who had watched the state visit on live television became dimly aware of something terribly wrong. The Marcoses' state visit revived painful memories of American domination of the Philippines, and Marcos's evident dependence on President Reagan's support gave the lie to his promises of Filipino independence. The visit eroded the historic goodwill between America and the Philippines and exposed long-forgotten memories of the bloody Philippine-American war. A hundred thousand sufferings long buried in the national psyche were pried loose when Reagan feted the hated dictator. Filipinos remembered the time when their fathers were free men, and recalled how, in a crucial moment of their history, they lost the opportunity to carve their own future.

It is possible that a nation, like an individual, reckons with its past as it unravels its fate. The experience of 1899 developed in Filipinos a sense of nation. This identity lay dormant and shapeless until it was recalled by Ronald Reagan and Ferdinand Marcos's ceremony on the South Lawn of the White House that autumn in 1982.

After the Marcoses returned home, Benigno Aquino became more and more convinced that staying in the United States was politically futile. His fellowship at the Massachusetts Institute of Technology had come to an end, and he decided then, against the advice of his family and close friends, that it was time he, too, returned home. He saw Imelda on one of her periodic shopping trips to New York in May 1983 and told her of his plan. She warned him that he faced death if he attempted to return. She also offered him a million dollars to start a new life in America. It seemed then to Aquino that she wanted to prevent his return at any cost. As Aquino later described the conversation, "she was frightfully single-minded."

Reagan's all-out support for Marcos had given Imelda fresh reserves of confidence. Yet paradoxically, she often felt insecure. Marcos was ill. The prospect that she would one day rule without him became more and more imminent. The rumors about his illness had ceased to be vague. It was now quite well-known that he suffered from systemic lupus erythematosus, an auto-allergenic disease, which had affected his kidneys. A kidney transplant was recommended by American specialists, but Malacanang disclosed only that Marcos would take a leave of absence, a kind of dry run to see how the government would run without him.

However, few were deceived. Marcos was at the end of his tether. He was hanging on precariously to power and was totally preoccupied with ensuring the succession he had planned. While he made a show of health and strength and stated that he was very much in command, the thrust of his actions and policies were directed toward making sure that Imelda succeeded him when he went. Through the years he had let her rule little by little, relinquishing responsibility to her in parts, while testing her acceptability to the public. She was Minister of Human Settlements, a ministry which functioned like a government within the government with access but no accountability to the funds of all other government departments. She was also governor of Metro Manila, politically the second most powerful position in the country, and was a member of the crucial Executive Committee, which would take over in the event of Marcos's death or disability.

To most, in those last years of the Marcos rule, she was President in everything but name. But what was obscured was that the basis for this power sharing had been laid down years ago. From their first electoral victory in 1965, when Imelda had fought so ardently for him to win the Presidency, she had been Marcos's partner and the bridge to his dynastic empire. The government and the country were spoils which they had divided between them. As Marcos became weaker, she assumed more and more responsibility for running the country, and by 1983, the year Aquino would be assassinated, she was carrying on most of Marcos's activities as an acolyte to the "mastermind." It is accurate to say that Marcos gave more and more power to Imelda because she acted in consonance with his wishes. If she deviated from his own policies, it was only on minor matters, and this is corroborated by their closest aides. Had political analysts understood this interpretation of their complex relationship, they would not have persisted in their attempts to convince Marcos that it was political suicide to name his wife his successor. Marcos could not discard Imelda for she was his faithful clone, his double.

At her zenith of wealth and power, Imelda began to look abroad for models on how to stay on top. She was not blind to the way royalty lived in other countries. During her travels abroad she had seen that kings and queens living lives of luxury and splendor were not necessarily hated by their people. She especially looked to the British royal family as an exemplar and hoped that at some time in the dim future the Marcos family would develop a similarly loving and ceremonial relationship with a grateful people.

Thus, when her youngest daughter Irene was bethrothed to Gregorio Araneta, scion of one of the most aristocratic families of the Philippines, Imelda saw an opportunity to indulge her fantasies and to provide a royal diversion for "the sake of the people." After all, if the world loved the pageantry of the wedding of Prince Charles and Princess Diana, why not a Filipino royal wedding? That seemed to be the only rationale for the otherwise mad frenzy with which Imelda created a seventeenth-century regal wedding setting out of Marcos's backwater birthplace in Sarrat. To work, the town had to have history and the buildings to prove it. No matter that its single claim to historicity was a massive baroque red-brick church, built in 1724 amid weathered houses of wood, stone, and bamboo. Sarrat is a typical Filipino provincial town reflecting the modest lives of its 20,000 residents. The mayor described the town thus, "It is second only to Bacarra in the number of U.S. balikbayans [Filipinos who have returned after working in America]." Most Sarratenos work in government offices in Manila, and those left behind eke out a living by planting rice, vegetables, garlic, and tobacco.

But when Irene chose her father's birthplace as the venue for her wedding, Imelda had it transformed overnight into a town of what she imagined to be seventeenth-century European splendor. And all this done between the day Mr. Araneta asked for Irene's hand and the day of the wedding. Two weeks before the wedding the town's main street was still strewn with everything from bricks and cement to potted bougainvilleas and imported holly bushes and all the rest of the paraphernalia needed to re-create the town for the wedding of the century. Imelda's forty-five-day deadline included the construction of five new buildings, all of them built according to the Spanish colonial style to match the church. Among them were guest houses and a massive reception building to impress Imelda's jet-set friends. A new international airport was built, as well as a five-star hotel complete with swimming pool, jacuzzi, and a lavish casino. In addition the old stone and brick schoolhouse where Marcos had studied was refurbished to look more "European and medieval." The townspeople relate how the entire town worked into the night in preparation for the grand wedding. To landscape the surroundings, more than 3,000 workers were brought in from outlying provinces. From a scruffy, sleepy village, Sarrat became a splendid, magnificent "royal" town with reproductions of Spanish aristocrats' town houses and streets lined with potted flowers. It was a creation of Imelda's Cinderella magic: instant success and instant wealth grafted onto a seventeenth-century background to reflect the "old money" of the Marcos and the Romualdezes.

Just as Princess Diana had her royal carriage, Irene Marcos, too, had a silver carriage from Austria, drawn by seven white horses which were flown in from Morocco. With dear friends like Kurt Waldheim of Austria and King Hassan of Morocco, Imelda quickly arranged such amenities. She had overruled her daughter's wish for a more private wedding, saying, "Irene is so naïve. She actually thinks she can get away with a private wedding!" What Imelda wanted was a wedding that would establish once and for all to the Philippine aristocracy that she was better than they.

Six hundred invitations for only the closest friends were issued for the church wedding. Among the wedding guests was Enrique Zobel, said to be one of the richest bankers in the world and the scion of the fabled Zobel family, whose wealth dates back to the Spanish conquistadors in the Philippines.

The Zobels symbolized the extraordinary power and wealth of the rich in the otherwise impoverished island nation. The Zobels' guarded villages in Makati—villages that rival Belgravia or Beverly Hills—stand as monuments to their influence.

Upper-class Filipinos, and Imelda of late, had emulated the Zobels' life-style. They were the "in" crowd, the Makati crowd. Marcos and Imelda referred to the Makati crowd as the "oligarchs" when addressing the electorate. Yet they came six-hundred-strong to Irene's wedding. The Aranetas were old friends of this crowd, and the Marcoses, well, were "new" friends. But even as they toasted the couple with Dom Pérignon and partook of the sumptuous food catered by the Via Mare, the old oligarchs were not taken in by the show of Marcos wealth. It was, they sneered among themselves, "stolen" wealth. Moreover, it was new.

Irene's father-in-law, the architect and antique collector Luis Araneta, made it known to friends that although he was very fond of his new daughter-in-law, his hierarchy of values were God, country, and family, and in that order. He was also said to have been mortally offended that the antique candelabras he had lent to grace the altar were painted white. It was in such poor taste. Imelda, the parvenu from Ulot, could not do right. She wore a beautiful gown designed by Italian couturier Balestra, and a single diamond brooch. Nothing else. She had deliberately worked at being a picture of subdued elegance, as the truly rich are wont to be. But it was whispered about that the deceptively simple jewelry was the Idol's Eye—the coveted diamond she had bought for $5.5 million. Still, she was not accepted. To the Zobels and Aranetas et al., she remained an outsider, and if they deferred to her, it was only because she held political power. Then, too, with all her money Imelda had never learned the cardinal rule of social acceptance: to blend and harmonize with the crowd. No matter what she did, in the end her past always seemed to take over—her compulsion to be a star, to stand out, to show off —when all she ever wanted was to be accepted.

People came away from the wedding revolted by the bacchanalian feast, and some vomited not just with disgust but also because the food was rotten. A news item later reported there had been large-scale food poisoning at the wedding, caused by salmonella from food that had traveled too long from Manila to Sarrat. It could have been worse. A few days after the wedding, the massive church collapsed when a strong earthquake shook the little town. It was said that had the earthquake taken place during the wedding, the country would have lost its entire elite, including some of the world's richest men and women, under a pile of red Vigan bricks. (Imelda, in her desire to prettify the church, had had it sandblasted so the true color of the brick would come out. That had weakened the structure.) But the end never comes before its time. It is precise to the minutest milli-second. Irene's wedding was Imelda's swan song. A last performance before curtain time.

The shadows were lengthening in the bright firmament of the Marcoses' twenty-year rule. The country entered its third year of recession, its gross national product up by a mere 2 percent, the lowest among the five members of the Association of South East Asian countries. Its debt was a massive $18 billion, the highest per capita level in the region. The country was teetering on the verge of economic collapse, and Marcos's appeal to the people to make sacrifices after the sumptuous Sarrat wedding was the unkindest blow. But if the people held fast and bottled up their resentment, it was only because the end seemed near. It was only a matter of time. With the economy in shambles and Marcos terminally ill, something had to give.

The Marcoses focused their dread and fear of the coming debacle on one man: Aquino. More than a decade after Marcos declared martial law to stop him from wresting the Presidency, Aquino was still perceived to be Marcos's chief nemesis. When Aquino announced he was coming home at this time of falling fortunes, the news touched a raw nerve in Marcos. He had come to believe that Aquino was the only man capable of uprooting him from power, of destroying his dynastic dream. He would have to use all the powers at his command to stop Aquino. From their intelligence sources the Marcoses had heard that Aquino was determined to come home. August 7 was his chosen date for arrival.

Once more, Marcos dispatched Imelda to New York. Aquino saw her, but this time she issued no threats. His passport had expired, and she promised she would renew it for him. He genuinely believed that she would, since the signs from the government, at least initially, were favorable to his return. After all, one of the stipulations of his move to the United States had been that he return to the Philippines after his operation. Even as late as July 3, Minister of Defense Juan Ponce Enrile had passed word through an opposition leader in Manila that "there was no legal basis to imprison Aquino should he return home." As for the death sentence Marcos had imposed, this too had become "moot and academic" when Aquino was allowed to leave, according to an official of the Supreme Court.

It was only later that Aquino realized why Imelda had so willingly volunteered to "renew" his passport for him. He never got it back. When he tried to get travel documents from the Philippine consulate, he was told of an assassination plot against him and that he should postpone his trip for another month to give the government the chance to "neutralize" this plot. In order to travel, Aquino used a passport issued in the name of Marcial Bonifacio by sympathetic consular personnel somewhere in the world. The first name stood for martial law, and the second for the camp in which Aquino had been imprisoned for more than seven years. The name also recalled a rebel and hero in the Filipino war of independence.

On July 31 Marcos reinstated the death sentence on Aquino. Defense Minister Enrile followed this hint with a cable which said: "We are convinced beyond a reasonable doubt that there are plots against your life. . . . We request you therefore to suspend your return to the Philippines for at least one month. . . . Your avowed intention to answer the call for national unity and reconciliation will not be advanced by any attempt against your life which will exacerbate the present situation."

Aquino believed Enrile. Little did he know that in changing the date of his arrival, he was following his perfect sense of timing for his appointment with fate. As a concession to Marcos, he changed the date of his arrival, but not for the full month that Enrile had requested. He thought the "month" was an arbitrary time, and that after it passed, they would ask for another month and still another until it was too late and the momentum of his return would be lost. He set a new arrival date: August 21, no more, no less.

On August 5 the government announced that Marcos was going into a three-week seclusion to write a book. Manila was rife with rumors that Marcos would undergo a kidney transplant during this three-week period. The seclusion bit was a camouflage. In retrospect, the time Marcos requested was not arbitrary after all. Indeed, it was learned later that this was about the time when two American kidney specialists visited Manila. But to Aquino, Marcos's announcement only made his decision to return more compelling. As he said to UPI reporter Max Vanzi, "We're racing against time . . . we must convince the President to bring democracy back. I'm appealing to him to grant me an interview. He is the only man who can return the Philippines to democracy peacefully. Otherwise, we're down the road of an El Salvador." He wanted to be there before Marcos died. The race to the finish line was on.

Throughout Aquino's journey, which began in New York on August 13, he was dogged with warnings not to return home—he would be killed. But he continued on, refusing to look back. His friend and lawyer, former Senator Jovito Salonga, had burned the telephone wires to reach him, pleading that if Marcos was indeed sick, how would Aquino ever talk to him, even assuming that he granted Aquino an audience? And what difference would it make anyway?

But Aquino was unreachable. He had been told that he might be shot at the airport and that the assassin would be shot in return. More ominous, one of the "security precautions" prohibited his family and friends from going beyond the airport reception area.

In Taipeh, just a few hours before his flight to Manila, Aquino was shown a wire story that said that General Ver, Marcos's right-hand military leader, had warned that Aquino might be assassinated at the airport. "Oh, my God!" Aquino said. This was one warning he could not take lightly. Ver was passionately loyal to Marcos and would do anything for his master. But Aquino stayed on course, never deviating from the path of death. Seven years and seven months in jail, years of humiliation, suffering, and despair, had prepared him for this moment.

Aquino made a last phone call to his wife, Corazón, before leaving for the Taipeh airport. He told his brother-in-law, ABC News correspondent Ken Kashiwara, who was accompanying him on the trip, "One regret I have is that Cory has had to suffer so much." Corazón Cojuangco Aquino had supported him in all these years of travail. She was the wife he left behind while at the hustings, the wife who was his eyes and ears while he languished in jail, and now, once again, the wife he left to face what might be his death.

As the China Air Lines Boeing 727 circled the familiar blue mountains and dark green fields of his country, Aquino told Kashiwara, "I think it's a victory if we just land. Everything else is a bonus." On a moment's impulse and without much thought, he gave his favorite Rolex watch to Kashiwara as a token of their friendship and adventure together. His unconscious, or whatever it is that propels a man to his fate, had taken over.

As soon as the plane landed, three khaki-clad soldiers entered the plane to fetch the celebrated passenger. All the other passengers were told to remain seated. Camera shutters clicked as the newsmen accompanying Aquino jostled to get the best vantage points. In an article written by Kashiwara for *The New York Times,* he reported: "The first soldier walked right past Ninoy, but it was the second one who recognized him . . . then Ninoy stood up and the three began to escort him out." Kashiwara tried to follow, but he was ordered by one of the soldiers to take his seat. The soldiers hustled the celebrated Marcos foe through the service door while plain-clothes security guards pushed back the rest of the photographers and newsmen who tried to follow, and immediately shut the door. The photographers and newsmen tried to push the door open, but the security guards pushed back.

Nine seconds after Aquino went out the door, the first shot was heard. The victorious white-clad Aquino fell flat on his face to the ground, kissing the earth he so loved, his hands outstretched as if ready to fly. In a split second the political drama had become a morality play, and Aquino, lying on the burning-hot tarmac under the noonday sun, was the symbol of goodness.

Outside the terminal building was a welcoming crowd of about 20,000 people, assembled by Aquino's family and political colleagues. They had come with yellow buntings and placards, the color of their welcome, adapted from the popular song "Tie a Yellow Ribbon," and cheering "Ninoy, Ninoy!" But Ninoy never came. Instead came the announcement that he had been shot. There were pandemonium, confusion, and disbelief. The cheers turned to tears, and the crowd as one dispersed, each to his own manner of grief. Some ran to the nearest church to kneel and pray, while others rushed to the streets to pass the word to strangers and friends. Ninoy had been killed. The government-controlled stations said nothing of it. It was only through Radio Veritas, run by the Catholic Church, that Filipinos heard the news which by then was all over the world. No matter, the news spread like wildfire by word of mouth to hundreds and thousands and millions of Filipinos. Before long it seemed every Filipino radio was tuned to Radio Veritas.

In the days that followed, all roads led to the Aquino house on Times Street, where Filipinos queued to pay tribute to their hero and to see his bruised and bloodied face. At the request of his mother, Aquino's face was left as it was when he was felled by an assassin's bullet. "So the world could see what they had done to my son," she said. To Cory, the endless stream of people was a salve to her grief and pain. "I could not believe my eyes when I saw a huge crowd at our home in Times Street waiting patiently in line to view Ninoy's body. I was overwhelmed by this extraordinary display of love and devotion." In their lonely battle against the Marcos regime, she had become used to the sparse crowds made up of the brave few who ventured to show their support for Aquino, under the watchful eyes of military spies.

But if Cory had not expected such an outpouring of sympathy, neither did Marcos and Imelda, who carried on as if August 21, 1983, had been just another day. When the massive pro-Aquino demonstrations began, Marcos told a gathering of mayors and governors, "We will get over this. We will get over this." He then quoted General George C. Patton's words: "No bastard ever won a war by dying for his country. He won it by making the other poor bastard die for his country." They were brash but useless words.

Three million Filipinos came to Ninoy's funeral to show the world who was victor. It rained and stormed, and lightning struck, killing one and wounding nine others, but the millions who lined the funeral route stayed in place. It took the funeral cortege eleven hours to negotiate the twenty-one-kilometer route from Sto. Domingo church, where Aquino had lain in state for nine days, to the suburban cemetery where he would be interred. Placards blossomed everywhere, sending their message: "Ninoy, you are not alone." It was the biggest funeral in world history. It must have been humiliating and humbling for Marcos, echoing as it did the "funeral cortege" that had begun his political career so many years ago.

On the afternoon of September 19, 1935, his father's political rival, Julio Nalundasan, together with friends and followers, had paraded a mock coffin to symbolize Marcos's father's political death and had passed in front of the their house. Could it be that another funeral, albeit a real one, in strange metamorphosis, would also mark its end?

No one then could tell. How could a morality play be transformed into political action? It was dusk when Ninoy's hearse finally entered the Manila Memorial Park. As "Taps" played, the crowds pushed and surged, teetering on the edge of chaos. Then the gentle voice of his widow rose above the din. "Let us discipline ourselves. Let us show them that we do not need anybody to discipline us." Cory stilled the raging crowd. But the country's deliverance would come only on the third year following her husband's death.

Marcos soon appeared on television to deny, without being asked, that Imelda had anything to do with the assassination. Whatever the meaning of this bizarre statement, the implication was clear—he was above the ugly event. He, who had twice dispatched Imelda to stop Aquino from returning home, would now remove himself from the fray and would "gallantly" rise to defend his wife. Even hard-nosed political analysts and some members of the opposition fell for this trap. One of the first rumors to come out of Malacanang was that Marcos was unconscious hours before the assassination. But it has lately become known that this was not true. In an interview with *Newsweek,* Minister of Defense Juan Ponce Enrile recalled that he received two phone calls at about three o'clock in the afternoon of that fateful day. One was from U.S. Ambassador Michael Armacost and the other from Marcos. Imelda herself told a group of bankers that she had asked Marcos's permission to have lunch with friends at the Gloria Maris Restaurant, in case he wanted her on hand for Aquino's arrival. She left him at 12:30. If he had been in coma, it would have been between Imelda's departure and the phone call to Enrile at which time he would indeed have made a miraculous recovery. It is more believable that Marcos was in control.

But as the facts slowly reinforced their suspicions that the assassination had been planned, these parties came to believe that perhaps someone in the government had plotted the killing without Marcos's knowledge.

"Our analysis here is that Marcos would have absolutely zero incentive to have this happen," said one American official. "Marcos is too smart to do it this way," said another, echoing Marcos's own televised statement the night after the murder that "it was not the way to do it." If his government had been involved, the killing would not have been done so ineptly, Marcos said, emboldened. What's more, he was convinced that if any member of his government had been involved, even at a fairly low level, he would have known. He denied that his government had killed Aquino or that airport security had been lax. And the Reagan administration was inclined to believe him.

Regarding an earlier statement that the assassination could have been Communist inspired, he said: "What I have been saying all along is that this was such a bitter, passionate, and angry act of hatred that it must have been motivated by personal reasons of vengeance, for what reason I don't know. But the Communists took advantage of it. I think that what happened was that they discovered a man who had decided to revenge himself on Aquino and used him for their own purpose. This is one of the theories which you remember I spoke of at the beginning. Up to now I cannot believe that any man would want to kill a political leader knowing that he would be killed himself unless he was motivated by the deepest kind of hatred, personal hatred."

No more need have been said. To most Filipinos, no man was more punished by Marcos than Aquino had been. Marcos tried to break Aquino in prison, putting him in strict isolation in a four-by-five-meter cell in a faraway province. Perhaps, in the final analysis truth is irrational. It includes a panoply of unseen factors beyond the reach of even the most calculating and shrewd tactician. Even a Marcos. No investigation would ever explain why Ninoy was assassinated as he was, at high noon with a soldier on each side of him, with the whole world watching.

And Imelda, the ever-dutiful wife, now changed her version of her threat to Aquino. Despite testimony to the contrary from more than one source, she claimed that she did not tell Aquino that he was dead if he returned to the Philippines. She had passed the same threat to Aquino through Laurel, but said that what she really meant was "if he went home and got killed, all of us will be in trouble, including you" (referring to Laurel). At the same time that Marcos and Imelda were making their denials, another rumor floated around Manila allegedly from a nurse who worked in Malacanang, who said that Marcos was showering when he was told of the assassination and that he had dashed out and slapped Imelda. It was a thoroughly unbelievable story, but similar variations had also circulated when Manotoc was kidnapped. As in the past, Imelda provided a good foil to take the heat off Marcos and his Presidency.

But most Filipinos were not drawn in by the subterfuge. To them it mattered very little whether it was Imelda or Marcos who had ordered Aquino's death. As Imelda had often said they hardly ever disagreed on policy or principle. Only one rule now bound them together: stay in power.

During the weeks and months that followed Ninoy's assassination, the Philippines plunged into political turmoil. There were angry demonstrations every day, but more extraordinary was the fact that the protesters were no longer simply oppositionists, political radicals, or the dispossessed. Filipinos from every walk of life—students, priests, nuns, teachers, housewives, even businessmen—now joined in a mammoth, desperate attempt to force Marcos and Imelda out of Malacanang. Makati, the Wall Street of Metro Manila, became the base of the new protest movement that brought together businessmen and political ideologues. Business ground to a standstill as both executives and office workers marched day after day under showers of yellow confetti and balloons, the symbol of Aquino's return, chanting, "Marcos, resign." Millions of dollars fled the country as investors lost confidence in the debt-riddled economy. Marcos in turn threatened and seduced the businessmen in an attempt to make them stop the snowballing protest. But even as he was asking the businessmen to help restore order and confidence in the government, the London *Sunday Telegraph* ran a story headlined, "How Long Can Marcos Last?" The story said that "usually reliable sources in Switzerland report that $1 billion dollars had been deposited in the Marcos accounts and that Imee Marcos had purchased a New York property of ambassadorial grandeur."

Incredibly, the focus of the protesters' discontent was not Marcos but the flamboyant Imelda. For if Ninoy had become the symbol of goodness, it was Imelda who had become the symbol of evil. Not that Marcos was forgiven. But it was Imelda's prodigality that caught the public's imagination—her gowns, her jewelry, her projects, her houses, her traveling binges, her parties in the face of so much poverty and want. "Sacrifice the Queen," an allusion to the last gambit in a chess game, became the cry of protest heard across the country. The protesters dreaded the shadow cast by Imelda's succession to the Presidency when Marcos died, extinguishing any hope of an end to their imperial rule. Imelda's cruelty was another concern: she portrayed a woman impervious to the sufferings of others.

By New Year's Day, 1984, it seemed to the Marcoses that Ninoy's death and the demonstrations that followed had finally "blown over." Malacanang was back to its sumptuous and unforgettable parties. Imelda had the great idea that if she invited everybody to the New Year's Party, all would be forgiven and forgotten. The protests were "just envy," she told close friends. Three thousand people, including Cory Aquino, were invited to the biggest party in Malacanang history. Cory declined, but many others, including some of the disgruntled Makati businessmen, came to partake of what was described as "a party to end all parties"—560,000 pesos' worth of fried chicken, thirty roasted calves, and dozens of roasted pigs, cooking under a fairyland of lights on the Palace lawns. The Russian ambassador had no cause for complaint; he even won a capitalist Ford car and got to meet Mr. Ford's former wife, Christina, Imelda's bosom friend. As did the famous Italian haute couturier, Renato Balestra, who brought with him a new collection of gowns for Imelda. To Imelda, no party was complete without her "beautiful people," jetted in free of charge.

The year came and went, and still there was no visible

change in the Marcoses' fortunes or those of their country-men. Imelda kept spending. Marcos was getting sicker. And the economy was in its death throes. Outside of Malacanang and Makati, in the dark villages of the province where Imelda had once lived, poor folk were starving. In Negros, called sugarland, which had bred millionaires by the dozen at the peak of the sugar industry in the early American colonial period, a man-made famine threatened four hundred thousand workers, faced with the collapse of the sugar market. It was one of the Marcoses' milking cows. They had created a monopoly that dictated the prices at which sugar could be bought and sold, with the profits going largely into their pockets and those of their cronies. The London shopping trips of Imelda and her children were often paid for by the office of the Philippine Sugar Commission there. But these earnings were small compared to those from the huge international loans the Marcos regime had received over the years. In late 1984 the World Bank in a confidential report said that of the $13.7 billion Marcos borrowed in the years 1978 to 1982, $3.1 billion could not be accounted for, and ". . . it appears that borrowing may have indirectly financed the acquisition of real or financial assets abroad that were imperfectly recorded in the balance of payments. Speculative outflows appear to have been an element of this capital flight." These revelations notwithstanding, the Marcoses were firmly ensconced in Malacanang, and it seemed they would stay there until they were bodily removed.

In the parliamentary elections of 1984, Marcos successfully divided the opposition, with half of it supporting participation in the elections and the other half calling for a boycott. There were merits in both arguments. The boycott side, composed mostly of the more progressive elements of the opposition, held that participation would be an implicit acceptance of Marcos's rule. The participation side, led by the traditional politicians, argued that it was important to keep fighting Marcos, and elections, no matter how unsatisfactory, were a ready-made platform. Although the former was the more idealistic position, it was to the latter that the people responded. At a later and more crucial time, it would be shown once more that the more "reasonable" course of action is not always right.

But in 1984 the elections gave Filipinos a chance to express their personal commitment. The actual exercise of voting and making sure that the vote is properly counted carried immense psychological power that effectively politicized the people. Although only fifty-nine opposition candidates were elected, (roughly a third of the total contested number), the 1984 parliamentary election marked a watershed in the continuing battle to unseat Marcos. It was the dry run for another, more crucial election to follow.

Marcos had an entirely different test in mind, however. He wanted to test Imelda's capability at the polls. She had "won" an earlier vote against Aquino in 1978, but this was at a time when martial law was still enforced. Aquino had campaigned from jail, despite the international protest against such an uneven and unfair contest. No one was deceived that force and money had not assured her victory then. But to most Filipinos, it was not the spurious tally of the votes that mattered but the deafening sound of the noise made by Filipinos banging pots and pans, honking car horns or doing anything and everything to signify their protest against the result. There was no doubt that Aquino was then as now the people's candidate.

But in May 1984 Marcos needed to know just how Imelda would fare. There was still plenty of money and intimidation available, but this time it was measured for a "reasonable" assessment. He would give Imelda a free hand to run the Manila campaign. Indeed, she gave all she could muster, dancing, singing, and cajoling the crowds to make sure her candidates won. There was no one who could match her dedication in the fight for victory, and on the eve of the election she announced her candidates would make a clean sweep of the city's vote. In fact, two-thirds of her candidates sank without a trace. Among the few who managed to survive the debacle was the aging Arturo Tolentino, and only because he had made appropriate oppositionist sounds and at one point, although a Marcos man, had said, "The real problem of the country was Marcos and Imelda."

With Imelda's defeat, Marcos finally came to accept the fact that his successor was as unpopular as he was. Over the years, he had made her his mirror image, yet he still expected that she would be as popular as she had been when she first sang for his campaigns in 1965. Then she had been the sweet Rose of Tacloban. He could not see that he had destroyed her, that politics had warped the innocence that had once been so compelling that people had pushed for a glimpse of its beautiful face. In a sense, she had destroyed him, too.

People were already looking to the long-promised Presidential elections in 1987, and Marcos could not have escaped the growing clamor for Cory Aquino to accept the political mantle of her martyred husband. Cory versus Imelda was the fight the Filipino electorate was spoiling for. If Imelda was indeed the power behind the throne, then she should put herself to the people's vote before Marcos became incapable of ruling, and before Imelda, with the support of Army General Ver, could seize power.

It was time for Marcos to adopt a new tack. In a press conference not long after the May election, Marcos made a public repudiation of Imelda's so-called power. In reply to the obviously planted question "Is it true, sir, that the First Lady is running your government?" he replied, "Certainly not. If I may be immodest, she is just a Galatea to my Pygmalion. She did not know anything about politics when she married me, poor girl. I remember when she used to have headaches whenever there were more than two visitors at home. No, I am running things, and perhaps I may add that most if not all of her principal initiatives and decisions have always had to be cleared by me." Nothing could have been clearer.

Very soon thereafter Imelda disappeared from the Manila scene. She was not even present at the traditional Independence Day reception at the Palace. She was rumored to have been displeased with the President's press conference. Whatever was the truth, Marcos's repudiation of her was short-lived. Imelda had gone to Rome to drown her sorrows on the Via Condotti, but she would soon return to his arms in Malacanang. Marcos had dispatched a most poetic note of apology to the First Lady. It read:

> To Imelda My Love. My soul crawls in the . . . nightmare of my long night. . . . For there is darkness when you are away. . . . I have lost the light in my world. . . . Please return the sun into my life. . . . Andy.

For all the intrigue and rivalry and gossip, Marcos and Imelda were kindred souls whom nothing could put asunder. They were peas in a pod. And Imelda was no less poetic in describing the relationship that had confounded the rest of the world. In an eerie anniversary greeting written in May 1972, Imelda had eulogized their marriage:

> Dearest Ferdinand:
> For 18 years I've loved you, and after this a whole eternity. . . . Our life was filled with joys and madness . . . Showered too with success and sadness . . . our love has transcended human passions . . . the splendor of heaven it has known . . . so what today can I give you once more, a love faithful, loyal, and true! Happy anniversary, darling! . . . Imelda.

Outside this passion a whole country was up in arms. All through 1985 the opposition continued their assault on Malacanang. The economy did not improve; if it moved at all, it went from bad to worse. Factories were closing, and no one was investing in the economy. Although the official figure put unemployment at 14 percent, in truth nearly one in two Filipinos was out of work. More worrisome, the Philippines had defaulted in the debt payments; the rescheduled payments now totaled a shocking $27.5 billion.

In Washington meanwhile, the perception grew that, indeed, the Marcos regime was in its twilight and the Reagan administration had backed a loser. Unless some democratic reforms took place soon, America would witness another Iran and another foreign policy debacle. The 1987 elections were far too distant to save the situation. The moderate opposition in the Philippines was becoming increasingly irrelevant and was clearly unable to bring reforms or to throw Marcos out. More and more Filipinos now looked to the radical opposition, the Communist Party of the Philippines and the New People's Army, to resolve the Philippine dilemma. From an initial force of a few hundred guerrillas in 1972, the New People's Army had ballooned to a well-armed fighting force of 20,000 with a substantial base of civilian sympathizers.

Still, a Communist threat was not the crucial factor. The key to political salvation was the perception of the majority of the people, of the millions who stood in silence at Aquino's funeral and the thousands who joined the rallies against Marcos thereafter. If no significant political change took place soon, this silent majority would be carried away by the Communist propaganda that only a violent overthrow could remove the Marcoses. As time dragged on, more and more ordinary Filipinos found it was no longer difficult to believe that freedom-loving America was behind the dictatorship. If there had been resistance to the anti-imperialist and anti-American line of the radicals, it was because of a fear that this would be treading on Communist ground, and the majority of Filipinos did not relish being another Vietnam or Cambodia. They wanted Marcos out and freedom in but not at the cost of another dictatorship. Their anti-Americanism and anti-imperialism and anti-Communism all came from the same source—the wellspring of a passionate drive for freedom, the historical experience of 1899, and the events that began in August 1983. Yet it is doubtful that Americans really understood, for they themselves had repressed the truth about that past. Learned and erudite Reagan aides had come to believe that an experience of so long ago was irrelevant to current political perceptions. Perhaps if they had probed deeper and understood that, like individuals, nations too have a past and that this could only be ignored under peril, it might have made all the difference. For the past works in the strangest ways. It came back to haunt Filipinos and give them the courage to bring about the denouement that saw the end of the Marcos regime.

Marcos's declining health added further tension and urgency to the situation. In the event of his sudden demise, there would be little that anyone could do to stop the Philippines from spiraling into chaos. To take no action, as some advocated, was to lose the initiative to control events. Despite continuous denials from Malacanang, private sleuthing had borne out the fact that Marcos had survived two kidney transplants, one at about the time of Aquino's assassination and another in the fall of 1984. At the time of the second transplant terrifying rumors had swept the country. Marcos was said to have suffered heart failure in surgery. Another rumor claimed he had flown to America for an emergency operation and had died.

Most of the rumors came from Filipinos phoning in from abroad. In Manila there was a total news blackout. *Newsweek* reported that Marcos had phoned President Reagan to tell him that his doctors advised he seek medical treatment in the United States. Reagan, mindful of the Iranian experience, which quickly deteriorated when the Shah sought medical treatment in the United States, reportedly asked Marcos who would be in charge while he was away. There was speculation that a junta of three military officers and two civilian officials would run the country. In fact, under continued pressure from America, Marcos had amended the constitution. If Marcos died, the Speaker of the National Assembly would run the country until elections were held sixty days later. As expected, the current Speaker was an Imelda man. But this new succession was simply academic if Marcos's death was kept secret. Imelda and her allies would then have plenty of time in which to seize power.

In reply to the clamor for accurate information on the President's health, the Palace issued a picture of Marcos reading the latest issue of a pro-government newspaper. But independent journalists remained unconvinced, and said the photo could have been faked. Imelda, they said, was already running the country, using faked voices and faked signatures to issue decrees.

After a suspenseful week Marcos reappeared, looking wan and tired and saying he never felt better. As for Imelda, she said the report that he had had a serious operation was ridiculous. "All he had was an allergy, and that runs in the family."

In the midst of this Orwellian drama, an unexpected development occurred within the Palace power circle that would have dire consequences for the Marcos regime. A serious rift developed between Imelda and Defense Minister Juan Ponce Enrile, a key architect of martial law in 1972. Their fights in front of a fairly large assembly of Marcos loyalists had ended with Imelda accusing Enrile of incompetence in dealing with the growing Communist menace. Imelda pushed the defense minister out and replaced him with his archrival, General Fabian Ver. In the probable scenario for a showdown, Enrile could count on the disaffected General Fidel Ramos, who, although a Marcos relative, did not admire Ver. Moreover, he was a professional and favored by the Americans to revamp the military, which had become a tangle of abuse and corruption. But Ramos was acting chief of staff in name only. Ver was still very much in command, despite prodding from the White House and his reputed role in Aquino's assassination. The knives were drawn in the Marcos court; only the time and setting of battle remained.

American policy makers, alarmed at the deteriorating situation, set their hopes on a credible election, to be held sooner than 1987. But they were still divided between those who supported Marcos and those who supported the long shot of an opposition victory. Philippine watchers now began talking of a political flashpoint within as little as a year, at which time the Communist Party could foment civil unrest which neither the military nor the police would be able to contain.

But Marcos was unmoved by any suggestions for change or reform. Imelda also continued to rule at his side. From his perspective, he had weathered the Aquino assassination and had a good laugh at suggestions that he resign. As for the Americans, he read them well, too. Or so he thought. He had survived four American administrations, and the current one was run by his good friend.

What he did not know was that Reagan, too, was under increasing pressure. Indeed, another Reagan friend, Singapore Prime Minister Lee Kuan Yew, had pointedly told the American President that Marcos was "living on borrowed kidneys," and had all but demanded that the Americans remove Marcos or imperil democracy in Southeast Asia. A procession of Reagan envoys soon hit the Manila trail, including then-U.N. envoy Jeane Kirkpatrick, Vernon Walters, CIA chief William Casey, and most importantly, Reagan's close friend and campaign manager Senator Paul Laxalt.

The solution to the election impasse came unexpectedly during Marcos's television interview with David Brinkley on November 3, 1985. Believing in his own brilliance, Marcos had consented to the interview as an opportunity to outwit his opponents before an audience of millions. In the course of the Brinkley interview, a Marcos supremely confident of his position had said he was willing to submit to a snap election to prove that he still enjoyed the mandate of his people. The challenge came literally out of the blue, but the opposition and their allies in the American State Department seized on Marcos's offer as an opportunity to save the Philippines. The main opposition candidate was Former Senator Salvador Laurel, president of the UNIDO Party, who was said to have enjoyed Aquino's support. Aquino, had he come out alive from the airport, would not himself have run for President, saying "whoever followed Marcos would inherit a host of problems and would stink in less than a year."

But Laurel was a controversial figure, having supported Marcos in the early years of martial law, and it was doubted that he could unite the opposition. This left Aquino's widow, Cory, but she was reluctant as ever to be drawn into political battle. When it had seemed she would not budge from her decision, she suddenly announced the conditions under which she might be persuaded to run—first, if Marcos called a snap election, and second, that one million people signed a petition drafting her to run. The first condition was soon met when Marcos announced snap elections in the beginning of the year and fixed the date as January 17, but he was later persuaded to give the opposition at least a month to prepare. The second condition was a cinch as her admirers banded together into the Cory Aquino Movement for President and combed the entire country for the required signatures in record time.

Marcos and his aides were increasingly discomfited by the prospect that Cory would run, for they had banked on Salvador Laurel as the easier opponent. Cory had been sanctified by her husband's martyrdom and, at least for the election, could not be sullied by the dirty game of politics. Any attack on her would only rebound to her benefit. This was a formidable obstacle to Marcos, whose effectiveness lay in his rough and dirty political style and his willingness to use any means necessary to achieve victory. To the opposition, Cory, pure, innocent, faultless, was his perfect match.

She announced her candidacy on December 3, 1985, a day after a Marcos-appointed court acquitted General Fabian Ver and twenty-five others accused in the assassination of her husband. A poetic battle loomed.

Like her husband, Cory seemed fixed on a course of action when she decided to run and win. Although for a time it looked like a three-pronged battle with Laurel also determined to run, Cory kept on fighting for a unified opposition ticket. When the negotiations seemed to fall through, the shy widow came into her own and, against the advice of her closest supporters, conceded to Laurel's wish that he would give way and be her vice presidential candidate only if they ran under his party's banner, the UNIDO.

This unified ticket, too, was achieved in breathtaking fashion, just an hour before the deadline for the registration of candidates for the election, which was signed into law by Marcos for February 7. Number 7 was this man of destiny's lucky number, and, being superstitious, he could not see how anyone other than him would be the 7th President of the Republic of the Philippines.

As Cory, the political neophyte, learned how to conduct her first campaign, Imelda, the seasoned campaigner, reverted to the tried and true tactics that had worked so well for her and Marcos in the past. But this time, the magic did not work.

Hampered by the lack of resources and time, Cory nevertheless conducted a spectacular campaign, drawing crowds beyond her expectations while the sick and ailing Marcos had to preserve his strength for the few occasions his doctors allowed. Once more, Imelda had to save his political career. To those who had seen her campaign in 1965, the change was remarkable. Imelda's steely determination remained, but it lacked the seductive innocence of her youth. "She would stand, legs apart like a man, on the platform, and although she sang the same songs, one knew this was a different Imelda—not the Imelda of those triumphant years when she was everybody's darling," said a friend.

Although the electoral battle was between Marcos and Cory, the comparison between the two women was inevitable. The pressure was on Imelda, who clung to the notion that her once-formidable beauty would still stand her in good stead. She deprecated Cory for not being beautiful, and said that, as such, she could never be President. Imelda was a drowning figure resisting the onrushing tide of change. "Our opponent does not put on any makeup. She does not have her fingernails manicured. . . . Filipinos are for beauty. Filipinos who like beauty, love, and God are for Marcos," she told an uncomprehending audience.

Imelda also lashed out against the American leaders who had abandoned her, saying, "The U.S. is a stupid country that doesn't respect women—especially tall and beautiful Filipino women who are smartly dressed. Just because you are a woman, they think you are frivolous. Just because you can sing a little, you are not to be taken seriously."

There had been a time when her beauty mattered, but its

worth had been tested and found wanting. She could not see that the adoring crowds of Marcos's first campaign had changed, nor could she see how she herself had hardened and had come to symbolize the cruelty and corruption of the Marcos regime.

The millions of Filipinos aching for change now only had eyes for Cory, with her quiet charm, her intelligence, and her simplicity. She was the real heiress, the woman born with a silver spoon in her mouth, whose family was one of the richest in the Philippines. If she did not show her wealth, it was because she did not need to. Cory Cojuangco could feel confident in clothes made by the neighborhood seamstress because there had never been a time when she was unwanted or rejected for lack of money. Her personal assets totaled more than 13 million pesos. Her jewels were truly heirlooms, not recent purchases from Van Cleef and Arpels. She was a true blue stocking, educated in the United States, and fluent in French. She represented all that Imelda had ever aspired to. Yet it was Cory, the blue stocking, with whom Filipinos of all classes identified, rather than with Imelda, the poor provincial girl. Cory exuded earnestness and sympathy for the poor, even if she had never been poor herself, while Imelda, who had suffered great poverty in her youth, showed poorly concealed disdain for those who reminded her of her true roots. Instead, she had preferred the role of the capricious "little rich girl."

The full consequence of her rejection of her past now came to the fore: Without the moorings of the child in General Solano, she had developed into a hated figure. In the distant future, when history shall judge the dramatis personae of this crucial period of Philippine history, Imelda's epitaph might read: She was the great what-might-have-been of Philippine politics.

Yet the outcome of the February elections and the extraordinary popular revolution that followed went beyond the differences between Cory and Imelda. It had to do with a people heaving mightily toward self-determination and marked the culmination of the political upheaval that began with Ninoy's assassination. Marcos's dictatorship was the tail end of nearly a century of Filipino subjugation. The people were fed up. When the elections came, the people were fully prepared to chain themselves to the ballot boxes so their true will and voice could be heard. In those moments they were a desperate people, fighting with a courage beyond themselves. Worldwide television coverage of the fight for an honest vote showed the Filipino people's reverence for the democratic process. For two decades it had been said that Filipinos were too easy-going, too uncaring, to take on the dictatorship that had impoverished the country. The people proved the rest of the world wrong. Marcos, on the other hand, showed the world a face of evil, using terror and outright fraud as he tried to steal the election by hook or by crook. The television cameras recorded scenes of Marcos's armed goons trying to drive voters away from the polls, juxtaposed against scenes of courageous citizens guarding ballot boxes and making sure they were safely deposited in town halls. Thousands of such morality plays were witnessed by foreign observers, including a sizable delegation from the United States headed by Republican Senator Richard Lugar, the Chairman of the Foreign Relations Committee. But Marcos was determined to win, and when the unofficial count of the NAMFREL electoral body showed Cory in the lead, the official government count shifted, and soon showed Marcos leading the returns.

Then a group of computer operators, mostly young frightened women, staged a walkout, charging that the count was being manipulated; what appeared on the tallyboards did not coincide with the figures they had recorded. Hemmed in, Marcos took the final step of his grand strategy and ordered that the count at both electoral bodies be stopped. The ballot boxes were moved to the National Assembly for the final tally. A superb tactician, he had earlier stipulated by decree that only the National Assembly, two-thirds of whose members were his men, was empowered to proclaim the final winner.

Predictably, the Assembly declared Marcos the winner, albeit with only a reasonable margin. Once again, it seemed

Marcos had survived, and quickly he moved to make concessional sounds, asking for unity and reconciliation so that the nation could go back to work. He did not reckon that Cory would respond to this hour of crisis by refusing to accept the results of an election marked by wholesale fraud and intimidation. Replying to President Reagan's suggestion that the opposition join a newly created Council of Presidential Advisers as a way out of the impasse, Cory said, "It would be a delusion to believe that the opposition, whose leaders and followers have been and are being killed, can suddenly settle down to a Western-style two-party system—too many would be dead the moment the world's head is turned."

Foreign observers as well as the hundreds of newspapermen from around the world who covered the event agreed with her—it had not been an honest or credible election and it was in Marcos's hands to secure that it was so. As Senator Richard Lugar returned to the United States to report on the elections, Cory called for public civil disobedience to protest the National Assembly count and to force Marcos out of Malacanang. Once again millions of Filipinos heard her speak of the long fight ahead. Marcos swung back with the threat that he would deal patiently but firmly with those who disobeyed the law, an implicit threat that he could order wholesale arrests and declare martial law once more. That was the drama on center stage.

But another drama was taking place, if less conspicuously, in the Palace. It involved a Malacanang plot which, if successful, could finally pave the way for Imelda's succession. Marcos issued orders for the arrest of Defense Minister Enrile and acting Chief of Staff Ramos, alleging that they were co-conspirators in an assassination plot against him and Imelda. They had caught the culprits and were about to present them on television when the ousted military men jumped the gun and announced they were breaking away from Marcos. The beleaguered President's own press conference would be televised two hours after.

On the evening of February 22, Radio Veritas announced

the news of Enrile's and Ramos's dramatic defection. Taking with them about five hundred followers, they had barricaded themselves in Camp Aguinaldo, a suburban army base. They called on their fellow officers and soldiers to join them. Before long, all of Manila was glued to Radio Veritas as they had been on that fateful day in August 1983. Then they had mourned a death that left them helpless and hopeless. Now they were hearing a message of hope that suggested that the change they had voted for was just possibly coming to fruition. To most who listened to Radio Veritas, the military rebellion provided an opportunity to take sides, to act out their cause. This was their forum at last to express their anger and resentment toward the now evil regime. On the day of confrontation the morality play shifted from a symbolic struggle to a real event, in which the spectators could take part.

Cardinal Sin, the Manila prelate who had campaigned vigorously for an honest election, called the people to the streets at nine o'clock on the evening of February 23, 1986. He said, "These two gentlemen need our help. They need food and support. People, please come." In a tremulous but firm voice he pleaded for every man, woman, and child to come and shield the military defectors from certain death. After talking to Ramos and Enrile, the Cardinal called on the nuns of Manila to fast and pray until the crisis was over, saying, "We are in battle and you are the powerhouses. And the moment we do not win the battle, you will have to fast until the end of your life." As God's man, he believed in the power of prayer to bring the miracle that was needed in those fearful February days.

Late that night, when it was uncertain how the crisis would be resolved, the cardinal received a surprise visitor: Imelda. She had slipped out of the Palace, impeccably dressed as ever, carrying a solid gold crucifix to give to the Cardinal. She had come to plead for his sympathy, and to reverse his support of the rebels. The Cardinal, who is also known for his sense of humor, admonished the distraught First Lady for visiting in the middle of the night, as this was the House of Sin and people might talk. She stayed two hours, pleading with him to reverse his position and promising to mend her ways. The kindly prelate then asked her to pray, and pray she did. Back in Malacanang she called some friends over to the Palace to pray for the preservation of the regime until it was time to go.

Cory returned to Manila on Sunday, February 23, and seconded the Cardinal's call to the people to support Ramos and Enrile, but firmly instructed them that peace, calm, and sobriety were to be observed at all times. The following day thousands of Filipinos heeded the Cardinal's call, and by the time Marcos ordered his tanks to assault the barricaded camp, a million people stood in the way, armed with nothing but rosaries, flowers, and chocolates.

In the end, the Filipino people's peaceful revolution would dazzle the world and stop Marcos's soldiers. The impact of a million people, dancing, singing, and praying for peace, disarmed the combative soldiers; one by one, they deserted Marcos and threw in their lot with the people. What held the people together was a mystical admixture of nationalism and religion—a combination with deep historical roots in the Philippines.

It was a unique protest. At one point, a mother stopped a soldier to say how much he resembled her son. Would the soldier shoot his mother, she asked. Another group of protesters sang native drinking songs and passed drinks to the soldiers, who were persuaded to join in the tumultuous clapping of hands. There were scenes upon scenes, but each Filipino who participated in that unbelievable show of people-power employed every ounce of charm and humor available to make it impossible for the soldiers to reach for their guns and fire.

Priests and nuns armed with rosaries and crucifixes were placed on the first line of defense. Entire families encircled the tanks, holding aloft images of the Lady of Fatima.

The fiesta-like atmosphere brought thousands more to the scene. In that sense, it was a non-Gandhian, nonconfrontational revolution. The crowds just laughed and sang and persuaded the soldiers to join them. All motives, political or otherwise, had fused into indefinable courage. "I don't know where I got my courage. Despite all the laughing, we knew that there could be a slight slip somewhere and we would all die. But I was a Filipino, whatever that means, and I truly believed that I had to save my country from the destruction and bloodshed that would have followed if we had not answered the call," said one housewife, distantly related to a general who had fought in the Filipino-American wars.

The most dramatic defection came from the fifteenth strike wing of the Air Force, led by Colonel Antonio Sotelo. Ordered by Marcos to fire at the rebels, the pilots promptly swung around and landed in the Ramos-Enrile camp, waving white flags of peace. The pall of defeat hovered over Malacanang, but still Marcos and Imelda fought on.

In simple ceremonies held on Tuesday morning, February 25, Corazón Aquino took her oath as the seventh President of the Republic of the Philippines. Marcos's inauguration took place a few hours later, after which he harangued a crowd of about 3,000 paid supporters from a Malacanang balcony. Imelda stood beside him in tears, and together they sang for the last time "Dahil sa Iyo" ("Because of You"), the love song with which they had enthralled barefoot audiences in the past. Those who saw Imelda during those last hours in the Palace saw a pathetic figure, walking mindlessly back and forth. Gone was the queenly and seemingly unflappable poise. In the past she had freely mixed with the newsmen who were covering the scene, but now she ignored them completely. She still had to perform her last duty as the efficient administrator of her husband's empire. She called together the employees who had stayed to the end and handed each a pay packet containing ten thousand pesos.

Marcos made one more desperate call to the White House, and bereft of dignity befitting the country's head of state, he pleaded with President Reagan for help. Amid the din of angry crowds pushing at the Palace gates, Marcos asked Senator Paul Laxalt what he should do. The senator and close confidant to President Reagan replied: "Mr. President, I am not bound by diplomatic restraint. I'm talking for myself. I think you should cut and cut cleanly. The time has come." A long silence followed, during which Laxalt thought Marcos had gone. "Mr. President. Mr. President. Are you there?" he asked.

Marcos's reply summed up how much had changed since he visited the White House in 1982. "I am so very, very disappointed," he told Laxalt. Even in that late hour, Marcos had hoped Reagan would bless a power-sharing arrangement with the opposition until the end of his term in 1987. The brilliant strategist who had finally run out of schemes prepared to face "heroic" death in Malacanang Palace. But in that final battle, Imelda's love for money overcame Marcos's lust for power and she convinced him to escape rather than die fighting.

A few hours later, Ferdinand and Imelda, their family and friends, began their flight to exile in Hawaii. Happiness broke loose in Manila, and Filipinos danced and embraced in the streets, singing Christmas songs.

The Shoes Matched

FOR THE FIRST time in twenty years Malacanang was opened to the public, and thousands queued patiently each day to see for themselves why Marcos and Imelda were reluctant to leave. They had enjoyed power like kings and queens. But if Marcos had been master in the Ortega house when he first married Imelda and disallowed her to change anything, Malacanang was her Palace. Its vulgar opulence and showy luxury are pure Imelda. She had transformed what was once a dignified residence for Philippine heads of state into a fantasy boudoir, replete with Persian carpets, French mirrors, Chinese vases, English antique furniture, and Aubusson tapestries. Her red-carpeted bedroom was the most luxurious in the Palace, with a magnificent double king-sized bed and a French baroque headrest topped with a huge carved wooden crown from which ninety yards of fine nylon tulle cascaded. It was marked the "Queen's Room." Below her room lay a veritable Aladdin's cave of a basement, filled with the treasures of twenty years of plunder, years that saw a once-promising country collapse into poverty.

The Cinderella who once lived in the Palace left behind

3,000 pairs of shoes in her flight to exile. The shoes, all size 8½, were lined up in neat racks. There were shoes of every shape and color, representing the most expensive name brands in the world. The shoes were a stark reminder that despite all her wealth, Imelda could not erase her past.

Why this fetish? What pinched, what hurt, what would not fit in her life of luxury and compelled her to ransack the shoe boutiques of Fifth Avenue, Rue Faubourg St. Honoré, and Via Condotti? From Hawaii, Marcos laughs at suggestions that 3,000 pairs of shoes were a bit much for one person to own when more than half of her countrymen worked themselves to the bone to afford just one pair. He said the shoes had been accumulated over the course of twenty years and that Imelda needed to change shoes more than once a day. Imelda herself laughs off the accusation that 3,000 pairs of shoes is proof of her mindless extravagance. She tripped and broke her shoe one day while walking on the streets of Honolulu. When a visitor gave her a new pair, she said wryly, "I should send this to Cory Aquino to make it three thousand and one pairs of shoes."

But apart from the 3,000 pairs of shoes which shocked the world, there were also 2,000 ball gowns, 500 bras, a trunkful of girdles, giant bottles of the most expensive perfumes in the world, gallons of anti-wrinkle cream, and boxes of handbags, still unopened. A walk-in safe held dozens of emptied jewelry cases. The sight of Malacanang moved even a jaded American congressman to say that it was the worst case of conspicuous consumption he had ever seen. "Compared to her, Marie Antoinette was a bag lady," said Stephen Solarz.

Yet Imelda's Malacanang exuded neither comfort nor beauty. Most visitors come away repulsed by the gloom and decay that pervade the Marcoses' living quarters. The Palace suffered from strongman's disease. Because of Marcos's allergies, the once-airy Palace had been fully air-conditioned and sealed to block the smell of pollution from the Pasig River. But the stench of the river, which takes waste from the city's factories and from the crowded slums that line its banks, seeped through the crevices of the centuries-old Presidential palace and permeated its rooms.

It must have been a constant battle to keep out the smell and the dirt. The signs of Marcos's disease were there as well—dialysis machines, oxygen tanks, medicines. Those who arrived at the Palace soon after the Marcoses fled said the whole family must have slept together bunker-style in the King's Room, which contained a hospital bed and several mattresses on the floor. An adjoining room contained a blackboard map showing the location and defenses of the army rebels. During the final hours before flight, Marcos was said still to hope he could stay, clutching at straws in the wind even as gunshots echoed in the distance. His children pleaded and cried while Imelda in the meantime went about saying good-bye and handing out money, in a zombe-like fashion. Friends said that minutes before they flew to exile she was fully made up, her hair perfectly coiffed, and that she was still wearing the white gown she had donned for the morning's inauguration. She was said also to have sung "New York, New York" all the way to Hawaii.

When investigators for the Aquino government rifled through the thousands of financial documents the Marcoses left behind, they discovered loot beyond any of their expectations. The documents outlined the Marcoses' formula for systematic plunder. They had amassed their wealth through bribe-taking and kickbacks from crony monopolies; through the diversion of government loans and contracts; through the profits from overpriced goods and construction; through unaudited government revenue, usually raised from taxes; and through the expedient of taking over businesses by decree and the diversion of yet more funds from government-controlled entities. Nothing was spared. Even payments for fresh flowers delivered daily to the homes of Imee, Irene, and Ferdinand Marcos, Jr., were disbursed from government funds. Imelda and Marcos and their cronies seemed to have devised every conceivable way of making money through the use of absolute power since the declaration of martial law in 1972. The commission which has been assigned to recover the Marcos fortune still does not know how much money they stole, but initial estimates hover between $5 billion and $10 billion, most of it already stashed abroad, in U.S. real estate and Swiss bank accounts. More Marcos accounts under false names have been found by Swiss authorities. The revised figure is a staggering $15 billion, more than half of the entire national debt of the Philippines.

One of the most intriguing documents Marcos left behind, however, was a set of manuscripts bound in a plain brown-red folder. The manuscripts tell a fictional story of Salcedo, the last Spanish conquistador to rule the Ilocos region. He discovers a mountain of gold and becomes the happiest man on earth. But then he falls in love with a beautiful native girl and, as she lies naked beside him, waiting, the potent conquistador runs away in grief. At the story's end the unknown author asks, was the inability to love the price of the mountain of gold?

When Cory Aquino took over, some bookstores that still held stocks of yellowing copies of *The Untold Story of Imelda Marcos,* which had been banned after martial law was declared in 1972, put them on sale. One store sold its entire stock of 2,000 copies in a day. "It went like popcorn," one salesgirl said.

Filipinos who have read Imelda's untold story may better understand why her "ancestral" home in Leyte, the Santo Nino shrine, constructed in 1982, meant so much to her. She had built this combination shrine and palatial home on the same spot where her family's Quonset hut stood, with its kitchen with steel mats and its primitive toilet. In its place she built this monstrous shrine with twenty luxurious bedrooms. But she never lived there. Imelda spent only one night in the opulent pink bedroom decorated with French mirrors, fine lace bedcovers, and peacock feathers; this "ancestral house" was meant only to be viewed. A long table in the huge reception area holds hundreds of framed pictures of Imelda with the world leaders she met in her travels. The reception room is illuminated even during the day with twinkling lights that cover the entire ceiling. To many Leytenos, the lights seemed like the fireflies that are their children's favorite playthings. Imelda, too, must have enjoyed playing with them in her youth. On one occasion, when she gave a big party at her summerhouse by the beach in Ulot, she had thousands of them caught to decorate the trees.

Scattered about the shrine cum ancestral house are Chinese porcelain vases, French antique furniture, a hundred Russian icons, and dozens of Chinese ivory figurines, including a life-size statue of Limahong, a medieval Chinese pirate who had foraged Marcos's hometown of Ilocos and who was said to be a distant ancestor of the fallen dictator. But why should a pirate be garbed in imperial robes?

The grand staircase is the centerpiece of Imelda's "ancestral" house. Dominating the wall by the staircase is a huge mural of Vicente Orestes's family of two wives and eleven children, with Imelda at the top of the family tree. Was this the salve for past days, when the child Imelda had to mount the stairs to the Big House to receive the food allowance for the children of the garage?

Try as she might to obscure the devastating days in General Solano, they kept coming back. Even in faraway New York, where she lived amid incredible splendor, the past never left her.

The mute testimony of the past and its continuing hold on Imelda rests in a first-floor storeroom of Imelda's Fifth Avenue townhouse. Amid objets d'art and household paraphernalia sit massive portraits of Ronald and Nancy Reagan, looking like royalty themselves, as interpreted by artist Ralph Wolfe Cowan, portraitist to their Royal Highnesses Prince Rainier III and the late Princess Grace. This was the gift Imelda had meant to give her favorite friends for having been so kind as to invite them to the White House a second time. The paintings were to be ready when the Reagans visited Manila in 1983. But then Ninoy was killed and the visit was canceled. The Reagans never again visited the Marcoses, and Imelda was never able to give them the magnificent oil portraits.

Behind the huge Reagan portraits stands another Ralph Wolfe Cowan painting, a diminutive oil of another couple whose faces would not be familiar to many who see it. It is a portrait of happiness, depicting a woman with the dusky brown good looks of a Filipina, her head crowned with pretty pastel flowers, standing by the side of a handsome Castilian-looking gentleman. It is an interpretation of the wedding picture of Remedios Trinidad and Vicente Orestes Romualdez.

INDEX

226

228